revise

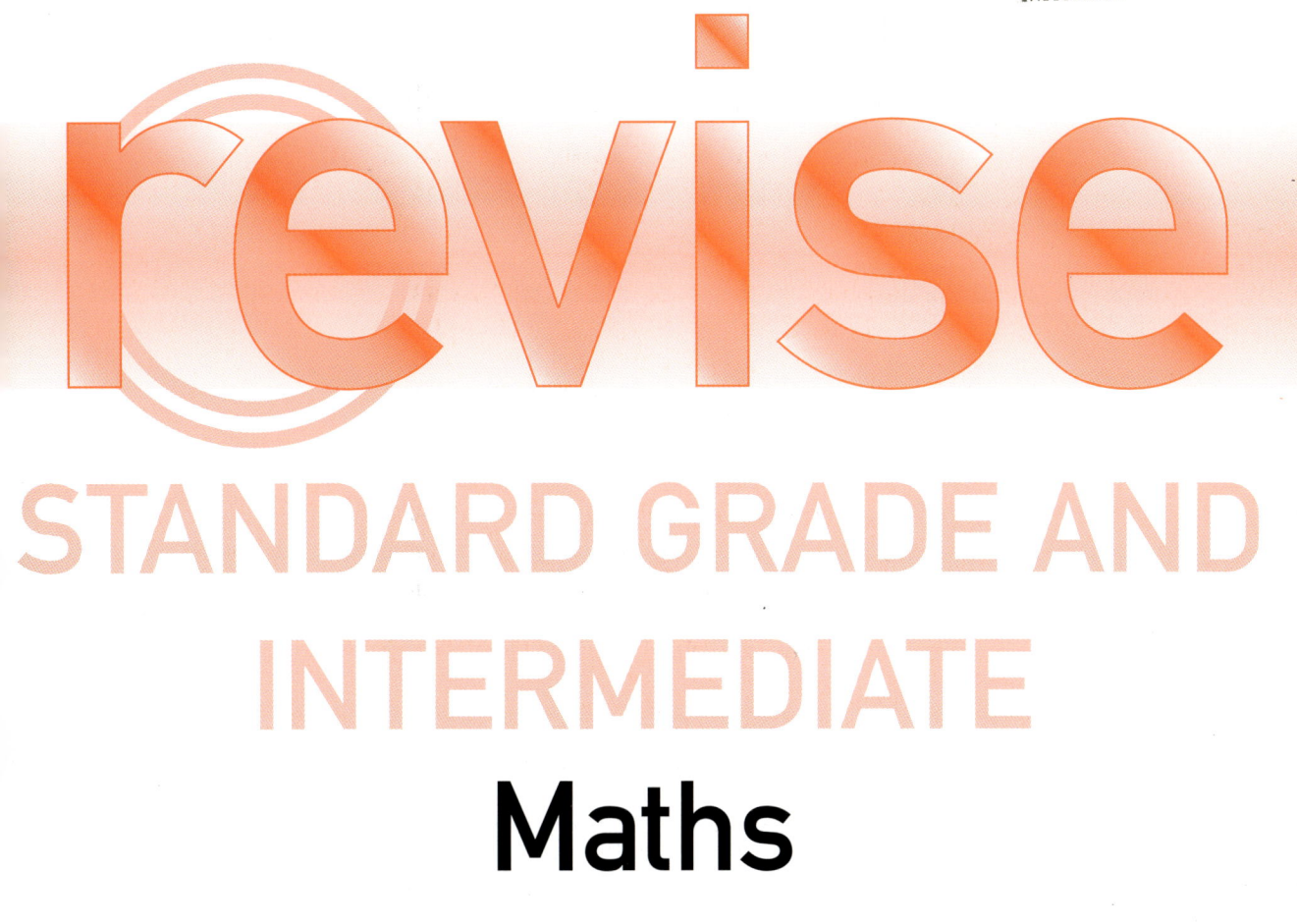

STANDARD GRADE AND INTERMEDIATE

Maths

Sheila Hunt and Philip Hooper

with Tony Buzan and Ken Hutchon

Hodder & Stoughton
A MEMBER OF THE HODDER HEADLINE GROUP

ISBN 0 340 78179 3

First published 2001
Impression number   10 9 8 7 6 5 4 3 2 1
Year   2005 2004 2003 2002 2001

The 'Teach Yourself' name and logo are registered trade marks of Hodder & Stoughton Ltd.

Mind Map® is the registered trade mark of the Buzan Organisation.

Copyright © 2001 Sheila Hunt, Philip Hooper and Ken Hutchon

Copyright © 2001 Tony Buzan

All rights reserved. No part of this publication may be reproduced or transmitted in any form or by any means, electronic or mechanical, including photocopy, recording, or any information storage and retrieval system, without permission in writing from the publisher or under licence from the Copyright Licensing Agency Limited. Further details of such licences (for reprographic reproduction) may be obtained from the Copyright Licensing Agency Limited, of 90 Tottenham Court Road, London W1P 9HE.

Typeset by Hardlines, Chalbury, Oxford
Printed in Spain for Hodder & Stoughton Educational,
a division of Hodder Headline Plc,
338 Euston Road, London NW1 3BH.

Mind Maps: Philip Chambers
Illustrations: Karen Donnelly, Andrea Norton,
  Mike Parsons, John Plumb, Chris Rothero
Cover design: Amanda Hawkes
Cover illustration: Paul Bateman

Contents

Revision made easy	v	
What's wrong with maths?	ix	
Keep this under your hat	ix	
The Mathematical Aid Circus	x	

1 Proportion, percentages and ratio — 1
- Proportion — 2
- Inverse proportion — 5
- Percentages — 6
- VAT questions — 7
- Ratio — 8

2 Number — 13
- Non-calculator numerical skills — 14
- Rounding — 16
- Indices — 17
- Converting time to a decimal number — 18
- Using formulae — 19

Number review — 22

3 Algebra — 23
- Simple equations — 24
- Linear inequalities — 27
- Simplifying expressions — 27
- Making expressions and equations from statements — 31
- Simultaneous equations — 33
- Multiplying out (expanding) double brackets — 35
- Factorising using double brackets — 36
- Solving quadratic equations — 41
- Rearranging formulae — 42
- Variation — 47

4 Graphs in algebra — 50
- Vases and vessels — 53
- Gradients — 53
- Finding the equation of a line — 55
- Interpreting the gradient and y-intercept — 56
- Graphical solutions to simultaneous equations — 56
- Curved graphs — 58

Algebra review — 61

5 Pythagoras' theorem and trigonometry — 65
- Pythagoras' theorem — 67
- Trigonometry — 70
- Angles of elevation and depression — 75
- Bearings — 75
- Trigonometry or Pythagoras' theorem? — 76
- Reasoning and enquiry/non-routine questions — 78
- Sin, cos and tan graphs — 82
- Solving trigonometric equations — 85

6 Length, area and volume — 89
- Perimeter — 90
- Circles — 90
- Area of shapes other than circles — 93
- Volume of a prism — 94

7 Shapes — 98
- Labelling angles — 100
- Polygons — 100
- Nets — 103
- Reflections — 103
- Rotations — 104

Shapes review — 106

8 Statistics	**108**	
Averages	110	
Measures of spread	110	
Median and quartiles	110	
Boxplots	111	
Stem-and-leaf charts	112	
Questions on pie charts	112	
Rules of probability	115	
Scatter diagrams	113	
Calculating probability	115	

Statistics review 118

Step-by-step revision 121
- Step 1 — 121
- Step 2 — 122
- Step 3 — 122

Checklist 123

Specimen examination papers 125
- Foundation level
  - Paper 1 (non-calculator) — 126
  - Paper 2 — 127
- General level (Intermediate 1)
  - Paper 1 (non-calculator) — 128
  - Paper 2 (non-calculator) — 129
- Credit level (Intermediate 2)
  - Paper 1 (non-calculator) — 130
  - Paper 2 — 132

Index 134

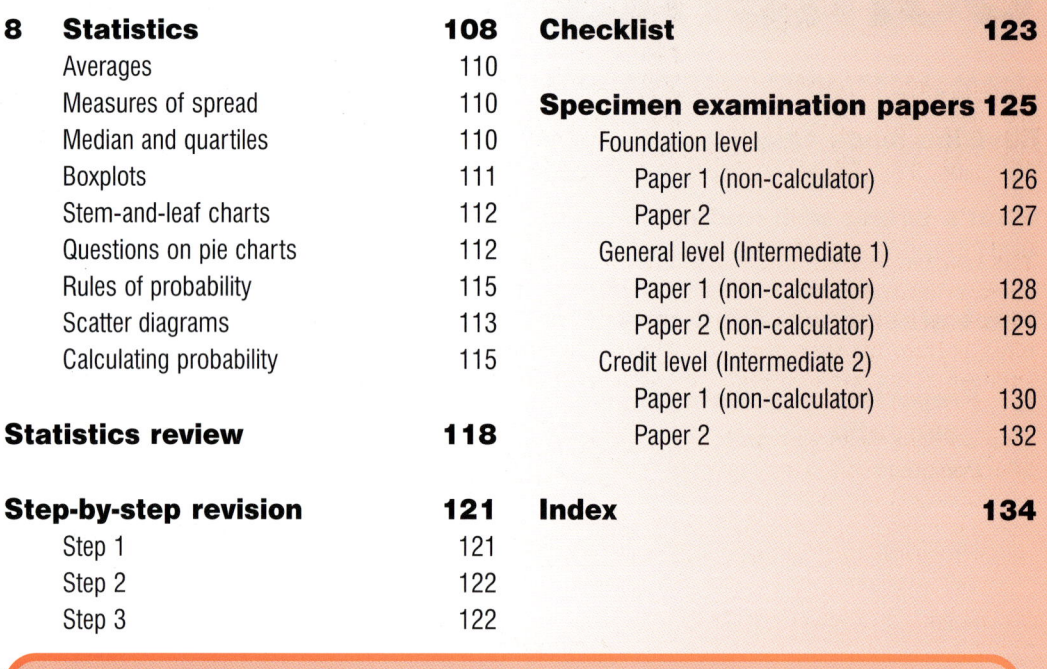

Roll up! Roll up!

To help you achieve that longed-for grade, we have great pleasure in introducing:

Ringo, our ringmaster, who will whip you safely past the

banana skins – those aspects of Mathematics that seem designed to bring you down.

He is aided and abetted by an amazing assortment of astonishing and astounding acts, including:

Gaynor Mark, whose down-to-earth dictionary defines difficult mathematical gobbledegook in sane, simple English,

Willie Droppitt, who will show you how to juggle formulae with ease,

the X-traordinary, X-ceptional X-Direct acrobats who, with their friend the relaxed, rational Ray Showroola will teach you a sense of proportion,

Hans Zoff, our Bavarian conjuror – marvel as his magical mastery makes algebraic anxieties all vanish into thin air – and last, but by no means least:

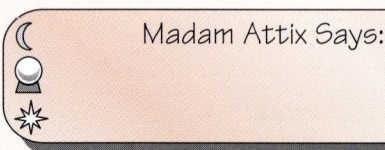

Madam Attix Says:

Madam Attix, our gipsy fortune-teller. Note well her wise sayings. She foretells that your predicted D or E could become a C, whilst a C might well turn into a B.

Also note that ‖ indicates Credit Level or Intermediate 2 material

Revision made easy

The four pages that follow contain a gold mine of information on how you can achieve success both at school and in your exams. Read them and apply the information, and you will be able to spend less, but more efficient, time studying, with better results. If you already have another Hodder & Stoughton revision guide, skim-read these pages to remind yourself about the exciting new techniques the books use, then move ahead to page 1.

This section gives you vital information on how to remember more *while* you are learning and how to remember more *after* you have finished studying. It explains

- **how to use special techniques to improve your memory**
- **how to use a revolutionary note-taking technique called Mind Maps that will double your memory and help you to write essays and answer exam questions**
- **how to read everything faster while at the same time improving your comprehension and concentration**

All this information is packed into the next four pages, so make sure you read them!

Your *amazing* memory

There are five important things you must know about your brain and memory to revolutionise your school life.

1 how your memory ('recall') works *while* you are learning

2 how your memory works *after* you have finished learning

3 how to use Mind Maps – a special technique for helping you with all aspects of your studies

4 how to increase your reading speed

5 how to zap your revision

1 Recall *during* learning – the need for breaks

When you are studying, your memory can concentrate, understand and remember well for between 20 and 45 minutes at a time. Then it *needs* a break. If you carry on for longer than this without one, your memory starts to break down! If you study for hours non-stop, you will remember only a fraction of what you have been trying to learn, and you will have wasted valuable revision time.

So, ideally, *study for less than an hour*, then take a five- to ten-minute break. During the break listen to music, go for a walk, do some exercise, or just daydream. (Daydreaming is a necessary brain-power booster – geniuses do it regularly.) During the break your brain will be sorting out what it has been learning, and you will go back to your books with the new information safely stored and organised in your memory banks. We recommend breaks at regular intervals as you work through the revision guides. Make sure you take them!

2 Recall *after* learning – the waves of your memory

What do you think begins to happen to your memory straight *after* you have finished learning something? Does it immediately start forgetting? No! Your brain actually *increases* its power and carries on remembering. For a short time after your study session, your brain integrates the information, making a more complete picture of everything it has just learnt. Only then does the rapid decline in memory begin, and as much as 80 per cent of what you have learnt can be forgotten in a day.

However, if you catch the top of the wave of your memory, and briefly review (look back over) what you have been revising at the correct time, the memory is stamped in far more strongly, and stays at the crest of the wave for a much longer time. To maximise your brain's power to remember, take a few minutes and use a Mind Map to review what you have learnt at the end of a day. Then review it at the end of a week, again at the end of a month, and finally a week before the exams. That way you'll ride your memory wave all the way to your exam – and beyond!

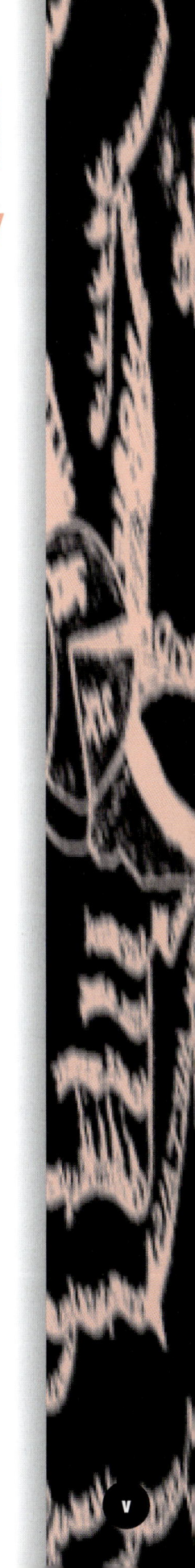

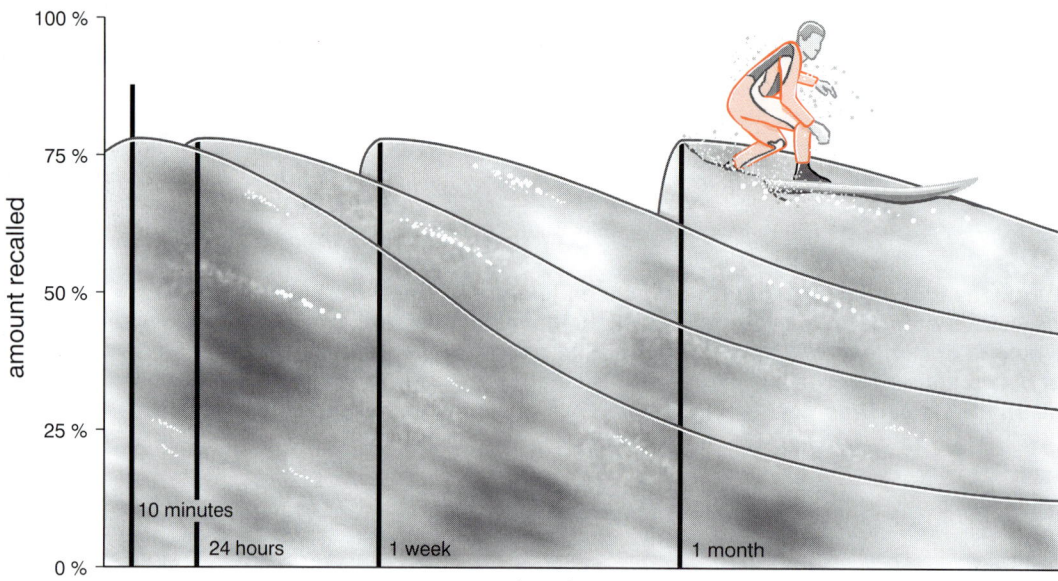

amount recalled: 100%, 75%, 50%, 25%, 0%
review time: 10 minutes, 24 hours, 1 week, 1 month

Amazing as your memory is (think of everything you actually do have stored in your brain at this moment) the principles on which it operates are very simple: your brain will remember if it (a) has an image (a picture or a symbol); (b) has that image fixed and (c) can link that image to something else.

3 The Mind Map® – a picture of the way you think

Do you *like* taking notes? More importantly, do you like having to go back over and learn them before exams? Most students I know certainly do not! And how do you take your notes? Most people take notes on lined paper, using blue or black ink. The result, visually, is *boring*! And what does your brain do when it is bored? It turns off, tunes out, and goes to sleep! Add a dash of colour, rhythm, imagination, and the whole note-taking process becomes much more fun, uses more of your brain's abilities, *and* improves your recall and understanding.

A Mind Map mirrors the way your brain works. It can be used for note-taking from books or in class, for reviewing what you have just studied, for revising, and for essay planning for coursework and in exams. It uses all your memory's natural techniques to build up your rapidly growing 'memory muscle'.

You will find Mind Maps throughout this book. Study them, add some colour, personalise them, and then have a go at drawing your own – you'll remember them far better! Put them on your walls and in your files for a quick-and-easy review of the topic.

How to draw a Mind Map

- Start in the middle of the page with the page turned sideways. This gives your brain the maximum room for its thoughts.
- Always start by drawing a small picture or symbol. Why? Because a picture is worth a thousand words to your brain. And try to use at least three colours, as colour helps your memory even more.
- Let your thoughts flow, and write or draw your ideas on coloured branching lines connected to your central image. These key symbols and words are the headings for your topic. The Mind Map at the top of the next page shows you how to start.
- Then add facts and ideas by drawing more, smaller, branches on to the appropriate main branches, just like a tree.
- Always print your word clearly on its line. Use only one word per line. The Mind Map at the foot of the next page shows you how to do this.
- To link ideas and thoughts on different branches, use arrows, colours, underlining, and boxes.

How to read a Mind Map

- Begin in the centre, the focus of your topic.
- The words/images attached to the centre are like chapter headings: read them next.
- Always read out from the centre, in every direction (even on the left-hand side, where you will have to read from right to left, instead of the usual left to right).

Using Mind Maps

Mind Maps are a versatile tool – use them for taking notes in class or from books, for solving problems, for brainstorming with friends, and for reviewing and revising for exams – their uses are endless! You will find them invaluable for planning essays for coursework and exams. Number your main branches in the order in which you want to use them and off you go – the main headings for your essay are done and all your ideas are logically organised!

MAD
COIN 1

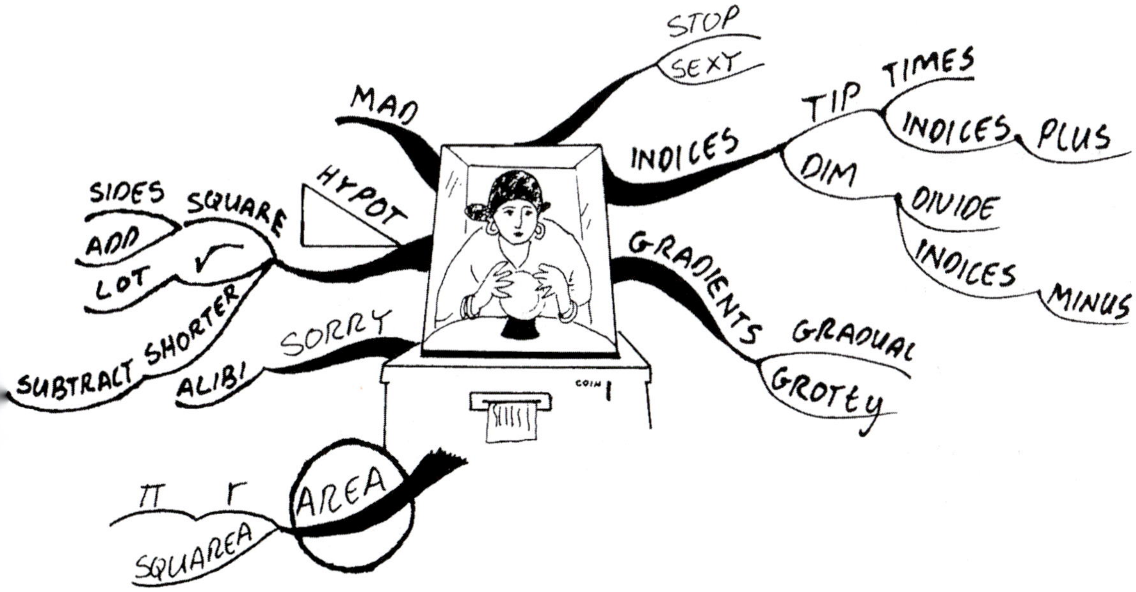
STOP
SEXY
MAD
TIP
TIMES
INDICES
PLUS
DIM
DIVIDE
INDICES
MINUS
HYPOT
SIDES
SQUARE
ADD
LOT
SHORTER
SUBTRACT
ALIBI
SORRY
GRADIENTS
GRADUAL
GROTTY
COIN 1
π
r
AREA
SQUAREA

4 Super speed reading

It seems incredible, but it's been proved – the faster you read, the more you understand and remember! So here are some tips to help you to practise reading faster – you'll cover the ground more quickly, remember more, *and* have more time for revision!

★ Read the whole text (whether it's a lengthy book or an exam paper) very quickly first, to give your brain an overall idea of what's ahead and get it working. (It's like sending out a scout to look at the territory you have to cover – it's much easier when you know what to expect!) Then read the text again for more detailed information.

★ Have the text a reasonable distance away from your eyes. In this way your eye/brain system will be able to see more at a glance, and will naturally begin to read faster.

★ Take in groups of words at a time. Rather than reading slowly and 'carefully' read faster, more enthusiastically.
Your comprehension will rocket!

★ Take in phrases rather than single words while you read.

★ Use a guide. Your eyes are designed to follow movement, so a thin pencil underneath the lines you are reading, moved smoothly along, will 'pull' your eyes to faster speeds.

5 Helpful hints for exam revision

Start to revise at the beginning of the course. Cram at the start, not the end and avoid 'exam panic'!

Use Mind Maps throughout your course, and build a Master Mind Map for each subject – a giant Mind Map that summarises everything you know about the subject.

Use memory techniques such as mnemonics (verses or systems for remembering things like dates and events, or lists).

Get together with one or two friends to revise, compare Mind Maps, and discuss topics.

And finally...

● *Have fun while you learn* – studies show that those people who enjoy what they are doing understand and remember it more, and generally do it better.

● *Use your teachers* as resource centres. Ask them for help with specific topics and with more general advice on how you can improve your all-round performance.

● *Personalise your revision guide* by underlining and highlighting, by adding notes and pictures. Allow your brain to have a conversation with it!

Your brain is an amazing piece of equipment – learn to use it, and you, like thousands of students before you will be able to master your maths with ease. The more you understand and use your brain, the more it will repay you!

What's wrong with maths?

How often have you said ...

1 ✗ Maths is boring.

✔ Our book is different. We can't absolutely guarantee not to bore you, but at least we'll try not to.

2 ✗ It has lots of long, strange words which I don't understand.

✔ It may amaze you, but maths can be simple and we promise to explain what we mean in ordinary, plain English.

3 ✗ You have to learn hundreds of formulae and methods and I can't remember them.

✔ You don't have to learn masses of material, and we've thought up all sorts of original ways to help you remember the bits which you just must know.

4 ✗ It takes up all your spare time, and I can think of loads of things I'd rather do.

✔ Our easy methods and short cuts should help you save time, effort and worry.

Just imagine – you can spend even more time lounging around doing nothing and end up with a better grade!

5 ✗ Why didn't I buy this book before?

Keep this under your hat!

If you skim through chapters 1 and 2, you'll find most of our secrets revealed there and *you could learn enough in those few pages to push your marks up a grade!*

After that, though, it's up to you, and you can work through the rest of this book in any order you like. For instance, if Trigonometry always trips you up, or you stumble over Statistics, you may want to tackle those chapters next. It doesn't matter.

However you choose to use this book, though, we hope that you'll find it easy to follow, and that our circus and fairground characters will help you make the grade.

Good luck!

Important note!

Sometimes you may be surprised to find that your answer is just slightly different from the one given – especially if you have used a calculator to work it out. Don't worry – this can happen when calculators are used. It all depends when you round your answers.

If you carry out a long string of calculations on your calculator, your answer will not be rounded until the very end. However, if you make lots of shorter calculations, you are likely to round each time. This will give you a slightly different answer. The examiner will understand this.

Always read the question carefully and follow the instructions exactly, just in case you are told at which points to round your answers.

Sheila Hunt and Philip Hooper

The Mathematical Aid Circus

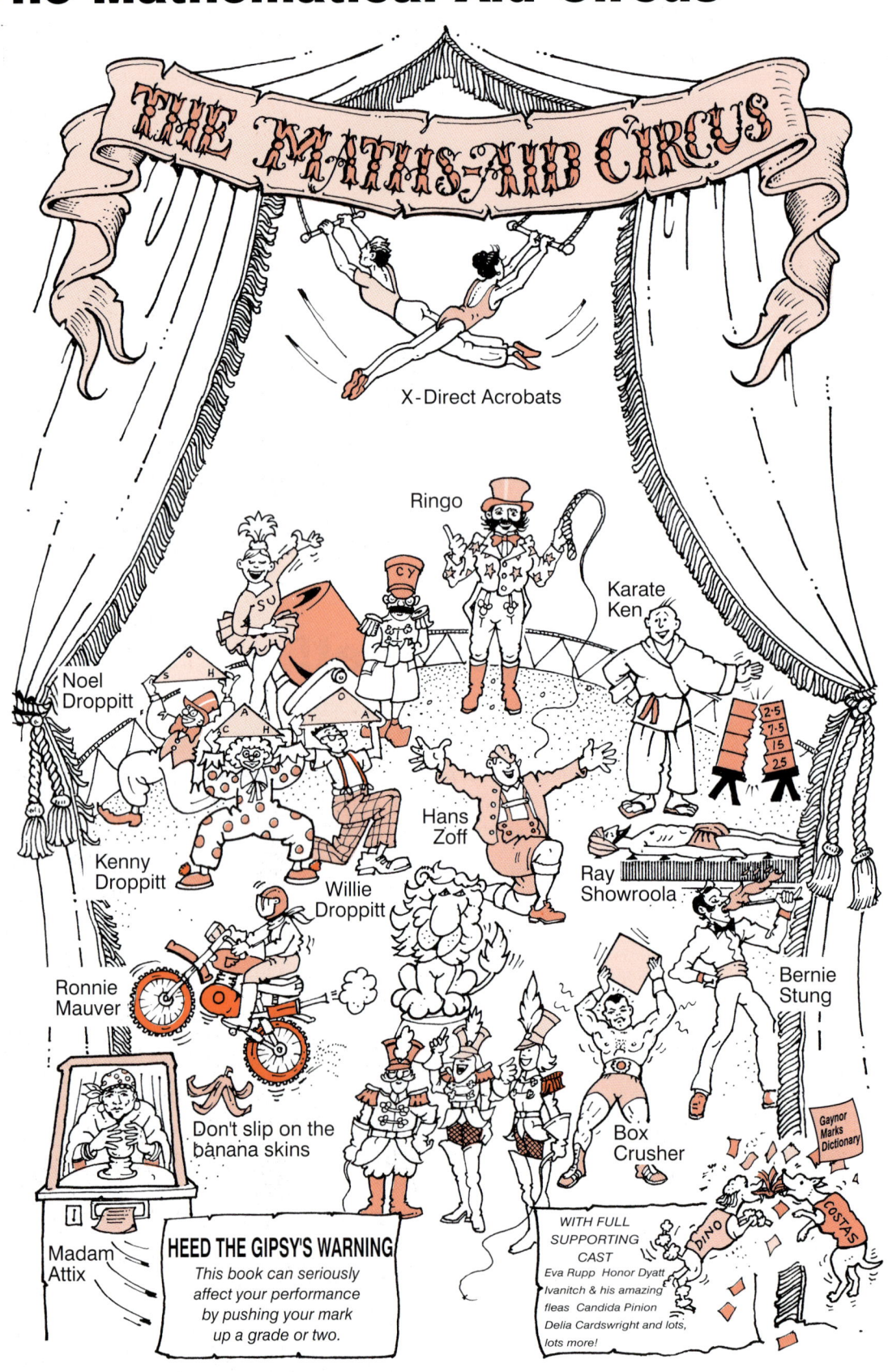

THE MATHS-AID CIRCUS

X-Direct Acrobats

Ringo

Noel Droppitt

Karate Ken

Kenny Droppitt

Willie Droppitt

Hans Zoff

Ray Showroola

Ronnie Mauver

Bernie Stung

Don't slip on the banana skins

Box Crusher

Madam Attix

HEED THE GIPSY'S WARNING
This book can seriously affect your performance by pushing your mark up a grade or two.

WITH FULL SUPPORTING CAST
Eva Rupp Honor Dyatt Ivanitch & his amazing fleas Candida Pinion Delia Cardswright and lots, lots more!

1

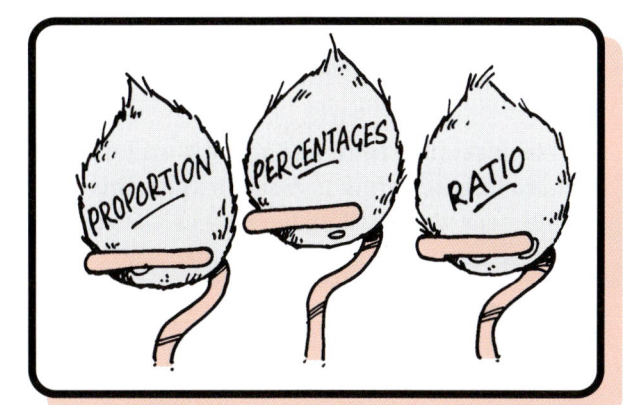

Proportion, percentages and ratio

preview

By the end of this chapter you will be able to:

- answer questions on direct and inverse proportion
- find one number as a percentage of another
- find a given percentage of a number
- increase or decrease a price or amount by a given percentage
- calculate the percentage discount on a price
- calculate the VAT-inclusive price of an article, given the pre-VAT price
- calculate the pre-VAT price, given the VAT-inclusive price
- divide a given number or amount in a given ratio
- calculate individual shares of a number or amount divided in a given ratio
- state ratios in their lowest terms
- state ratios in the form 1 : n or n : 1
- work out the lengths involved in scale drawing

How many of these coconuts would you shy away from?

By the end of this chapter, thanks to that death-defying duo, the X-Direct Acrobats, our very own ratio expert, Ray Showroola, and a huge supporting cast, these problems will be a thing of the past!

Meet the ringmaster

Ringo the ringmaster is the first person you will meet in this chapter. He's a mine of useful information and he'll keep you on the right track. Look out for his helpful tips and reminders.

1

Revise Standard Grade and Intermediate Maths

How much do you know already?

Exercise 1.1

1. 1 kilogram is approximately 2.2 pounds (1 kg ≈ 2.2 lbs).
   a) Big Hilda Klime weighs 75 kg. How much is that in pounds?
   b) A bag of rice weighs 1.1 lb. Express this in grams.

2. What is 40% of 60?

3. A pie chart is drawn to represent 300 members of the audience. How many degrees represent 80 members?

4. Two litres of a solution contain 850 grams of a chemical.
   a) How many litres would contain 1500 g?
   b) How many grams are there in 3.3 litres? Give your answer to the nearest hundred grams.

5. In a test, a student scored 45 out of a possible 70 marks. What percentage was this?

6. The plan of a new house and garden is drawn, using a scale of 1 : 25.
   a) The length of the kitchen as drawn on the plan is 15 cm. What is its actual length, in metres?
   b) The actual garden is 12.5 metres long. How long will it be on the plan?

7. The lengths of the labels of two jars are in the ratio of 5 : 2.
   a) If the larger label is 8 cm wide, how wide is the smaller?
   b) If the smaller label is 5 cm high, find the height of the larger.

8. Mike Harr bought a van for £9500 and sold it a year later for £7800. Find its depreciation as a percentage of the cost price.

Answers

1 a) 165 lbs b) 500 g
2 24
3 96°
4 a) 3.53 litres
  b) 1402.5 g = 1400 g to the nearest hundred grams
5 64%
6 a) 3.75 m b) 50 cm
7 a) 3.2 cm b) 12.5 m
8 18%

How did you get on?

All of them right?

Well done! Questions of this type are common at Standard Grade and Intermediate level. If you found them easy, you probably have methods which work well for you, and you don't need to change them. However, you may find that we can show you some shortcuts that could save you valuable minutes in the exam, so it's worth looking through our methods which we show you below. You just might pick up a tip or two.

Most questions right, but a few blunders?

You are just the sort of person for whom this chapter was written. With the help of X-Direct or Ray Showroola, you should score 100% next time.

Don't even ask?

Don't despair. Just work through this chapter and you'll see just how easy it is to score 100%!

Proportion

Introducing our fabulous X-Direct Acrobats

Here they are, in a really easy example.

Example 1.1 – A Really Easy Example!

Five books cost £15. Find the cost of seven books.

This is probably the method you used in the past.

> 5 books cost £15
> 1 book costs £15 ÷ 5 = £3
> 7 books cost £3 × 7 = £21

Proportion, percentages and ratio

Solution
Using the X-Direct method

Step 1
Set out the information in a table.

	Books	Cost (£)
What does the question tell me?	5	15
What do I need to know?	7	

Make sure you put the numbers under the right heading!

Step 2

Books   Cost (£)
5   15
7

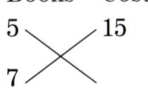

Draw in the diagonal X as shown.

The acrobat with two numbers is Times.

The other acrobat, with one number, is Divide.

Just Times the two, Divide by the other.

Books   Cost (£)
5   15
7

Cost of 7 books = $\frac{7 \times 15}{5}$ = 21

Seven books cost £21.

Once you get the hang of this, it's really quick and easy, as you'll discover when you see it in action.

Example 1.2

A box of chocolates was bought in the USA for $4.58, when the exchange rate was £1 = $1.42. Give the cost in pounds sterling to the nearest penny.

Solution

	£	$
What does the question tell me?	1	1.42
What do I need to find?		4.58

Using X-Direct, you can see that the calculation is
$\frac{1 \times 4.58}{1.42}$ = £3.23

Since you are multiplying by 1, you can of course leave it out of your written working without affecting the answer, but many people prefer to write everything in until they get used to X-Direct.

*Tip! Try to get into the habit of making a rough estimate **before** you carry out the calculation, just to give you some idea of what answer to expect.*

Example 1.3

Paul E. Payde worked for 42 hours and received £48.30. How much would he receive for working 20 hours at the same rate?

Solution

Estimate: 20 is about half of 42, so he should receive about £24.

	Hours	£
What does the question tell me?	42	48.30
What do I need to know?	20	

Amount = $\frac{20 \times 48.30}{42}$ = £23.00

Example 1.4 – Using X-Direct more than once

1 litre ≈ 1.75 pints

(≈ means 'approximately equals')

8 pints = 1 gallon

How many litres are approximately equal to 30.5 gallons?

Solution

You need to work backwards on this one.

	pints	gallons
What do I know?	8	1
What must I find?		30.5

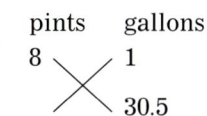

$\frac{8 \times 30.5}{1}$ = 244 pints

Revise Standard Grade and Intermediate Maths

Now consider the relationship between pints and litres.

	pints	litres
What do I know?	1.75	1
What must I find?	244	

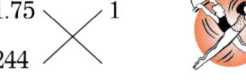

$$30.5 \text{ gallons} \approx \frac{244 \times 1}{1.75} = 139.4 \text{ litres}$$

Now you try your luck!

Exercise 1.2

1 a) 3.5 m of tape cost £4.20. What would 8 m cost?
b) How much would you get for £15?

2 30 cm ≈ 1 foot
3 feet = 1 yard
1760 yards = 1 mile

How many metres are approximately equal to 1 mile?

3 Ivanitch the flea tamer buys honey for his fleas in different sized pots. The larger jar weighs 850 grams and costs £4.50 and the smaller costs £1.75 for 300 grams.
a) Which is better value and why? Show your working.
b) Why might Ivanitch's mother choose the other size instead?

Answers

1 a) £9.60 b) 12.5 m
2 1584 m
3 He can buy 189 g for £1.00 if he buys the larger size. He gets 171 g for £1.00 if he buys the smaller size. The larger is better value, but his mother might buy the smaller if she did not use much honey.

Meet Gaynor Mark

It's time for you to meet another character who features widely in this book. Gaynor Mark has written a very useful dictionary which translates English into the weird and wonderful language of Maths exams. This makes it much easier for candidates to understand what the question is asking, and so it gives them a better chance of actually answering it.

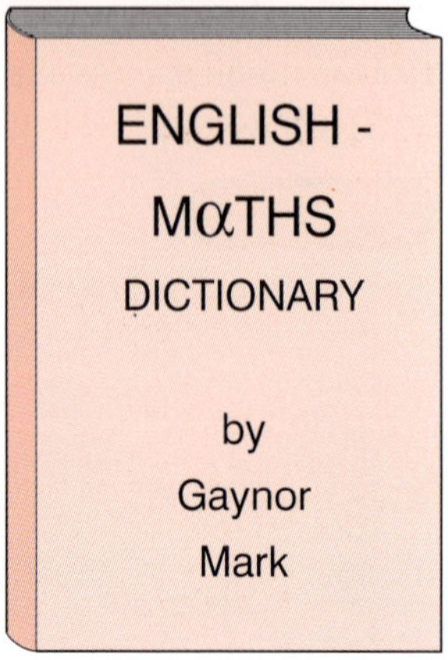

Whenever you see this sign, you know that Gaynor Mark is about to give you a useful hint.

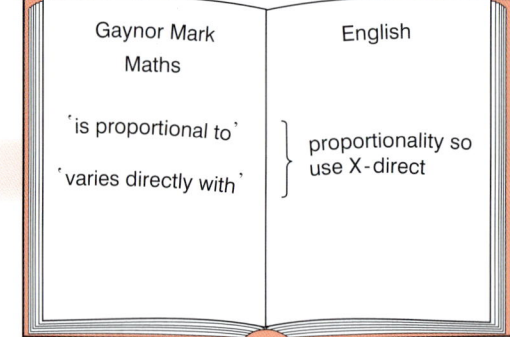

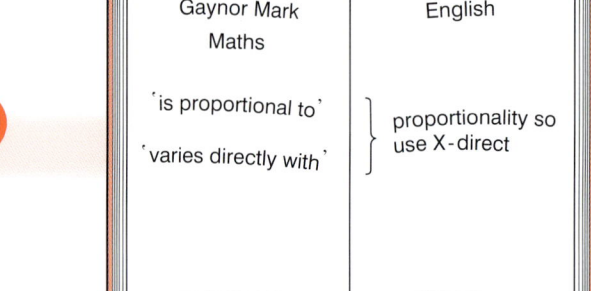

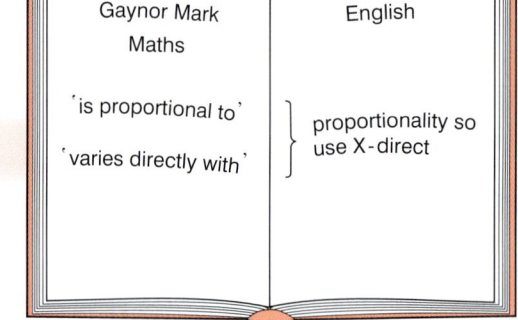

Gaynor Mark Maths	English
'is proportional to' 'varies directly with'	proportionality so use X-direct

TAKE A BREAK

This is a good point to take a break.

When you come back, look again at the principles of X-Direct. Start to make a list of situations when you could use the technique. You will be surprised how often it crops up.

Avoiding pitfalls

We have used the symbol of the banana skin to point out potential hazards which could trip you up. Whenever you see the banana skin you know there is something that could cause you a problem. It's a warning to be careful and to try to avoid common mistakes. Its first appearance in this book is to help you distinguish X-Direct problems from those involving inverse proportion.

ENGLISH - MαTHS DICTIONARY
by Gaynor Mark

Inverse proportion

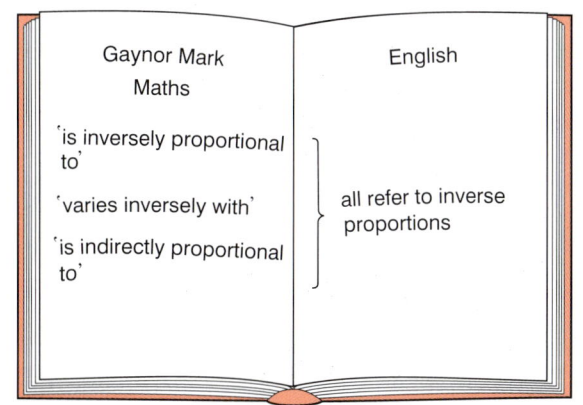

Gaynor Mark Maths:
- 'is inversely proportional to'
- 'varies inversely with'
- 'is indirectly proportional to'

English: all refer to inverse proportions

A problem involving inverse proportion is one of the very rare cases where X-Direct must *not* be used.

Example 1.5

A journey takes 6 hours at 40 km/h. How long does it take at 80 km/h?

*Common sense tells you that the faster you go, the less time you take, so you must use **inverse proportion** (i.e. one variable gets bigger as the other gets smaller and vice versa). X-Direct only applies to questions where both variables increase at the same rate, or both decrease at the same rate.*

Solution

Multiply what you are given	$6 \times 40 = 240$
And then	
Divide by the other number.	$240 \div 80 = 3$

The journey takes 3 hours.

Introducing Madam Attix

Madam Attix is a wise old woman. Her sayings will help you remember formulae and rules.

> **Madam Attix Says:**
> *Inverse proportion can drive you MAD!*
> **M**ultiply **A**nd then **D**ivide.

Caution!

Do not use X-Direct for inverse proportion.

Inverse proportion questions are not nearly as common, but we have inserted them here, so that you don't muddle them with X-Direct.

Exercise 1.3

1 If Dinah Tate and four friends share the bill at a restaurant, the cost per head is £24.00. How much should each person pay if the cost is shared among eight people?

2 Andy Chapterno and two other odd-job people can put up the Big Top in three hours. How long would six people take?

Answers
1 £15.00
2 1.5 hours

TAKE A BREAK

Now's the time for a break! You probably feel you need it. Don't make it too long, though, because we still have to tackle percentages.

Revise Standard Grade and Intermediate Maths

Percentages

Percentages feature very prominently throughout Standard Grade and Intermediate level papers, so this section could help you pick up some useful marks. If you have a method which works for you, then by all means, continue to use it. However, the mere fact that you are reading this section probably means that you are having problems, so try X-Direct!

Percentages using X-Direct

Important! *One hundred per cent, or 100%, means the whole, original or total amount.*

This, unbelievably, is all you have to know to use this method.

Type 1: Finding the percentage of a number

Example 1.6

What is 20% of £200?

Solution

100% is the original amount of £200.

It is the amount of money which equals 20% of £200 that we need to know.

Pounds (£)   Percentage (%)
200   100
                    20

Using X-Direct:

$$\frac{200 \times 20}{100} = 40$$

So your answer, as it should be in the pounds column, is £40.

Type 2: Expressing one number as a percentage of another

Example 1.7

In a fairground survey, 25 stallholders, out of 125 who were asked, said that they were running their stalls at a loss. Express this as a percentage.

Solution

100% refers to the total number of people asked, i.e. 125.

We need to find 25 as a percentage of 125.

People   Percentage (%)
125   100
25

Using X-Direct:

$$\frac{25 \times 100}{125} = 20$$

As this answer would go in the percentage column, the answer is 20%.

Example 1.8

Stew Pidd bought a radio for £80.00 and sold it again for £60.00. Find the percentage loss.

Solution

Start by finding the actual loss.
(i.e. £80.00 − £60.00 = £20.00)

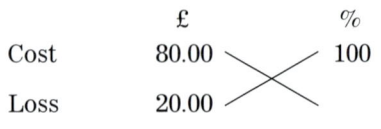

                £   %
Cost   80.00   100
Loss   20.00

$$\text{Percentage loss} = \frac{20 \times 100}{80}$$

$$= 25\%$$

Proportion, percentages and ratio

Type 3: When the figure that you are given does not refer to 100%

Example 1.9

Ivor Bargin buys a camera. The price is reduced by 20%, and it is discounted by £7.50. Find the original price.

Solution

The original price is 100%.

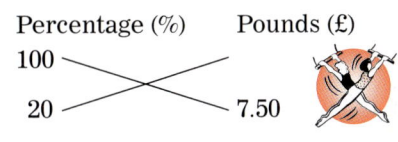

Percentage (%)   Pounds (£)
100   7.50
20

Using X-Direct: $\dfrac{100 \times 7.50}{20} = 37.5$

The answer is £37.50 (not £37.5 – money is never written like this!).

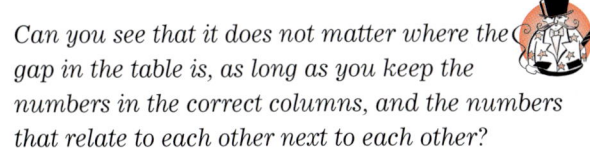

Can you see that it does not matter where the gap in the table is, as long as you keep the numbers in the correct columns, and the numbers that relate to each other next to each other?

Example 1.10

The price of a camera is reduced by 25% to £30. Find its original price.

Solution

This question is practically the same as the one before, but is worded slightly differently. This time the price after the discount has been given, rather than the discount itself.

If 25% has been taken off the original of 100%, then we have 75% left. So £30 relates to 75%.

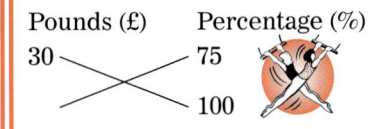

Pounds (£)   Percentage (%)
30   75
                        100

Using X-Direct: $\dfrac{30 \times 100}{75} = 40$

So the original price was £40.00.

Exercise 1.4

1. As an experiment to encourage larger audiences, the price of all tickets to the circus is reduced by 15%. If the original price of a ticket was £5.70, find the new price.

2. In an audience of 240 people, 108 were children.
   a) What percentage of the audience were children?
   b) What percentage were adults?

3. Mark M. Upp increased the site rent for the fair by 20% one year. If the new rent is £300, find the original charge.

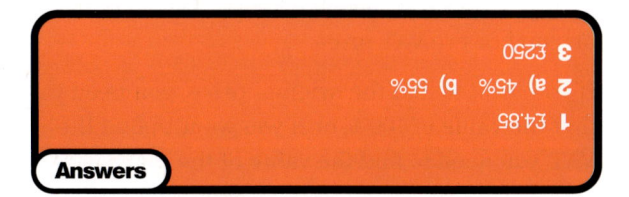

Answers

1 £4.85
2 a) 45% b) 55%
3 £250

VAT questions

At the time of writing this book, VAT is 17.5%. This is a tax put on most items that you would buy in the shops. VAT questions are very common in exams.

Adding on VAT

Example 1.11

The pre-VAT price of a toy is £58.40. Find the price including VAT.

Solution

There are two ways of solving this problem: either work out 17.5% and add it on to the original price, or use the complete 'VAT-inclusive' percentage, which will be 100% + 17.5% = 117.5%.

Method 1

Price (£)   Percentage (%)
58.40   100
                         17.5

VAT = $\dfrac{58.40 \times 17.5}{100} = 10.22$

The price including VAT = £58.40 + £10.22 = £68.62.

Method 2

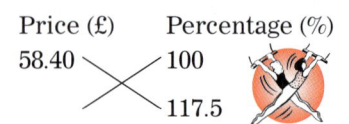

Price (£)   Percentage (%)
58.40   100
              117.5

Total price including VAT = $\frac{58.40 \times 117.5}{100}$ = £68.62.

Removing the VAT from the 'VAT-inclusive' price

As you saw in the example above, the 'VAT-inclusive' price is 100% + 17.5% = 117.5% of the original or pre-VAT price.

If you want to find the original price, you need to find the value of 100%, or if you want to find the VAT, you need to find the value of the 17.5%.

Example 1.12

A coffee-maker is priced at £31.49 including VAT. Find its price before VAT was added.

Solution

Price (£)   Percentage (%)
31.49   117.5
              100

Pre-VAT price = $\frac{31.49 \times 100}{117.5}$ = 26.8

The original price was £26.80.

Remember: Not £26.8!

Example 1.13

Find the VAT on a calculator if the price including VAT is £16.92.

Solution

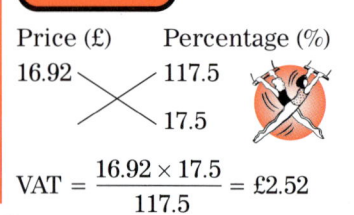

Price (£)   Percentage (%)
16.92   117.5
              17.5

VAT = $\frac{16.92 \times 17.5}{117.5}$ = £2.52

Exercise 1.5

In this exercise, take VAT to be 17.5%.

1. Adam Upp, the book-keeper for the circus, calculates the VAT. If the pre-VAT price of a ticket is £11.50 for adults and £8.50 for children, find the price including VAT.

2. Zena Fobier booked a foreign holiday for £1001.10 including VAT. What would the price be without VAT?

3. Phyl Theeritch paid £426.76 for a coat including VAT. How much VAT did she pay?

Answers

1. Adult's ticket = £13.51, child's ticket = £9.99
2. £852.00
3. £63.56

Ratio

Ratio is a way in which quantities can be divided.

How much do you know already?

Exercise 1.6

1. Lottie Ree distributed £600 among three people in the ratio 2 : 3 : 7. How much did each receive?

2. Huw Jeego wanted his photo on the circus poster enlarged in all dimensions in the ratio 2 : 5. If the original length is 45 cm, find the new length.

Answers

1. £100, £150 and £350
2. 112.5 cm

Did you realise you can use X-Direct?

Proportion, percentages and ratio

How did you get on?

If you managed those questions without any difficulty, you obviously have a method which works for you. However, if you had any problems, see if Ray Showroola and his bed of nails combined with X-Direct, might help.

Meet Ray Showroola

Use this ruler and you'll have ratio nailed!

Ray Showroola in action

Look carefully at these rulers. Count the number of parts in each one. Add up the two numbers in the ratio. Get the idea?

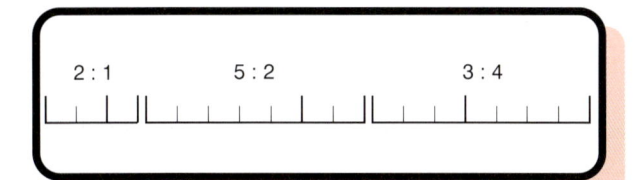

2 : 1   5 : 2   3 : 4

Type 1: The question gives a quantity that relates to the whole of the ruler

Example 1.14

Shirley Knott visited the circus and gave £300 to her two favourite lion tamers, Terry Fyde and Petra Fyde in the ratio of 3 to 2. How much did each receive?

Solution

Write £300 above the whole of the 3 : 2 ratio ruler.

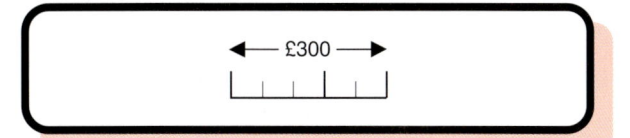

← £300 →

Use X-Direct to find Terry's share.

Share (£)   Sections
300   5
              3

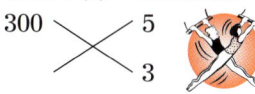

Terry's share = $\dfrac{300 \times 3}{5}$ = £180.

Or work out the money relating to each section. i.e. £300 ÷ 5 = £60.

Terry receives 3 sections   £60 × 3 = £180

Petra receives 2 sections   £60 × 2 = £120

Check: All the amounts must add up to the original £300.

Example 1.15

Mister Catch, a retired juggler, gave £750 to his successors, Willie, Kenny and Noel Droppitt in the ratio of their years of experience i.e. 7, 6 and 2 respectively. How much did each receive?

Solution

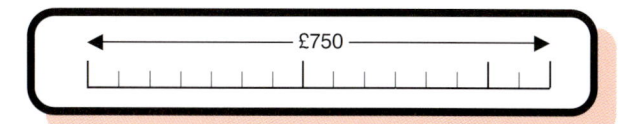

← £750 →

Use X-Direct to find Willie's amount of money.

Share (£)   Sections
750   15
              7

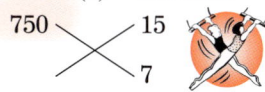

Willie's amount = $\dfrac{750 \times 7}{15}$ = £350

or

Each section represents £750 ÷ 15 = £50.

Willie gets £50 × 7 = £350

Kenny gets £50 × 6 = £300

Noel gets £50 × 2 = £100

Check: 350 + 300 + 100 = 750

9

Revise Standard Grade and Intermediate Maths

Type 2: The quantity given in the question relates to part of the ruler

Example 1.16

Picture frames are made in two sizes. The width of the smaller is 16 cm. The lengths on the larger size are bigger in the ratio 4 : 5. Find the width of the larger frame.

Solution

Start by marking out a ratio ruler with nine divisions, in the ratio 4 : 5.

This time you do not have a total, so do not write anything along the top.

Write the 16 as shown in the diagram.

Now it is a simple matter of using X-Direct to get the answer.

4 : 5

16 :

$$\frac{5 \times 16}{4} = 20 \text{cm}$$

Giving ratios in their lowest form

Example 1.17

Give the ratio 2 : 8 : 12 in its lowest form.

Solution

Look for common factors other than 1.

(These are numbers which divide into 2, 8 and 12. If you have forgotten about factors, you need to refer to Chapter 3, Algebra.)

The only common factor of 2, 8 and 12 is 2, so dividing through by this gives 1 : 4 : 6.

Example 1.18

A ratio is given as 5 : 8.

a) Express this ratio in the form $n : 1$.
b) Express this ratio in the form $1 : n$.

Solution

Once again, X-Direct can come to the rescue. Leave a space where the n should come.

a) 5 : 8
       : 1

$$\frac{1 \times 5}{8} = 0.625$$

Answer in the form $n : 1$ is   0.625 : 1

b) 5 : 8
    1 :

$$\frac{8 \times 1}{5} = 1.6$$

Answer in the form $1 : n$ is   1 : 1.6

Just to recap

Ray Showroola says:

1. Mark out a ruler showing you all the parts.

2. If you have a total (i.e. the whole amount) which has to be shared, write the amount over the top. You can then see that dividing the total by the number of parts will give you the 'size' of one share. Then it is just a matter of using X-Direct to calculate the other shares.

3. If you do not have the total, but just an increase or decrease in one part, write this underneath the ruler and solve *either* by using X-Direct *or* by working out the size of each section.

Proportion, percentages and ratio

Exercise 1.7

1. Share £750 in the ratio 5 : 7 : 13.

2. Money has been shared in the ratio 3 : 2. If the larger amount is £450.00, find the smaller.

3. a) A party from Pause Pelling Grammar School plans to visit the circus. If the ratio of teachers to students must be 2 : 15, how many teachers would be needed to accompany a party of 45 students?
   b) If 12 teachers were available, what is the maximum number of students who could accompany them?

Answers
1 £150, £210 and £390
2 £300
3 a) 6 teachers   b) 90 students

6. In a college, 80 people were asked what grade they expected to get in Maths. Sadly, 22 of them said that they would be lucky not to get a 'U'. Express this number as a percentage of the whole group asked.

7. A packet contains 24 biscuits. Half of the biscuits are put aside, and the remainder are shared by Ava Garribaldi, Big Di Gestive and Chris Crinkle in the ratio 3 : 4 : 5.
   a) What fraction of the original packet does Big Di receive?
   b) Chris eats two biscuits. What fraction of his share does he still have?
   c) Ava eats one of her biscuits and does not like it, so divides her remaining biscuits equally between Big Di and Chris. What fraction of the original packet has Big Di received altogether?
   d) What fraction of the packet of biscuits did Ava eat?

8. The sides of two pictures are in the ratio 5 : 3.
   a) If the larger is 35 cm wide, how wide is the smaller?
   b) If the smaller is 10.5 cm long, find the length of the larger.

Exercise 1.8

1. Gaye Vaway sells paper plates at 5p each, or in packets of 10 for 40p, or in packets of 50 for £1.85. Find the cheapest way to buy:
   a) 9 plates   b) 20 plates   c) 110 plates.

2. In a closing down sale, a shop reduces all its prices by 15%. What is the sale price of an item which originally cost £380.00?

3. A gift of £1800 is to be shared among Anne Doubt, Jack Pott and Wynne de Faul in the ratio of their ages: 3, 4 and 2 respectively.
   a) How much will each receive?
   b) If, instead, the present is deferred for a year, but still divided in the ratio of the ages of the recipients, how much would each receive?

4. A job is advertised as paying an hourly rate of £7.50.
   a) How much would be paid for working a 40 hour week?
   b) Overtime is paid at a rate of time and a half. How much extra would be paid for six hours overtime?
   c) If one week a man earned £401.25, how many hours overtime did he work?

5. The price of an item has been reduced in a sale by 20%. If it now costs £70.00, find its original price.

Answers
1 a) In a packet of 10
   b) 2 packets of 10
   c) 2 packets of 50 and one packet of 10
2 £323.00
3 a) Anne gets £600, Jack gets £800, Wynne gets £400
   b) Anne gets £600, Jack gets £750, Wynne gets £450
4 a) £300   b) £67.50   c) 9 hours
5 £87.50
6 27.5% or 28 %
7 a) $\frac{4}{24} = \frac{1}{6}$ b) $\frac{3}{5}$ c) $\frac{5}{24}$ d) $\frac{1}{24}$
8 a) 21 cm   b) 17.5 cm

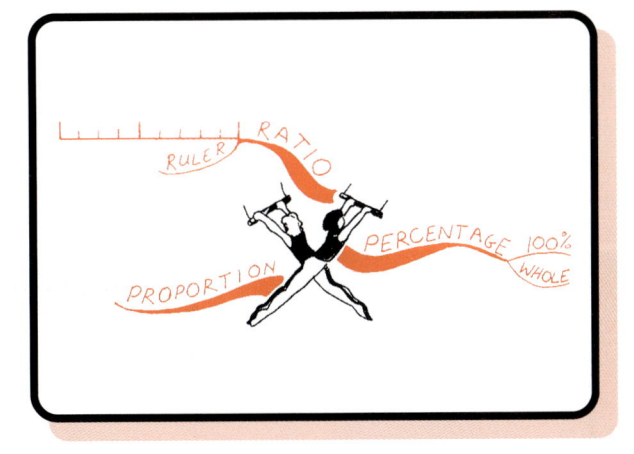

Revise Standard Grade and Intermediate Maths

1 review

How much have you learnt?

Tick off each topic in the list when you are confident you can cope with it.

- Answer questions on direct proportion.
- Answer questions on inverse proportion.
- Find one number as a percentage of another.
- Find a given percentage of a number.
- Increase a price or amount by a given percentage.
- Decrease a price or amount by a given percentage.
- Calculate the percentage discount on a price.
- Calculate the VAT on an article, given the pre-VAT price.
- Calculate the VAT on an article, given the VAT-inclusive price.
- Calculate the VAT-inclusive price of an article, given the pre-VAT price.
- Calculate the pre-VAT price, given the VAT-inclusive price.
- Divide a given number or amount in a given ratio.
- Calculate individual shares of a number or amount divided in a given ratio.
- State ratios in their lowest terms.
- State ratios in the form $1 : n$.
- State ratios in the form $n : 1$.
- Work out the lengths involved in scale drawing.

Number preview

How much do you know already?

Exercise 2.1

1. Write 23.897 correct to two decimal places (2 d.p.).
2. Write 5468 to two significant figures (2 sig. figs.).
3. Change $\frac{2}{5}$ to **a)** a decimal **b)** a percentage.
4. Write the following numbers in standard form (scientific notation).
   a) 5 240 000 000 **b)** 0.000 005 24
5. Evaluate and write the answer in standard form.
   $(3.2 \times 10^9) \times (2.1 \times 10^{12})$
6. Evaluate and write the answer in standard form.
   $(1.4 \times 10^{15}) \div (6.8 \times 10^8)$
7. Write the following numbers in order of size starting with the smallest.
   1.3×10^{12}, 6.2×10^8, 1.7×10^{11}, 8.6×10^9, 7.3×10^8
8. Without using a calculator, calculate
   a) 15×9 **b)** $6 - 2.35$ **c)** $\frac{3}{4}$ of 36
   d) 20% of £7 **e)** $(-3) - 6$
9. Give your answers to the following as a power of 5 where possible.
   a) $5^5 \times 5^2$ **b)** $5^5 + 5^2$ **c)** $5^5 \div 5^2$

By the end of this chapter you will be able to:

- carry out calculations without a calculator
- round a decimal fraction to a given number of decimal places or significant figures
- round to the nearest 0.5, 1, 10, 50, 100, etc.
- apply the rules of powers or indices
- express a decimal number in standard form
- answer questions involving rates, such as speed
- express time as a proper decimal

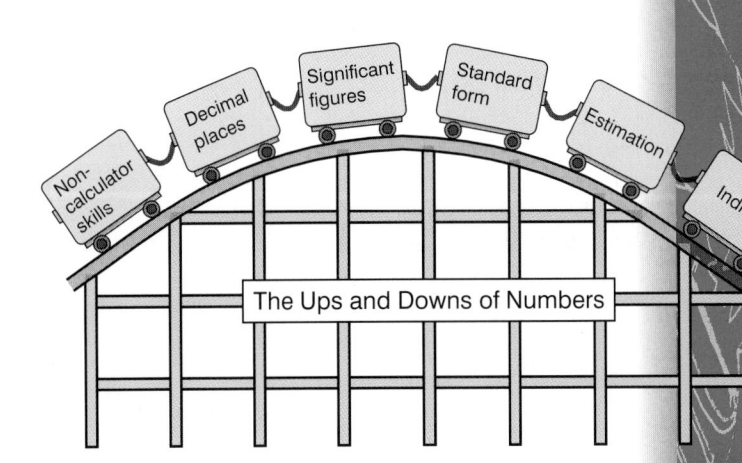

Revise Standard Grade and Intermediate Maths

10 a) A car travels at 96km/h. How far does it go in 3 hours 40 minutes?

b) How long would it take the car travelling at this speed to travel 120km? Give your answer in hours and minutes.

11 Evaluate $(-7) \times (-3)$, without using a calculator.

12 Evaluate $-14 \div 2$, without using a calculator.

Answers

1. 23.90
2. 5500
3. a) 0.4 b) 40%
4. a) 5.24×10^9 b) 5.24×10^{-6}
5. 6.72×10^{21}
6. 2.06×10^6
7. $6.2 \times 10^8, 7.3 \times 10^8, 8.6 \times 10^9, 1.7 \times 10^{11}, 1.3 \times 10^{12}$
8. a) 135 b) 3.65 c) 27 d) £1.40 e) -9
9. a) 5^7 b) You cannot simplify this as a power of 5.
   c) 5^3
10. a) 352 km b) 1 hour 15 minutes
11. 21
12. -7

How did you get on?

All questions right?
Well done! Skim through the rest of the chapter because we have some new methods which might appeal to you.

Less than full marks?
This chapter is not very long, and you shouldn't find it too difficult.

Non-calculator numerical skills

In one of the papers in the examination (Paper 1) you will not be allowed to use a calculator. You will need to carry out calculations involving whole numbers (sometimes called integers), decimals, fractions and percentages, without the help of a calculator. The following exercises will give you practice in answering non-calculator questions. If you have any problems Ringo is here to help you.

Example 2.1

a) Find 25% of £60.
b) Find the total cost of 5 CDs at £3.99 each.
c) Evaluate $7.3 + 2.1 + 3.9$

Solution

a) Learn that
$10\% = \frac{1}{10}$
$20\% = \frac{1}{5}$
$25\% = \frac{1}{4}$
$33\frac{1}{3}\% = \frac{1}{3}$
$50\% = \frac{1}{2}$

25% of £60 = $\frac{1}{4}$ of £60 = £15

b) *The CDs cost roughly £4. Then take away the extra 1p for each CD.*

$5 \times £3.99$ is roughly $5 \times £4 = £20$

£20 less $(5 \times 1p) = £19.95$

Note: You will need to learn your multiplication tables up to at least 9×9.

c) *Add the 2.1 and 3.9 first of all and the calculation will be easier.*

$7.3 + 2.1 + 3.9 = 7.3 + 6 = 13.3$

Exercise 2.2

1 a) $461 + 75 + 219$ **b)** $2460 - 926$
   c) 2015×6 **d)** $72 \div 8$

2 a) $6.11 + 3.45$ **b)** $7.2 - 3.8$
   c) 8.25×3 **d)** $18.6 \div 2$
   e) 13.5×100 **f)** $27.3 \div 10$

3 a) $\frac{1}{3}$ of £12   **b)** $\frac{1}{2}$ of £2.30
   c) $\frac{1}{5}$ of £10.20   **d)** $\frac{1}{7}$ of 21 metres

4 a) 10% of 80km   **b)** 20% of £56
   c) 25% of 116mm   **d)** $33\frac{1}{3}\%$ of £60
   e) 50% of £7.24

5 The temperature at 8pm was 2°C. By midnight it had fallen by 6°C. What was the temperature at midnight?

Answers

1 a) 755 b) °1534 c) 12 090 d) 9
2 a) 9.56 b) 3.4 c) 24.75 d) 9.3 e) 1350 f) 2.73
3 a) £4 b) £1.15 c) £2.04 d) 3 metres
4 a) 8km b) £11.20 c) 29mm d) £20 e) £3.62
5 −4°C

Example 2.2

a) 46×19
b) $\frac{3}{4}$ of 280
c) $5 \times 17 \times 2$
d) $4.2 - 1.9 + 0.8$
e) $17\frac{1}{2}\%$ of £56

Solution

a) It would be easier to pretend the 19 was a 20 and then subtract 46×1.

$46 \times 20 = 920$

$920 - (46 \times 1) = 874$

b) Divide by 4 first and then multiply by 3 because it is easier to work with smaller numbers.

$\frac{3}{4}$ of $280 = 3 \times 70 = 210$

c) Multiply the 5 by the 2 first because it is much easier to divide by 10.

$5 \times 17 \times 2 = 10 \times 17 = 170$

d) Add the 0.8 to the 4.2 to make it a whole number.

$4.2 - 1.9 + 0.8 = 5 - 1.9 = 3.1$

e) First find 10%, 5% and 2.5%.

10% of £56 = $\frac{1}{10}$ of £56 = £5.60
5% of £56 = $\frac{1}{2}$ of £5.60 = £2.80
2.5% of £56 = $\frac{1}{2}$ of £2.80 = £1.40
                                    ─────
                                    £9.80

Exercise 2.3

1 a) 28×11 b) 15×29
2 a) $1.217 + 3.206$ b) $7 - 2.165$
   c) 6.225×4 d) $1.008 \div 2$
   e) 0.119×1000 f) $1.765 \div 10$
3 a) $\frac{3}{5}$ of £70 b) $\frac{4}{5}$ of £2.25
   c) $\frac{2}{3}$ of 60p d) $\frac{3}{4}$ of 20 metres
   e) $\frac{1}{2} - \frac{1}{4}$ f) $\frac{7}{8} - \frac{1}{4}$
   g) $\frac{1}{2} \times \frac{1}{4}$ f) $10 \times 6\frac{1}{2}$
4 a) 60% of £20 b) 30% of £14.50
   c) 5% of £4.80
5 a) $2 + (-3)$ b) $(-4) + (-11)$
   c) $(-2) - 3$ d) $(-11) + 4$
   e) $4 \times (-5)$
   f) The temperature in Elgin is −10°C. The temperature in Glasgow is −1°C. How much colder is it in Elgin than in Glasgow?

Answers

1 a) 308 b) 435
2 a) 4.423 b) 4.835 c) 24.9 d) 0.504 e) 119 f) 0.1765
3 a) £42 b) £1.80 c) 40p d) 15 metres e) $\frac{1}{4}$ f) $\frac{5}{8}$ g) $\frac{1}{8}$ h) 65
4 a) £12 b) £4.35 c) £0.24 or 24p
5 a) −1 b) −15 c) −5 d) −7 e) −20 f) 9°C colder (or a difference of −9°C)

Example 2.3

a) $3 + 4 \times 6$ b) $18 - 6 \div 2$

Solution

a) You must do the multiplication first.

$3 + 4 \times 6 = 3 + 24 = 27$

b) You must do the division first.

$18 - 6 \div 2 = 18 - 3 = 15$

Revise Standard Grade and Intermediate Maths

Exercise 2.4

1. $14.5 + 6.2 \times 8$
2. $3 - 2\frac{1}{2} \times 9$
3. $17 + 14.4 \div 3$
4. $15 \div 2.5 + 2$
5. $2\frac{1}{4} + 5\frac{1}{3}$
6. $4\frac{1}{5} - 1\frac{1}{2}$
7. $\frac{2}{3} \times \frac{3}{4}$
8. $\frac{3}{5} \div \frac{1}{3}$
9. $(-4) \times (-7)$
10. $(-8) \div 2$
11. $18 \div (-3)$

Answers

1. 62
2. −15
3. 21
4. 7
5. $7\frac{7}{12}$
6. $2\frac{7}{10}$
7. $\frac{6}{12}$ or $\frac{1}{2}$
8. $\frac{9}{5}$ or $1\frac{4}{5}$
9. 28
10. −4
11. −6

Rounding

Decimal places

The number of decimal places is the number of digits (figures) that there are in a number, **to the right of the decimal point**.

Example 2.4

Write 4.782 correct to 1 d.p.

Solution

Write the number, and put a ring round the digit which is **one figure to the right** of the required decimal place e.g. 4.7⑧2.

Now decide whether to round up or down by looking at the number which you have ringed. If it is less than 5, you usually round *down*, but if it is 5 or more, you usually round *up*.

4.782 = 4.8 correct to 1 d.p.

Example 2.5

Write 7.304 correct to 2 d.p.

Solution

7.304 = 7.30 correct to 2 d.p.

As the question asks for 2 d.p. you must include the zero.

If the question asks you to give an amount of money to the nearest penny, you are really rounding to two decimal places. If you have to round to the nearest 0.1 cm, you need one decimal place.

Significant figures

The first significant figure is the first digit greater than zero starting from the left.

Example 2.6

Write 28.3762 correct to 3 sig. figs.

Solution

Ring the figure **to the right** of the required number of significant figures. If it is 5 or more, round up; if it is 4 or less round down.

28.3⑦62 = 28.4 to 3 sig. figs.

Example 2.7

Write 7 143 680 correct to 2 sig. figs.

Solution

It may helpful to notice that large numbers, bigger than 9999, are usually written with spaces before every third number, starting from the right.

7 1④3 680

The original number is approximately 7 million, so you must be careful to indicate this in your answer by including appropriate zeros. Try writing the original number with a decimal point at the end, and write the approximation directly below.

7 143 680.

7 100 000.

7 143 680 to 2 sig. figs. is 7 100 000.

Remember the zeros. Don't write your answer as 71.

Example 2.8

Write 0.000 759 6 correct to:

a) 1 sig. fig.   b) 2 sig. figs.   c) 3 sig. figs.

Solution

Note that 7 is the first significant figure as it is the first non-zero digit starting from the left.

a) 0.000 759 6 = 0.0008 to 1 sig. fig.

b) 0.000 759 6 = 0.000 76 to 2 sig. figs.

c) 0.000 759 6 = 0.000 760 to 3 sig. figs.

Remember to include the final zero as it is the third significant figure.

Indices

In the number 2^3, the 3 is called the **power** or the **index**. (The plural of index is indices.) 2^3 means $2 \times 2 \times 2$, **not** 2×3.

Remember: $2 \times 2 = 2^2 = 4$

Rules of indices

1. You can only simplify indices when the base number is the same.

2. When dividing or multiplying powers of the same number remember TIP and DIM.

Madam Attix has a card for it.

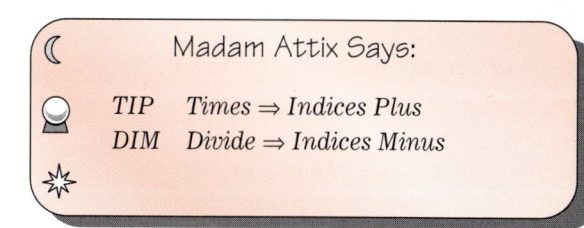

> Madam Attix Says:
>
> TIP Times ⇒ Indices Plus
> DIM Divide ⇒ Indices Minus

Example 2.9

Simplify the following.

a) $3^2 \times 3^5$ b) $3^7 \div 3^2$ c) $3^2 + 3^5$

d) $4^3 - 4^2$

Solution

a) $3^2 \times 3^5 = 3^7$

b) $3^7 \div 3^2 = 3^5$

c) $3^2 + 3^5$ cannot be simplified as a power of 3.

d) $4^3 - 4^2$ cannot be simplified as a power of 4.

Standard form or scientific notation

This is a shorthand method of writing very large or very small numbers. It involves rewriting the number as a number between 1 and 10, multiplied by a power of 10.

Remember:

$10^1 = 10$

$10^2 = 100$

$10^3 = 1000$

$10^8 = 100 000 000$

and so on.

Be careful! $10^0 = 1$

Revise Standard Grade and Intermediate Maths

Example 2.10

Write 34 200 in standard form (scientific notation).

Solution

Rewrite your original number, inserting a decimal point after the first non-zero digit.

3.4200

Note that the decimal point was originally at the right-hand end of the number.

34 200.

3.4200   How many places has the point moved?

Ronnie Mauver the dare-devil rider, moves the decimal point four places in the positive direction.

$34\,200 = 3.42 \times 10^4$

The simplest way is to count the number of decimal places you need to return the decimal point to its starting position and write this as a power of 10.

Example 2.11

Write 0.000 067 in standard form.

Solution

Ronnie Mauver jumps back five places.

This means that the power will be negative.

Rewriting the original and inserting the required decimal point gives:

000006.7

0.000067

$0.000\,067 = 6.7 \times 10^{-5}$

If your original number is smaller than zero (as it is in this case), write the power of 10 with a negative sign. Remember that if you need to travel back to the start in a negative direction, you need a negative sign.

Exercise 2.5

1. Write 1 700 000 in standard form (scientific notation).
2. Write 0.0000035 in standard form (scientific notation).
3. Evaluate $(2.3 \times 10^6) \times (4.1 \times 10^5)$. Give your answer in standard form.
4. Evaluate $(3.4 \times 10^{22}) \div (1.6 \times 10^9)$. Give your answer in standard form, correct to three significant figures.
5. The speed of light is approximately 2.998×10^8 metres per second. How many metres does it travel in half a minute?

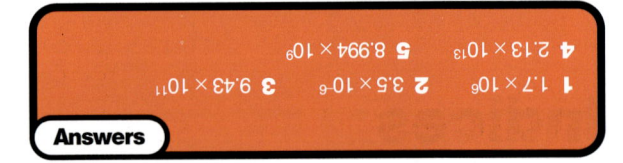

Answers

1. 1.7×10^6 2. 3.5×10^{-6} 3. 9.43×10^{11} 4. 2.13×10^{13} 5. 8.994×10^9

Converting time to a decimal number

A common mistake with hours and minutes is to write 2 hours and 45 minutes as 2.45. **This is wrong!**

Remember: There are 60 minutes in an hour.

Think of 45 minutes as $\frac{45}{60}$ of an hour.

So 45 minutes = $45 \div 60 = 0.75$ of an hour (three-quarters of an hour) and 2 hours 45 minutes is 2.75 hours.

Or use the fraction button!

2 hours 45 minutes

= [2] [a^b/$_c$] [4] [5] [a^b/$_c$] [6] [0]

If you press [=], it simplifies the fraction. Then you need to convert this to a decimal. Most calculators will do this if you press the fraction key [a^b/$_c$] again, but on some you need to press the [2nd f] or [inv] key followed by a different button.

Introducing our famous juggler, Willie Droppitt

And now we invite you to marvel at our latest attraction, the one and only Willie Droppitt, who can help you to juggle formulae. He is here to help you with the next section.

Using formulae

The infallible Willie Droppitt method

To find the value of a letter firstly cover it or cross it out. If the uncovered letters are:

a) on the same level, multiply them

b) on different levels, divide the top one by the bottom one.

Willie Droppitt in action!

Distance, speed, time

$D = S \times T$ $S = \dfrac{D}{T}$ $T = \dfrac{D}{S}$

*Remember **D**owning St.*

Amount, rate, time

$A = R \times T$ $R = \dfrac{A}{T}$ $T = \dfrac{A}{R}$

Remember ART.

Example 2.12

Ella Von Urri drives at 120 km/h. How far does she travel in 3 hours and 25 minutes?

Solution

Firstly, **do not** write 3 hours 25 minutes as 3.25.

3 hours 25 minutes = $3 + \dfrac{25}{60}$ or

[3] [a^b/$_c$] [2] [5] [a^b/$_c$] [6] [0]

You are asked for the distance. Cover or cross out D.

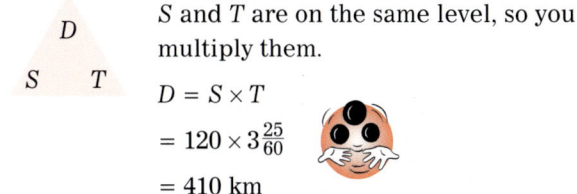

S and T are on the same level, so you multiply them.

$D = S \times T$

$= 120 \times 3\dfrac{25}{60}$

$= 410$ km

Example 2.13

Hywel Menditt's tap is leaking at a rate of 25 cm³ per second. How long does it take to fill a 1 litre bowl? (1 litre = 1000 cm³)

Solution

$T = \dfrac{A}{R}$

$= \dfrac{1000}{25}$

$= 40$ seconds

Don't mix units. The rate is in cm^3, so change the litre into cm^3.

Similarly, if the question involves cm and m, change the metres into centimetres.

Example 2.14

Jenny Da Lifte has to travel 210 kilometres in 3 hours and 30 minutes. Find her average speed in kilometres per hour.

Solution

3 hours 30 minutes = 3.5 hours (not 3.3 hours)

$$S = \frac{D}{T}$$

$$= \frac{210}{3.5}$$

$$= 60 \text{ km/h}$$

Keep this to yourself, but you may find these techniques useful in Physics, too!

Exercise 2.6

In this exercise you have the chance to practise some of the techniques that are covered in chapters 1 and 2. If there is a question that you cannot answer, look back through both chapters for some clues.

1 a) Write a time of 3 hours 24 minutes in decimal form.
  b) Write the decimal form of 5.7 hours in hours and minutes.

2 A teenager plans to spend 40% of each weekday either at school or studying at home.
  a) How many hours a day is this?
  b) Express your answer to **a)** in hours and minutes.
  c) If she counts the school day as lasting 6 hours 30 minutes altogether, how many hours per day does she plan to spend studying at home?
  d) What percentage of the day is spent studying at home, to the nearest 1%?

3 a) A car travels at a speed of 96 km/h. How long does it take to complete a journey of 796.8 km?
  b) Another car completes the same journey in 7 hours 15 minutes. What is its average speed?

4 Water flows out of a leaking tank at the rate of 5.2 litres per second. If the tank originally holds 135 litres, how long would it take for it to empty?

5 A car travels 18.6 km on 4.4 litres of petrol.
  a) How far does it go on 20 litres?
  b) How many litres would it use to travel 100 km?

6 Write the following numbers in standard form.
  a) 2 380 000 000 000
  b) 0.000 000 007 23
  c) 14 678.3 (Write this answer correct to three significant figures.)

Answers

1 a) 3.4 hours **b)** 5 hours 42 minutes
2 a) 9.6 hours **b)** 9 hours 36 minutes
  c) 3 hours 6 minutes or 3.1 hours **d)** 13%
3 a) 8.3 hours = 8 hours 18 minutes **b)** 110 km/h (3 s.f.)
4 26 seconds (2 s.f.)
5 a) 84.5 km (1 d.p.) **b)** 23.7 litres (1 d.p.)
6 a) 2.38×10^{12} **b)** 7.23×10^{-9} **c)** 1.47×10^4

(**Remember:** Any number written to the power of zero is 1.)

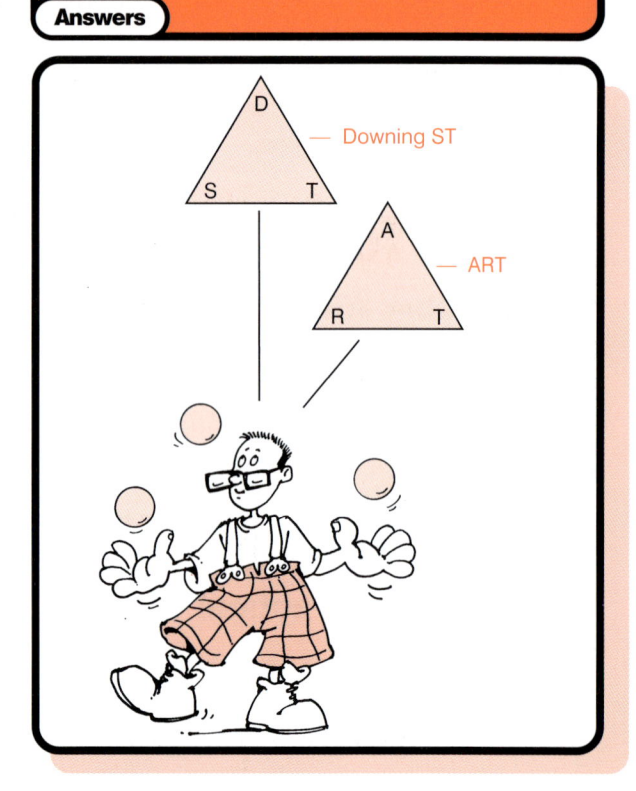

Number

review
How much have you learnt?

Tick off each topic in the list when you are confident you can cope with it.

- ⬤ Carry out calculations without a calculator.
- ⬤ Round a decimal fraction to a given number of decimal places.
- ⬤ Round a number to a given number of significant figures.
- ⬤ Round to the nearest 0.5, 1, 10, 50, 100 etc.
- ⬤ Apply the rules of powers or indices.
- ⬤ Express a decimal number in standard form.
- ⬤ Answer questions involving rates, such as speed.
- ⬤ Express time as a proper decimal.

If you have mastered this chapter and Chapter 1, Proportion, percentages and ratio, it is time for you to tackle the Number review, on page 22.

Number review

1. Evaluate the following without using your calculator.
   a) 2.3 × 9
   b) 7.06 − 0.5
   c) $\frac{1}{7}$ of 91
   d) $\frac{1}{2} + \frac{2}{3}$
   e) $\frac{3}{7} \times \frac{2}{5}$
   f) $33\frac{1}{3}\%$ of £45
   g) (−2) + (−4)
   h) $(−3)^2$

2. Two people score points in the ratio of 7 : 2. If the higher score was 42, what was the lower?

3. Express $\frac{33}{60}$ as a percentage.

4. When going on holiday, a man converts £620 into 4700 French francs.
   a) If his friend changes £590, how many francs will he receive?
   b) If they have a total of 1210 francs at the end of the holiday, what would this be worth in pounds?

5. A train travels 288 kilometres in 2 hours 10 minutes. What was its average speed in km/h?

6. Write 0.000 007 02 in standard form.

7. A club of 130 people hires coaches for an event. If each coach can hold 30 people, how many coaches must be hired?

8. The price of a jacket, usually set at £75, is reduced by 15% in a sale. Find the sale price.

Answers

1 a) 20.7 b) 6.56 c) 13 d) $1\frac{1}{6}$ e) $\frac{6}{35}$ f) £15 g) −6 h) 9
2 12
3 55%
4 a) 4472.58 francs b) £159.62
5 133 km/h (3 s.f.)
6 7.02×10^{-6}
7 5 (Remember to round up!)
8 £63.75

3 Algebra

preview

By the end of this chapter you will be able to:

- solve simple linear equations in one unknown
- explain the meaning of the words coefficient, constant and variable
- solve simple linear inequalities
- make expressions and equations from statements
- solve simultaneous equations in two unknowns
- multiply out double brackets
- factorise algebraic expressions
- solve quadratic equations by factorising
- solve quadratic equations by use of formula
- rearrange formulae
- solve problems involving inverse or joint variation

How much do you know already?

Exercise 3.1

1 Solve for x.
$7x + 2 = 10x - 13$

2 Solve for x and y.
$4x + 3y = 41$
$5x - 2y = 34$

3 Solve this equation for x.
$x^2 - 17x - 18 = 0$

4 Rearrange the formula below to make c the subject.
$t = ad - c^2$

5 Solve the inequality.
$2x + 3 \geq 17$

6 Find the value of $x(xy^2 - 3)$ when $x = 5$ and $y = -2$.

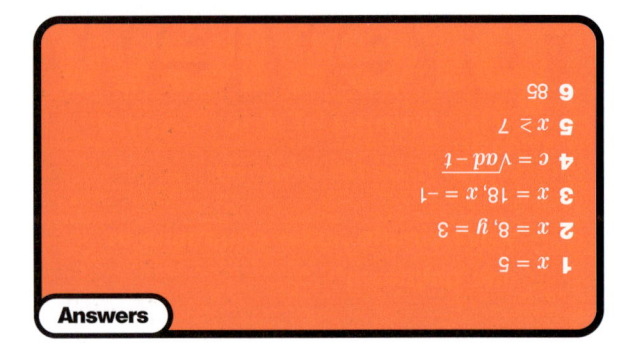

Answers
1. $x = 5$
2. $x = 8, y = 3$
3. $x = 18, x = -1$
4. $c = \sqrt{ad - 1}$
5. $x \geq 7$
6. 85

How did you get on?

All of them right?
Have you considered taking a Maths degree?

Four or more right?
You must do Higher Maths next year!

Fewer than four right?
The bad news is that this is probably the most difficult chapter in the book. The good news is that our easy methods will make it less difficult and will boost your marks.

Don't let Algebra spook you – our methods are guaranteed ghost busters.

Just to recap
$ab = a \times b$

$\dfrac{a}{b} = a \div b$

$3a = 3 \times a$

$3a^2 = 3 \times a^2 = 3 \times a \times a$

$(3a)^2 = 3a \times 3a = 9a^2$

$-a \times -a = a^2$

$-a \times b = -ab$

Non-calculator skills in algebra

Example 3.1

a) Find the value of $12y - 7$ when $y = 8$.

Solution
$12y - 7 = 12 \times 8 - 7$
$= 96 - 7$
$= 89$

b) Find the value of $6ab$ when $a = 5$ and $b = -4$.

Solution
$6ab = 6 \times a \times b$
$= 6 \times 5 \times -4$
$= 30 \times -4$
$= -120$

c) Find the value of $2t^2$ when $t = -7$.

Solution
$2t^2 = 2 \times t \times t$
$= 2 \times -7 \times -7$
$= 2 \times 49$
$= 98$

Simple equations

How much do you know already about equations?

Here are some straightforward equations for you to try, just to see how much algebra you have taken in during all those Maths lessons you have sat through over the years.

Exercise 3.2

Evaluate (find the value of) x in the following equations.

1 $x + 2 = 20$

2 $x - 3 = 15.5$

3 $2x + 1 = 15$

Algebra

4 $5x - 2 = 33$

5 $16 = 24 - 2x$

6 $5x + 20 = 5$

7 $\frac{x}{2} = 10$

8 $\frac{x}{3} + 1 = 5$

9 $5x + 2 = 3x + 18$

10 $2x - 1 = 5x - 28$

Answers

1 18
2 18.5
3 7
4 7
5 4
6 −3
7 20
8 12
9 8
10 9

If you managed to get the whole exercise right without our help, you can skip the next section, and turn to 'Simplifying expressions' on page 27. However, if things did not go so well, don't despair, because all the way from Bavaria, to help with solving equations, we are proud to introduce our conjuror, the one and only Hans Zoff.

Meet Hans Zoff
Whatever Hans Zoff does to one side of the equation, he does to the other.

Example 3.2

Find x if $5x + 3 = 23$.

Solution

$$5x + 3 = 23$$
$$\underline{\quad -3 \quad -3 \quad}$$ Take 3 from both sides.
$$5x = 20$$
$$\underline{\quad \div 5 \quad \div 5 \quad}$$ Divide both sides by 5.
$$x = 4$$

Check: Put your answer into the original equation to see if your answer is correct.

$5 \times 4 + 3 = 23$

Example 3.3 – Using a subtraction sign

Find x if $2x - 5 = 17$.

Solution

$$2x - 5 = 17$$
$$\underline{\quad +5 \quad +5 \quad}$$ Add 5 to both sides.
$$2x = 22$$
$$\div 2 \quad \div 2$$ Divide both sides by 2
$$x = 11$$ Remember to **check** your answer!

Example 3.4 – With a negative coefficient of x

Solve the equation $4 = 16 - 3x$ to find x.

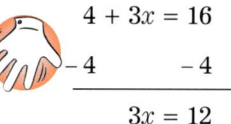

Solution

$$4 = 16 - 3x$$
$$\underline{\quad +3x \quad +3x \quad}$$ Add $3x$ to both sides.
$$4 + 3x = 16$$
$$\underline{\quad -4 \quad -4 \quad}$$ Subtract 4 from both sides.
$$3x = 12$$
$$x = 4$$ **Check** your answer!

Revise Standard Grade and Intermediate Maths

Example 3.5 – Negative answer

Find x if $3x + 10 = 4$.

Solution

$$3x + 10 = 4$$
$$ -10 \quad -10 \qquad \text{Subtract 10 from both sides.}$$
$$3x = -6$$
$$\div 3 \quad \div 3 \qquad \text{Divide both sides by 3.}$$
$$x = -2 \qquad \text{Because } -6 \div 3 = -2!$$

Check your answer!

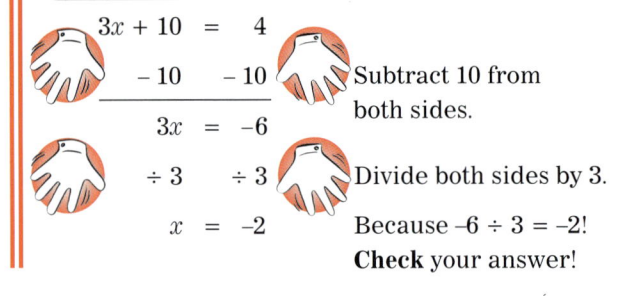

Example 3.6 – Fractional answer

Find x if $6x - 1 = 2$.

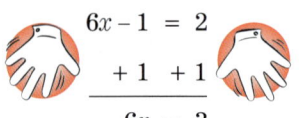

Solution

$$6x - 1 = 2$$
$$+1 \quad +1 \qquad \text{Add 1 to both sides.}$$
$$6x = 3$$
$$\div 6 \quad \div 6 \qquad \text{Divide both sides by 6 (not } 6 \div 3\text{).}$$
$$x = \tfrac{1}{2} \qquad \text{Check your answer!}$$

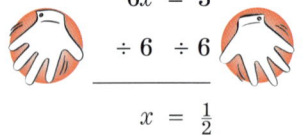

A common error here would be to have an answer of 2. This is one reason why we tell you to check your answer. You should always divide by the **coefficient** of x (which in this case is 6) at this point.

Here are two words to impress your teacher! A variable is a letter used to stand for an unknown number. In many examples the letter used is x, but you can use any letter. A coefficient is simply a number in front of a variable. For example, the coefficient of x in 4x is 4, the coefficient of a^2 in $-5a^2$ is -5.

Example 3.7 – Using fractional coefficients

Given that $\dfrac{x}{2} + 1 = 11$, find the value of x.

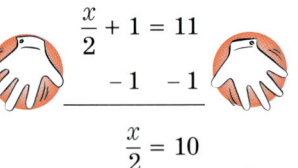

Solution

$$\frac{x}{2} + 1 = 11$$
$$-1 \quad -1 \qquad \text{Subtract 1 from both sides.}$$
$$\frac{x}{2} = 10$$
$$\times 2 \quad \times 2 \qquad \text{Multiply both sides by 2.}$$
$$x = 20 \qquad \text{Check your answer!}$$

Balancing act: questions with variables on both sides

In this type of question, you need to take the variables (usually x) on to one side and the rest of the numbers on to the other.

Example 3.8

Find the value of x which satisfies $4x + 7 = 2x + 37$.

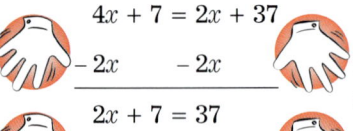

Solution

$$4x + 7 = 2x + 37$$
$$-2x \qquad -2x \qquad \text{Take } 2x \text{ from both sides.}$$
$$2x + 7 = 37$$
$$-7 \quad -7 \qquad \text{Subtract 7 from both sides.}$$
$$2x = 30$$
$$\div 2 \quad \div 2 \qquad \text{Divide both sides by 2.}$$
$$x = 15 \qquad \text{Check your answer!}$$

Linear inequalities

Inequalities are very similar to equations, but with two important differences.

1. If you swap the entire left and right-hand sides then the inequality reverses.
2. If you multiply or divide by a negative number, the the inequality sign is reversed.

Example 3.9

Solve the inequality. $3 - 2x < 7$

Solution

Method 1 – taking the $2x$ over to make the coefficient positive.

$3 < 2x + 7$

$2x + 7 > 3$ Swapping the sides and reversing the inequality (Rule 1)

Method 2 – dividing by -2

$3 - 2x < 7$

$-2x < 4$

$x > -2$ The inequality reverses when dividing by a negative number (Rule 2)

TAKE A BREAK

It's probably time for a break now. This is a long chapter, so don't try to do too much at any one sitting.

Simplifying expressions

Remember: When simplifying expressions, you can only add or subtract like with like. Our pet lions Fee Roshus and Nora Nedoff will demonstrate why.

If a lion is x and a lion tamer is y, then 2 lions and 2 lion tamers can be represented by

$2x + 2y$

Then 2 lions and 2 lion tamers *minus* 1 lion tamer can be represented by

$2x + 2y - y = 2x + y$

Example 3.10

Simplify the following.

a) $x + x$
b) $x + x + y + 3$
c) $x^2 + x$
d) $x^2 + x^2 + x + 2x$
e) $x^2 + xy + xy + y + 3$

Solution

a) $x + x = 2x$
b) $x + x + y + 3 = 2x + y + 3$
c) $x^2 + x$ cannot be simplified
d) $x^2 + x^2 + x + 2x = 2x^2 + 3x$
e) $x^2 + xy + xy + y + 3 = x^2 + 2xy + y + 3$

How good are you at simplifying expressions?

Exercise 3.3

Simplify the following expressions where possible.

1. $3a + 2a + 5a + b$
2. $10c + 5a - 2a$
3. $2a^2 - a$
4. $6t + 5t^2 - 8t$
5. $5b^2 + 3b - 7b^2$
6. $12x - x^2 - 3x + 10x^2$

Answers
1. $10a + b$
2. $10c + 3a$
3. Cannot be simplified.
4. $5t^2 - 2t$
5. $3b - 2b^2$
6. $9x^2 + 9x$

Expansion of single brackets

Multiply the number outside the bracket with each term inside. Exam questions say "Multiply out the brackets" or "Expand".

Example 3.11

Multiply out the brackets $3(2x + 5)$.

Solution

$3(2x + 5) \quad 3(2x + 5)$

$3(2x + 5) = 3 \times 2x + 3 \times 5$

$3(2x + 5) = 6x + 15$

You only need the last line – the others are optional.

Example 3.12

Expand $a(b - c)$.

Solution

$a(b - c) \quad a(b - c)$

$a(b - c) = a \times b + a \times -c$

$a(b - c) = ab - ac$

Remember: The sign is always attached to the number that follows it – which is why we have ringed $-c$.

Example 3.13

Multiply out the brackets $-4(3x + 2y)$.

Solution

$-4(3x + 2y) \quad -4(3x + 2y)$

$-4(3x + 2y) = -4 \times 3x - 4 \times 2y$

$-4(3x + 2y) = -12x - 8y$

Remember: The negative sign is attached to the 4.

Algebra

Example 3.14

Simplify $2x(y-4) - 3(2x-1)$.

Solution

$2x(y-4) - 3(2x-1) = 2xy - 8x - 6x + 3$
$ = 2xy - 14x + 3$

Example 3.15

Simplify $2x - (x-4)$.

Solution

As there is no number immediately outside the brackets, it is a good idea to put in a 1. That way there is less chance of getting the sign wrong when you expand the brackets.

$2x - (x-4) = 2x - 1(x-4)$
$ = 2x - x + 4$
$ = x + 4$

Remember: $-1 \times -4 = +4$

Exercise 3.4

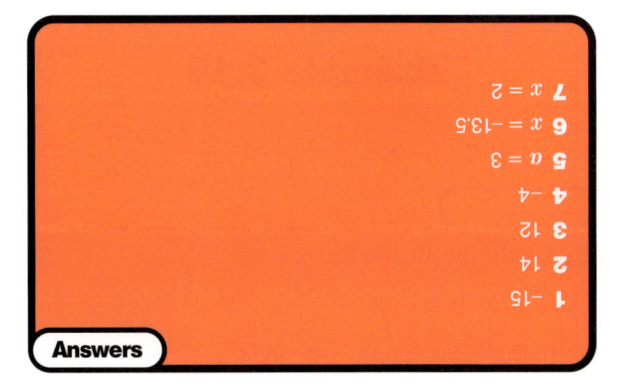

Simplify the following expressions.

1. $3(2x + 4) + 2(x + 3)$
2. $2(x + y) + 3(x + 2y)$
3. $2x(y + 4) + y(x - 3)$
4. $a(2 + a) - 3(a - a^2)$
5. $3(2a + 3) - (a - 3)$

Answers
1. $8x + 18$
2. $5x + 8y$
3. $3xy + 8x - 3y$
4. $4a^2 - a$
5. $5a + 12$

Simple equations with brackets

To find x, expand the brackets, simplify and solve (or evaluate) as we did before.

Example 3.16

Find x where $3(2x-1) - 4(x-1) = 15$.

Solution

$3(2x-1) - 4(x-1) = 15$
$6x - 3 - 4x + 4 = 15$
$2x + 1 = 15$
$2x = 14$
$x = 7$

Exercise 3.5

Solve each equation for x.

1. $5(x + 20) = 25$
2. $4(x - 2) = 2(x + 10)$
3. $2 - (x - 3) = -7$
4. $2(x - 1) = 5(x + 2)$
5. $7 - (a - 3) = 3a - 2$
6. $3(x - 4) = 5(x + 3)$
7. $4(x - 2) + 2(x + 5) = 14$

Answers
1. -15
2. 14
3. 12
4. -4
5. $a = 3$
6. $x = -13.5$
7. $x = 2$

Factorising using single brackets

Factorising means splitting a number into its factors. For example, the factors of 12 are 1, 2, 3, 4, 6 and 12. When you factorise you need to find the **highest common factors**, i.e. the biggest numbers or letters that 'go into' all the terms.

Example 3.17

Find the highest common factors of each pair of numbers.

a) 4 and 10

b) 20 and 5

c) a and a^2

d) y^2 and y^3

Solution

a) 2 $4 = 2 \times 2$, $10 = 5 \times 2$

so the highest common factor, or HCF of 4 and 10 is 2.

b) 5 $20 = 4 \times 5$, $5 = 1 \times 5$

so the HCF of 20 and 5 is 5.

c) a $a^2 = a \times a$

so the HCF of a and a^2 is a.

d) y^2 $y^2 = y \times y$ and $y^3 = y \times y \times y$

so their HCF is $y \times y = y^2$.

Example 3.18

Factorise $10z^2b - 6za$.

Solution

Start with the 10 and the 6.

Their HCF is 2.

Write the 2 outside the brackets.

2( )

If you were simplifying, as you did in the section above, you would have to have 5 and 3 in the brackets in order to multiply out correctly.

$2(5z^2b - 3za)$

Inside the brackets you still have z^2 and z. Their HCF is z, so you can write that outside the brackets as well. As you must be able to multiply out the factorised expression to find the original again, the solution is:

$10z^2b - 6za = 2z(5zb - 3a)$

The letters a and b appear in one term only, so they stay inside the brackets.

Example 3.19

Factorise $6x^2y + 18xy^2$ fully.

Solution

The HCF of 6 and 18 is 6.

$6x^2y + 18xy^2 = 6(x^2y + 3xy^2)$

If it helps, you can cross out the factors as you go along:

$6x^2y + 18xy^2 = 6(x^2y + 3xy^2)$

or

$6x^2y + 18xy^2 = 6(x^2y + 3xy^2)$

The HCF of x^2 and x is x.

$6(x^2y + 3xy^2) = 6x(xy + 3y^2)$

or

$6(x^2y + 3xy^2) = 6x(xy + 3y^2)$

The HCF of y and y^2 is y.

$6x(xy + 3y^2) = 6xy(x + 3y)$

or

$6x(xy + 3y^2) = 6xy(x + 3y)$

So $6x^2y + 18xy^2 = 6xy(x + 3y)$

Check your answer by multiplying out the brackets to make sure that both sides are the same.

Algebra

Example 3.20

Factorise $12a^2b^2 - 4ab$ fully.

Solution

The HCF of 12 and 4 is 4.

$12a^2b^2 - 4ab = 4(3a^2b^2 - ab)$

or

$\overset{3}{\cancel{12}}a^2b^2 - \cancel{4}ab = 4(3a^2b^2 - ab)$

The HCF of a^2 and a is a.

$4(3a^2b^2 - ab) = 4a(3ab^2 - b)$

or

$4(3a\cancel{^2}b^2 - \cancel{a}b) = 4a(3ab^2 - b)$

The HCF of b^2 and b is b.

So $4a(3ab^2 - b) = 4ab(3ab - 1)$

or

$4a(3ab\cancel{^2} - \overset{1}{\cancel{b}}) = 4ab(3ab - 1)$

If all the factors of a term are taken outside the brackets, you have to replace them inside the brackets with a 1, so that when you multiply out the brackets you will get back to your original expression.

Exercise 3.6

Factorise the following expressions.

1 $24x - 12$

2 $16ab + 10bc$

3 $4c^2 - 2ac$

4 $10a^2b^2 - 5a$

5 $2a - 10ab$

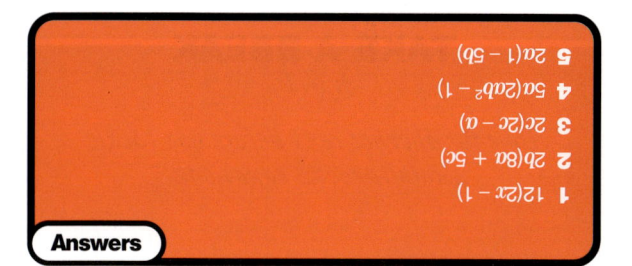

Answers

1 $12(2x - 1)$
2 $2b(8a + 5c)$
3 $2c(2c - a)$
4 $5a(2ab^2 - 1)$
5 $2a(1 - 5b)$

Making expressions and equations from statements

Expressions

Before you look at the solutions of the next example, see if you can work out the expressions by yourself.

Example 3.21

a) Noelle Mett, the stuntsperson, knows that her best friend is eight years younger than she is. If Noelle is x years old, write down an expression for the age of her friend.
(**Remember**: If you are asked for an expression, your answer will be in terms of a variable, such as x.)

Solution

a) $x - 8$

b) Lou Kout and Bea Ware are lion tamers. Lou Kout is very experienced – he has survived three weeks – so he is paid three times as much per week as Bea Ware. If Bea Ware earns y pounds per week, find Lou Kout's weekly wage.

Solution

b) $3y$

c) Paul E. Payde earns £5 per hour for his Saturday job.
   i) If he works n hours, how much does he get paid?
   ii) If he also gets £10 in tips, how much money will he take home?

Solution

c) i) $5n$ ii) $5n + 10$

31

Example 3.22

Eva Rupp is too heavy for acrobatics. She now weighs twice as much as her friend Honor Dyatt, who weighs x kg.

a) Write an expression for Eva's weight.

b) Write an expression for their combined weight.

   Simplify your expression.

c) If their combined weight is 138 kg, write an equation in x and solve it to find the weight of each of them.

Solution

Gaynor Mark's dictionary states that whenever you can write 'is' or 'are' in a sentence, you can replace the word by '='. In plain everyday English, it would make sense to say, 'Eva is twice as heavy as' instead of, 'Eva weighs twice as much as', so Eva's weight = 2 × Honor's weight.

a) As Honor's weight is x kg, Eva's = $2x$.

b) Their combined weight = $x + 2x = 3x$.

c) $3x = 138$ kg

   $x = 46$ kg so $2x = 92$ kg

   Honor Dyatt weighs 46 kg, Eva Rupp weighs 92 kg.

Exercise 3.7

1 Serge O'Hedd and Liza Round took a test. Serge O'Hedd scored ten marks more than Liza.
   a) If Liza's mark was y, find in terms of y:
      i) Serge's mark   ii) their total mark.
   b) If their total score was 65, write an equation in y and solve this to find their individual marks.

2 Vic Taurius and Bjorn Looza had several goes on the hoopla stall. Vic won three times as many prizes as Bjorn.
   a) If Bjorn Looza won n prizes, write an expression for the number won by Vic Taurius.
   b) Write an expression for the total number of prizes won.
   c) If, between them, they collected 68 prizes, how many prizes did Vic receive?

3 Besides being too heavy, Eva Rupp is now too old for the high wire. She is 20 years older than the current star, Honor Dyatt. Take Eva's age as x years.
   a) Write an expression in x for Honor Dyatt's age.
   b) In terms of x, how old will each be in two years' time?
   c) In two years' time Eva will be twice as old as Honor. Write this statement as an equation, and solve it to find their current ages.

4 Wanda Lust and her friend Sandie Beech are saving up to go on holiday. They find that Sandie has £30.00 less than Wanda. After six months of really saving hard, each has managed to save an extra £20.00. Take the amount that Wanda starts with as £x.
   a) Write an expression for the amount of money in pounds that Sandie has at the start.
   b) Write an expression for the amount of money in pounds that Wanda has after six months.
   c) Write an expression for the amount of money in pounds that Sandie has after six months.
   d) After six months Wanda has twice as much money as Sandie. Write this as an equation and solve it.

Answers

1 a) i) $y + 10$ ii) $2y + 10$
  b) $2y + 10 = 65$, $2y = 55$, $y = 27.5$, so Serge scored 37.5, Liza scored 27.5.
2 a) $3n$ b) $4n$ c) $4n = 68$, $n = 17$, Vic won 51 prizes.
3 a) $x - 20$ b) $x + 2$, $x - 18$
  c) $x + 2 = 2(x - 18)$, ages 18 and 38
4 a) $x - 30$ b) $x + 20$
  c) $x - 10$ because $x - 30 + 20 = x - 10$
  $x + 20 = 2(x - 10)$ so $x = 40$

TAKE A BREAK

Time for another rest before you tackle Simultaneous equations.

Simultaneous equations

Simultaneous equations are two equations involving two variables (usually x and y), and you are asked to find the values of x and y which satisfy both equations at once, or simultaneously.

> **Madam Attix Says:**
>
> **S**imultaneous **e**quations are **SEXY** because for **S**imultaneous **E**quations you need to find x and y.

There are several ways of solving simultaneous equations by algebra, but don't worry, we'll only show you one in this chapter.

Elimination

This is the most common method, and one that always works as long as you make sure all the variables are on the same side of the equations. If, for instance, you have $4x = 22 - 2y$, you must first rearrange it to get $4x + 2y = 22$.

Example 3.23 – The coefficients of either x or y are the same

Solve the following simultaneous equations.

$4x + 2y = 22$

$3x + 2y = 19$

Solution

Remember:

1. You must have the same coefficient in both equations for one of the letters (ignoring whether it is positive or negative). In our example there is a $2y$ in each of the equations.

2. If the signs of these are the same, you take away one equation from the other, and if the signs are opposite you add (plus) them.

> **Madam Attix Says:**
>
> **STOP** – **S**ame **T**ake, **O**pposite **P**lus.

3. In our example, both $2y$s are positive (same sign and 'same take, opposite plus'), so we must take away.

Box the terms that will cancel out.

$4x + \boxed{2y} = 22$
$3x + \boxed{2y} = 19$
$\overline{}$
$\qquad x = 3$

($4x - 3x = x$, $22 - 19 = 3$)

Remember: **S**imultaneous equations are *sexy* – you need to find both x and y.

Use the easier equation.

$3x + 2y = 19$
$9 + 2y = 19 \quad$ because $3x = 3 \times 3 = 9$
$2y = 10$
$y = 5$

Check: Use the other equation ($4x + 2y = 22$).

$4 \times 3 + 2 \times 5 = 22$

The answer is $x = 3$, $y = 5$.

Example 3.24

Find the values of x and y which satisfy these equations.

$3x + 2y = 16$

$x + y = 5$

Solution

$3x + 2y = 16 \quad$ 1

$x + y = 5 \quad$ 2

Ignoring the signs, are the coefficients of either variable (letter) the same? No.

Revise Standard Grade and Intermediate Maths

It is usually easier to multiply the equation with the lower coefficient to make the coefficients of either x or y the same (ignoring signs). As we have chosen to eliminate y, we have multiplied the second equation by 2. (If instead you chose to eliminate x, you would have to multiply the equation by 3.)

Remember: You need to multiply the whole equation.
If $x + y = 5$ then $2x + 2y = 10$.

$$\begin{array}{ll} 3x + 2y = 16 & 1 \\ 2x + 2y = 10 & 2 \times 2 \\ \hline x = 6 & \end{array}$$

The signs of the ys are the same, so we've taken one equation from the other.   **STOP**

Having found x we need to find y, so substitute x back into the easier of the two original equations.   **SEXY**

$x + y = 5$
$6 + y = 5$
$y = -1$

Check in equation 1: $3 \times 6 + 2 \times -1 = 16$

This is true so your answers for x and y are true.

Exercise 3.8

Find x and y in the following equations.

1 $x + 8y = 17$
    $x + y = 10$

2 $5x + 2y = 26$
    $3x + 2y = 18$

3 $6x + 5y = 67$
    $6x + 3y = 45$

Answers
1 $x = 9, y = 1$
2 $x = 4, y = 3$
3 $x = 2, y = 11$

Example 3.25

Solve these equations.

$5x - 4y = 32$

$3x + 4y = 0$

Solution

Ignoring the signs, the coefficients of y are the same.

The signs are opposite for the $4y$s so the equations must be added.

$$\begin{array}{l} 5x - 4y = 32 \\ 3x + 4y = 0 \\ \hline 8x = 32 \\ x = 4 \end{array}$$

STOP: 'same take, opposite plus'

Having found x you must find y.

Remember: *Simultaneous equations are sexy!*

Using the simpler second equation, $3x + 4y = 0$

$12 + 4y = 0$
$4y = -12$
$y = -3$

Check your answers by substituting them into the original formulae.

Just to recap
1 Make the coefficients for either the x or y terms the same, ignoring signs. Multiply if necessary.
2 Use STOP to find either x or y.
3 Remember SEXY and find the other value.
4 Check.

Exercise 3.9

Find x and y in the following equations.

1. $x + 5y = 35$
   $2x + 3y = 14$
2. $7x - 2y = 110$
   $x + 2y = 50$
3. $5x + 4y = 47$
   $2x + 3y = 23$
4. $3x + 4y = 65$
   $2x + 5y = 76$

Answers

1. $x = -5, y = 8$
2. $x = 20, y = 15$
3. $x = 7, y = 3$
4. $x = 3, y = 14$

Remember: You can solve simultaneous equations graphically by finding the point where two lines cross. You can find out more about that on page 56.

TAKE A BREAK

Time for tea? Take a break before tackling quadratics.

Multiplying out (expanding) double brackets

We are using FOIL (**F**irst **O**uter **I**nner **L**ast) to expand double brackets. If you've learnt another method, feel free to use it.

Example 3.26

Expand $(x + 1)(2x + 3)$.

Solution

Using FOIL   First   Outer   Inner   Last

$(x + 1)(2x + 3) = x \times 2x + x \times 3 + 1 \times 2x + 1 \times 3$

$ = 2x^2 + 3x + 2x + 3$

$ = 2x^2 + 5x + 3$

A common mistake is to add the last terms instead of multiplying them.

You can leave out the first line of working – we included it just to show how we got the terms.

Exercise 3.10

Expand the following.

1. $(x + 3)(x - 2)$
2. $(x - 1)(x + 1)$
3. $(4 - x)(x + 7)$
4. $(2x - 1)(3x - 5)$
5. $(2x - 5)^2$

Answers

1. $x^2 + x - 6$
2. $x^2 - 1$
3. $-x^2 - 3x + 28$
4. $6x^2 - 13x + 5$
5. $4x^2 - 20x + 25$

Hint: Write it out as $(2x - 5)(2x - 5)$

Factorising using double brackets

In this section we shall show you how to rewrite a quadratic expression (i.e. one containing an x^2), putting it into two brackets. As you have just spent the last section making a quadratic expression out of two brackets, this may seem a rather curious activity, but the exam may test either skill, and a few more marks are always worth having!

There are, as usual, several approaches. Try the exercise that follows, and if you can do it go on to the section on 'Rearranging formulae' on page 43.

Exercise 3.11

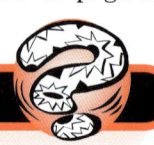

Factorise the following expressions.

1. $x^2 + 6x + 8$
2. $x^2 + 9x + 20$
3. $x^2 - 9x + 20$
4. $x^2 + 11x - 12$
5. $x^2 - 7x - 30$

Answers

1. $(x + 4)(x + 2)$
2. $(x + 5)(x + 4)$
3. $(x - 5)(x - 4)$
4. $(x + 12)(x - 1)$
5. $(x - 10)(x + 3)$

How to factorise when the coefficient of x^2 is 1

When you multiply out double brackets, you usually finish up with three terms – an x^2 term, an x term and a term without x, sometimes called a **constant**, e.g. $(x + 3)(x + 2) = x^2 + 5x + 6$.

This is another word you can use to impress your teacher!

Factorising is the reverse of FOIL.

1. The x^2 term is usually made by putting an x in the first place in each bracket.

    $(x \quad)(x \quad)$

2. The other two numbers will involve the factors of the constant. Split the constant into pairs of factors. For the expression $x^2 + 5x + 6$, the constant is 6. The pairs of factors are:

1	2
6	3

3. Separating the terms will be two signs. These could be two positives, two negatives, or one of each.

    $(x + ?)(x + ?)$ $(x - ?)(x - ?)$
    $(x + ?)(x - ?)$ $(x - ?)(x + ?)$

To decide which type you have, firstly look at the *second sign* in the original equation.

$x^2 + ?x \; + \; ?$ $x^2 - ?x \; - \; ?$
$x^2 + ?x \; - \; ?$ $x^2 - ?x \; + \; ?$

In the example $x^2 + 5x + 6$, the second sign is positive.

Type 1: The second sign in the expression is positive

If the second sign is positive, both signs in the brackets will be the same. (*Plus* and *same* both have four letters.)

If the first sign is positive, both signs in the brackets are positive.

If the first sign is negative, both signs in the brackets are negative.

Now go back to the pairs of factors which you wrote down and put positive or negative signs in front of each number, according to which sign you are going to need.

$x^2 + 5x + 6$

Algebra

Since the first sign is positive:

+1   +2
+6   +3

One pair of factors when added must total the coefficient of x, in this case 5.

When you add up the columns, you can see that only 2 + 3 gives the required total 5, so the answer is

$x^2 + 5x + 6 = (x + 3)(x + 2)$

Check your answer using FOIL.

Example 3.27

Factorise $x^2 + 12x + 20$.

Solution

The pairs of factors making up 20 are:

1   2   4
20   10   5

The second sign is + (positive), so both signs are the same.

The first sign is +, so both signs will be +.

Inserting the +s and totalling the pairs gives:

+1   +2   +4
+20   +10   +5
─────────────────
21   12   9

As the original expression has $12x$, the answer is:

$x^2 + 12x + 20 = (x + 10)(x + 2)$

Example 3.28

Factorise $x^2 - 9x + 20$.

Solution

List the factors of 20.

1   2   4
20   10   5

The second sign is positive, so both signs are the same.

The first sign is negative, so both signs will be negative.

−1   −2   −4
−20   −10   −5
─────────────────
−21   −12   −9

$x^2 - 9x + 20 = (x - 5)(x - 4)$

Exercise 3.12

Factorise the following expressions.

1 $x^2 + 11x + 10$

2 $x^2 - 6x + 8$

3 $x^2 - 13x + 36$

4 $x^2 + 11x + 24$

Answers

1 $(x + 10)(x + 1)$
2 $(x - 4)(x - 2)$
3 $(x - 9)(x - 4)$
4 $(x + 8)(x + 3)$

Type 2: The second sign in the expression is negative

If the second sign is negative, both signs in the brackets will be different. (*Different* and *minus* both have i as their second letter.)

Example 3.29

Factorise $x^2 + 11x - 12$.

Solution

List the factors of 12.

1   2   3
12   6   4

37

Revise Standard Grade and Intermediate Maths

The second sign is negative, so the signs will be different.

To decide which way round to put the factors, look at the first sign in the expression.

If it is positive, this means that the larger factor is positive.

If it is negative, this means that the larger factor is negative.

As 11 is positive, put + in front of the larger number in each pair of factors, and – in front of the smaller. Then total them in the usual way.

–1	–2	–3
+12	+6	+4
11	4	1

$x^2 + 11x - 12 = (x + 12)(x - 1)$

Example 3.30

Factorise $x^2 - 7x - 30$.

Solution

List the factors of 30.

1	2	3	5
30	15	10	6

The second sign is negative, so the signs in the brackets will be different.

The first sign is –, so the larger factor is negative.

1	2	3	5
–30	–15	–10	–6
–29	–13	–7	–1

$x^2 - 7x - 30 = (x - 10)(x + 3)$

Just to recap

1. Look at the sign of the constant term (the *second* sign).
   plus ⇒ same sign
   minus ⇒ different signs
2. List the pairs of factors.
3. By looking at the x term, give the factors the appropriate signs.
4. Complete the brackets.

Exercise 3.13

Factorise each of these expressions.

1. $x^2 + 8x - 9$
2. $x^2 + 7x - 18$
3. $x^2 - 3x - 28$
4. $x^2 - 24x - 25$

Answers
1. $(x + 9)(x - 1)$
2. $(x + 9)(x - 2)$
3. $(x - 7)(x + 4)$
4. $(x - 25)(x + 1)$

Unfortunately, examiners won't tell you whether you have a Type 1 or Type 2 expression. However, if you always start by looking at the second sign and then following the above procedure, you should be able to cope with anything they might throw at you.

Here are some mixed examples for you to try.

Exercise 3.14

Factorise these expressions.

1. $x^2 + 14x + 45$
2. $x^2 + 5x - 6$
3. $x^2 - 11x + 24$
4. $x^2 - x - 12$

Answers
1. $(x + 9)(x + 5)$
2. $(x + 6)(x - 1)$
3. $(x - 3)(x - 8)$
4. $(x - 4)(x + 3)$

The bare bones of factorisation

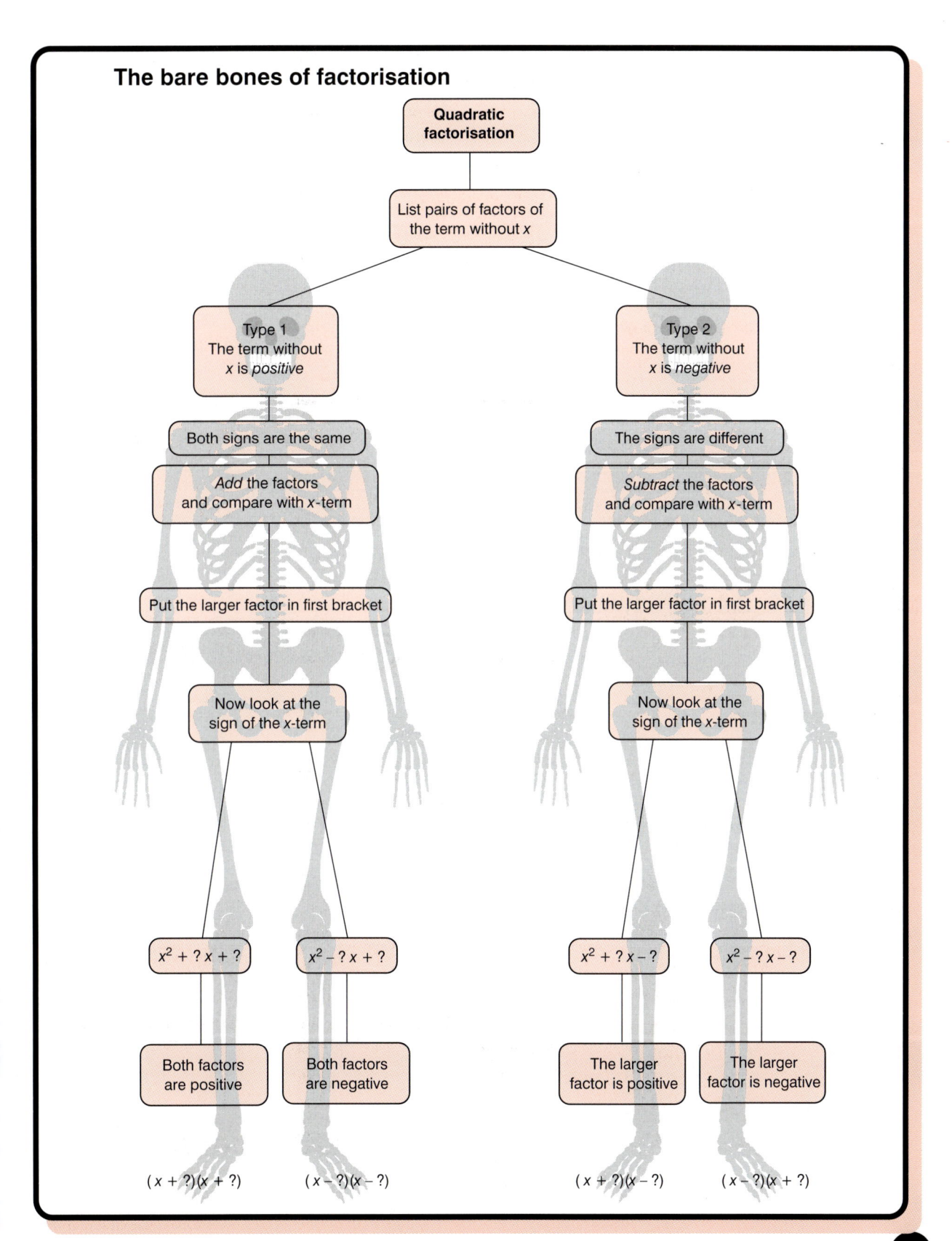

Quadratic factorisation

List pairs of factors of the term without x

Type 1 — The term without x is *positive*

Both signs are the same

Add the factors and compare with x-term

Put the larger factor in first bracket

Now look at the sign of the x-term

$x^2 + ?x + ?$ → Both factors are positive → $(x + ?)(x + ?)$

$x^2 - ?x + ?$ → Both factors are negative → $(x - ?)(x - ?)$

Type 2 — The term without x is *negative*

The signs are different

Subtract the factors and compare with x-term

Put the larger factor in first bracket

Now look at the sign of the x-term

$x^2 + ?x - ?$ → The larger factor is positive → $(x + ?)(x - ?)$

$x^2 - ?x - ?$ → The larger factor is negative → $(x - ?)(x + ?)$

Factorising quadratic expressions into two brackets when the coefficient of x^2 is greater than 1.

Example 3.31

Factorise $3x^2 + 13x - 10$.

Solution

The coefficient of x^2 can only be the product of $3x$ and x. So write these at the start of the brackets.

$(3x\quad)(x\quad)$

Now write all the pairs of numbers with product 10: 1×10; 2×5.

Experiment to see which makes the coefficient of x equal to 13.

$3x^2 + 13x - 10 = (3x - 2)(x + 5)$

Exercise 3.15

Factorise the following expressions.

1. $5x^2 - 7x - 6$
2. $3x^2 + x - 10$
3. $2x^2 - 11x + 12$
4. $3x^2 + 11x + 6$
5. $2x^2 + x - 10$
6. $4x^2 + 4x + 1$

Answers

1. $(5x + 3)(x - 2)$
2. $(3x - 5)(x + 2)$
3. $(2x - 3)(x - 4)$
4. $(3x + 2)(x + 3)$
5. $(2x + 5)(x - 2)$
6. $(2x + 1)^2$

Difference of two squares

These are quadratic expressions, but they have no term in x, and the two terms are separated by a minus sign.

Example 3.32

Factorise these expressions.

a) $x^2 - y^2$
b) $100a^2 - 49b^2$
c) $a^2 - 1$
d) $18x^2 - 8y^2$

Solution

a) $x^2 - y^2 = (x - y)(x + y)$, or of course $(x + y)(x - y)$
b) $100a^2 - 49b^2 = (10a - 7b)(10a + 7b)$
c) $a^2 - 1 = (a - 1)(a + 1)$
d) $18x^2 - 8y^2 = 2(9x^2 - 4y^2)$
   $\qquad\qquad\;\; = 2(3x - 2y)(3x + 2y)$

Exercise 3.16

Factorise the following expressions.

1. $b^2 - a^2$
2. $1 - 9x^2$
3. $4a^2 - 25$
4. $3x^2 - 12a^2$

Answers

1. $(b - a)(b + a)$
2. $(1 - 3x)(1 + 3x)$
3. $(2a - 5)(2a + 5)$
4. $3(x^2 - 4a^2) = 3(x - 2a)(x + 2a)$

TAKE A BREAK

Solving quadratic equations

Quadratic equations are of the form $ax^2 + bx + c = 0$.

For example, $2x^2 + x - 4 = 0$ is a quadratic equation.

Solution of quadratic equations

The three most common ways of solving quadratic equations are:

1 factorising

2 quadratic formula

3 graphically (see Chapter 4, Graphs in algebra for this method).

Solution of quadratics – method 1

After taking all terms on to one side and factorising, equate each bracket to zero and solve.

For example $x^2 + 6x + 5 = 0$

$(x + 5)(x + 1) = 0$

When the product of two numbers is zero, one or the other must be zero.

So either $x + 5 = 0$ or $x + 1 = 0$

$x = -5$ $x = -1$

You must have a zero on the right-hand side of the equation to use this method.

Also, if you have a negative coefficient of x^2, take all terms on to the other side of the equation to make the coefficient positive.

Solution of quadratics – method 2

You may have to use the formula for solving quadratics.

$$x = \frac{-b \pm \sqrt{b^2 - 4ac}}{2a}$$

Don't worry, you do not need to learn this – it'll be on the *Formulae list* of your exam paper.

Use this method if:

- the question asks you to give your answer to a certain number of decimal places
- the equation looks difficult to factorise.

Exercise 3.17

1 Find the values of x which satisfy these equations.
- **a)** $x^2 + 8x = -15$
- **b)** $2x^2 - 11x + 5 = 0$
- **c)** $x^2 + 24x = 25$
- **d)** $x^2 - 9 = 0$
- **e)** $x^2 = 25$

2 Find the values of x in the following questions, correct to two decimal places.
- **a)** $3x^2 - 11x + 4 = 0$
- **b)** $4x^2 - 17x + 1 = 0$
- **c)** $2x^2 + 8x = 3$
- **d)** $3x^2 + 1 = 9x$
- **e)** $6 - x^2 - 10x = 0$

Answers

1 a) $x = -5, x = -3$
b) $x = 0.5, x = 5$
c) $x = -25, x = 1$
d) $x = -3, x = 3$
e) $x = -5, x = 5$
2 a) $x = 3.26, x = 0.41$
b) $x = 4.19, x = 0.06$
c) $x = 0.35, x = -4.35$
d) $x = 0.12, x = 2.88$
e) $x = -10.57, x = 0.57$

TAKE A BREAK

Definitely time for another break! There's a bit more hard work coming up.

Rearranging formulae

Many students think that rearranging formulae (or formulas, you will find both words used) is going to be difficult. However, if you can solve simple equations like the examples at the beginning of the chapter, you shouldn't have any problems. In fact, if you have survived this far into this algebra chapter, you have learned more than enough techniques to solve any of the formula questions which the examiners might dream up.

How much do you know already?

Exercise 3.18

In each of the following questions, rearrange the formula to make the letter in brackets the subject.

1. $a = b + c$ (b)
2. $d = e - f$ (e)
3. $a = x - y$ (y)
4. $ab = z$ (b)
5. $\dfrac{a}{x} = z$ (a)
6. $\dfrac{s}{t} = p$ (t)
7. $b = ac + d$ (a)
8. $y(x - z) = s$ (x)
9. $t = b - ak$ (k)
10. $v = h^2 + t$ (h)
11. $s = c + \sqrt{b}$ (b)
12. $e = b - \sqrt{c}$ (c)
13. $b = \dfrac{c}{e - f}$ (e)
14. $c = 2\pi r$ (r)

Answers

1. $b = a - c$
2. $e = d + f$
3. $y = x - a$
4. $b = \dfrac{z}{a}$
5. $a = xz$
6. $t = \dfrac{s}{p}$
7. $a = \dfrac{b - d}{c}$
8. $x = z + \dfrac{s}{y}$
9. $k = \dfrac{b - t}{a}$
10. $h = \sqrt{v - t}$
11. $b = (s - c)^2$
12. $c = (b - e)^2$
13. $e = \dfrac{c}{b} + f$
14. $r = \dfrac{c}{2\pi}$

How did you get on?

All, or most of them right?
Well done! You should be able to cope with any formula rearrangement question which appears on a Credit level or an Intermediate 2 paper.

The first nine right, but the last few defeated you?
Your only problem is one of confidence. You solved the first nine formulae, didn't you? Well then, you have shown that you can think logically, and that is all you need to do to solve the more involved examples. As you get to grips with the routines that we're about to demonstrate, you will soon begin to wonder why you ever had any problems with formula rearrangement.

The first six right but the rest wrong?
You have the basic ideas well established, but you just need more practice in combining the processes.

Don't even ask?

If it's any comfort, most Credit level and Intermediate 2 level students (and a good many Higher level students too), start off in much the same position as you are now. However, almost everyone can rearrange formulae, given a little help from the next characters to be introduced.

Rearranging formulae with Simon Nova and Susannah Porter

To their friends they are known as Su and Cy (pronounced 'sigh').

Cy Nova and Su Porter work the human cannon ball.

Su Porter supports the letter which is to become the new subject of the formula, whilst Cy Nova shoots all the surplus letters and numbers over the = sign, changing their sign as he does so.

+ and − change with each other.

× and ÷ change with each other.

Of course, they don't *actually* do anything of the kind. Formulae behave just like any other equations, and you are really adding, subtracting, multiplying or dividing both sides of an equation, as shown on pages 24 – 26. However, you may find it easier to imagine Cy Nova firing symbols or numbers across the = sign, changing the sign as he does so.

Example 3.33

Rearrange this formula, making b the subject.

$a = b + c$

Solution

Su Porter supports the b.

Cy Nova fires the c across the =, changing it to $-c$.

$a - c = b$

$b = a - c$

It is usually a good idea to leave the term you want alone until the end, and start by getting rid of all the surplus letters and terms which are on the same side of the equation.

Example 3.34

Make e the subject of this formula.

$d = e - f$

Solution

Su Porter supports the e, whilst Cy Nova shoots the f over to the opposite side, changing its sign as he does so.

$d + f = e$

$e = d + f$

Example 3.35

Make y the subject of this formula.

$a = x - y$

Solution

Su Porter is not happy holding negative terms, so Cy Nova shoots the y over the = sign to make it positive.

This is not absolutely essential at this stage, but it does make the later operations much easier.

$a + y = x$

Now Su Porter can support the y whilst Cy Nova shoots the a across to give:

$y = x - a$

Example 3.36

Make b the subject of this formula.

$ab = z$

Solution

Su Porter supports the term containing the required letter. As there are no other terms in the equation, Cy Nova can shoot the a across.

As you already know, ab is the algebraic way of writing $a \times b$, so he turns the new expression into a division sum.

The answer is:

$b = \dfrac{z}{a}$

A common mistake is to write $b = \dfrac{a}{z}$.

You can avoid this by first writing down anything which hasn't been moved.

The z has remained in the same place, so start by writing $b = z$.

As the a is moving, it is a that changes sign (from × to ÷), and not z.

Example 3.37

Make a the subject of this formula.

$\dfrac{a}{x} = z$

Solution

This is much easier than it might first appear! Su Porter supports the a, so all Cy Nova has to do is to shoot the x up to join the z.

To 'undo' dividing by x, just multiply by x.

$a = zx$

If the required letter is on the bottom, you have to get it to the top as soon as possible.

Example 3.38

Make t the subject of this formula.

$\dfrac{s}{t} = p$

Solution

Su Porter does not like the t in the denominator of the fraction.

Cy Nova shoots the t across to give:

$s = tp$

Then he shoots the p down to the other side and the expression becomes:

$\dfrac{s}{p} = t$

or $t = \dfrac{s}{p}$

Short cut

Can you see that t and p have changed places? This is easier to understand if you use numbers.

$\dfrac{20}{10} = 2$ so $\dfrac{20}{2} = 10$

If you don't want to use this short cut you don't have to. Just continue using Su and Cy in the usual way.

Algebra

Example 3.39

Make a the subject of this formula.

$b = ac + d$

Solution

Su Porter supports the ac, whilst Cy Nova shoots over the d.

$b - d = ac$

Then he shoots over the c to give:

$\dfrac{b - d}{c} = a$

Example 3.40

Make k the subject of this formula.

$t = b - ak$

Solution

Su Porter holds the ak. As it includes the subject and it is negative, it is a good idea to make it positive at the outset.

Shoot it over to get:

$t + ak = b$

Then you can shoot over the t to get:

$ak = b - t$

As you need the k by itself, shoot across the a to leave:

$k = \dfrac{b - t}{a}$

Example 3.41

Make h the subject of this formula.

$v = h^2 + t$

Solution

Start in exactly the same way as before.

$v - t = h^2$

To 'undo' a squared number, you find its square root, so taking the square root of both sides, gives:

$\sqrt{v - t} = h$

Example 3.42

Make b the subject of this formula.

$s = c + \sqrt{b}$

Solution

Start in exactly the same way.

$s - c = \sqrt{b}$

To 'undo' the square root, you have to square both sides. As the term on the left-hand side is $s - c$, you get:

$(s - c)^2 = b$

Note: You do not get $s^2 - c^2 = b$.

Example 3.43

Make c the subject of this formula.

$e = b - \sqrt{c}$

Solution

As you have a negative subject, start by shooting it over into a positive value.

$e + \sqrt{c} = b$

Then you have to shoot the e over.

$\sqrt{c} = b - e$

Finally, squaring both sides gives:

$c = (b - e)^2$

Revise Standard Grade and Intermediate Maths

Example 3.44

Make e the subject of this formula.

$b = \dfrac{c}{e} - f$

Solution

Start in the usual way by shooting over the f.

$b + f = \dfrac{c}{e}$

Now, because the required subject is on the bottom, i.e. dividing, you must bring it to the top.

$e(b + f) = c$

Because you need e by itself, $(b + f)$ must be shot to the other side to give:

$e = \dfrac{c}{b + f}$

Example 3.45

Make r the subject of this formula.

$V = \frac{4}{3}\pi r^3$

Solution

This is about the most complicated example which you might get, but you have already practised all the necessary skills, so it shouldn't prove to be too much of a problem.

You may find it easier to rewrite the expression as:

$V = \frac{4}{3}\pi r^3 = \dfrac{4\pi r^3}{3}$

Start by bringing the 3 across to the top.

$3V = 4\pi r^3$

Then divide by 4π.

$\dfrac{3V}{4\pi} = r^3$

Just as you 'undo' a square number by finding the square root, you 'undo' a cube by finding the cube root.

$\sqrt[3]{\dfrac{3V}{4\pi}} = r$

It is worth persevering with this example, since it occurs quite often on exam papers.

How much have you learnt?

Exercise 3.19

In the following examples, rearrange the formula to make the letter in the bracket the subject.

1 $d = ab - r$ (r)
2 $A = \pi r^2$ (r)
3 $aw^2 = v$ (a)
4 $C = 20h + t$ (t)
5 $C = 20h + t$ (h)
6 $c^3 - a = b$ (c)
7 $ah - t = w$ (t)
8 $y - xw = t$ (x)

Answers

1 $r = ab - d$
2 $r = \sqrt{\dfrac{A}{\pi}}$
3 $a = \dfrac{v}{w^2}$
4 $t = C - 20h$
5 $h = \dfrac{C - t}{20}$
6 $c = \sqrt[3]{a + b}$
7 $t = ah - w$
8 $x = \dfrac{y - t}{w}$

TAKE A BREAK

Even we have to admit it – that was difficult! This time, you can comfort yourself with a short rest and the knowledge that it's downhill from here on.

Variation

$y \propto x$ means y is proportional to x

$y \propto x^2$ means y is proportional to x^2

$y \propto \dfrac{1}{x}$ means y is inversely proportional to x

$y \propto \dfrac{1}{x^2}$ means y is inversely proportional to x^2

Replace 'proportional to' with '$= k$'.

In 'inversely', change the i to a 1 and the n to an o, then the first five letters give '1 over'.

Thus $y \propto x$ becomes $y = kx$

$y \propto \dfrac{1}{x^2}$ becomes $y = k \times \dfrac{1}{x^2}$ or $y = \dfrac{k}{x^2}$

In questions like these you have to find the constant k using values given for x and y. Then the question will give another value for x or y and you will have to find the missing variable using the value of k that you have calculated.

Note: Variation is included in the General and Credit Level syllabus, but is not included at Intermediate 1 or 2 levels.

Example 3.46

y is proportional to x^3. When $x = 1.6$, $y = 17.2$. Find:

a) y when $x = 0.6$ b) x when $y = 196$.

Solution

$y \propto x^3$

First find the value of k using the given x and y values.

$y = kx^3$

$17.2 = k(1.6)^3$

$17.2 = 4.096k$

$k = \dfrac{17.2}{4.096} = 4.2$ correct to 1 d.p.

a) When $x = 0.6$ $y = 4.2x^3$

$\qquad\qquad\qquad\quad = 4.2 \times 0.6^3$

$\qquad\qquad\qquad\quad = 0.91$ correct to 2 d.p.

b) When $y = 196$ $y = 4.2x^3$

$\qquad\qquad\qquad 196 = 4.2x^3$

$\qquad\qquad\qquad \dfrac{196}{4.2} = x^3$

$\qquad\qquad\qquad x = \sqrt[3]{\dfrac{196}{4.2}}$

$\qquad\qquad\qquad\quad = 3.6$ correct to 1 d.p.

Remember that the inverse, or opposite, of cubing is cube rooting or working to the power of $\frac{1}{3}$.

Example 3.47

y is inversely proportional to x^2 and $x = 0.162$ when $y = 471$. Find:

a) y when $x = 1.34$

b) x when $y = 302$

giving all answers correct to three significant figures.

Solution

Firstly, find k.

$y \propto \dfrac{1}{x^2}$

So $y = \dfrac{k}{x^2}$

$471 = \dfrac{k}{(0.162)^2}$

$k = 471 \times (0.162)^2$

$\quad = 12.36$

To minimise later rounding errors, either use the calculator memory for k or round it to four or five significant figures.

a) When $x = 1.34$

$$y = \frac{k}{x^2}$$

$$y = \frac{12.36}{1.34^2}$$

$$= 6.88 \text{ correct to 3 s.f.}$$

b) When $y = 302$

$$302 = \frac{12.36}{x^2}$$

$$302x^2 = 12.36$$

$$x^2 = \frac{12.36}{302} = 0.040\,93$$

$$x = 0.202 \text{ correct to 3 s.f.}$$

Exercise 3.20

1 y is proportional to x^2. If $y = 21.3$ when $x = 7.2$, find:
 a) the value of y when $x = 1.7$
 b) the value of x when $y = 41.3$.

2 y is inversely proportional to x^3. If $y = 141.1$ when $x = 1.45$, find:
 a) y when $x = 2.74$
 b) x when $y = 444.3$.

3 y varies directly as the cube root of x. If $y = 3.44$ when $x = 71.2$, find:
 a) y when $x = 106.8$
 b) x when $y = 4.75$.

4 y varies inversely with the square root of x. If $y = 32.1$ when $x = 43.2$, find:
 a) y when $x = 55.7$
 b) x when $y = 20.1$.

Answers

1 $k = 0.41$ a) $y = 1.2$ b) $x = 10.0$
2 $k = 430.2$ a) $y = 20.9$ b) $x = 0.99$
3 $k = 0.83$ a) $y = 3.94$ b) $x = 187.5$
4 $k = 211$ a) $y = 28.3$ b) $x = 110.2$

Joint variation

Example 3.48

The volume of a shape, v, varies directly as its height, h, and as the square of its base radius, r.

a) The volume of the shape is $1571\,\text{cm}^3$ when h is 5 cm and r is 10 cm.
 Find a formula connecting v, h and r.
b) Find the volume when $h = 8$ and $r = 5$ cm.

Solution

a) $v \propto hr^2$

$$v = khr^2$$

$$\text{vol } 1571 = k \times 5 \times 10^2$$

$$k = 3.142$$

$$v = 3.142 hr^2$$

b) $v = 3.142 \times 8 \times 5^2$

$$= 628.4$$

volume $= 628.4\,\text{cm}^3$

Exercise 3.21

1 A varies directly as h and as b. $A = 160$ when $h = 16$ and $b = 4$.
 a) Find a formula for A in terms of h and b.
 b) Calculate A when $h = 20$ and $b = 6$.

2 S varies directly as the square root of t and indirectly as p. $S = 86.5$ when $t = 9$ and $p = 23.5$.
 a) Find a formula for S in terms of t and p.
 b) Calculate S when $t = 25$ and $p = 14.7$.

Answers

1 a) $A = 2.5\,hb$
 b) $A = 300$
2 a) $S = 7.2\frac{\sqrt{t}}{p}$
 b) $S = 51.4$

review
How much have you learnt?

Tick off each topic in the list when you are confident you can cope with it.

- ○ Solve simple linear equations in one unknown.
- ○ Explain the meaning of variable, coefficient and constant.
- ○ Solve simple linear inequalities.
- ○ Make expressions and equations from statements.
- ○ Solve simultaneous equations in two unknowns.
- ○ Multiply out double brackets.
- ○ Factorise algebraic expressions.
- ○ Solve quadratic equations by factorising.
- ○ Solve quadratic equations by use of formula.
- ○ Rearrange formulae.
- ○ Solve problems involving inverse or joint variation.

If you had trouble with Algebra before you started on this chapter, try Exercise 3.1, on page 23, again to see if you find it easier.

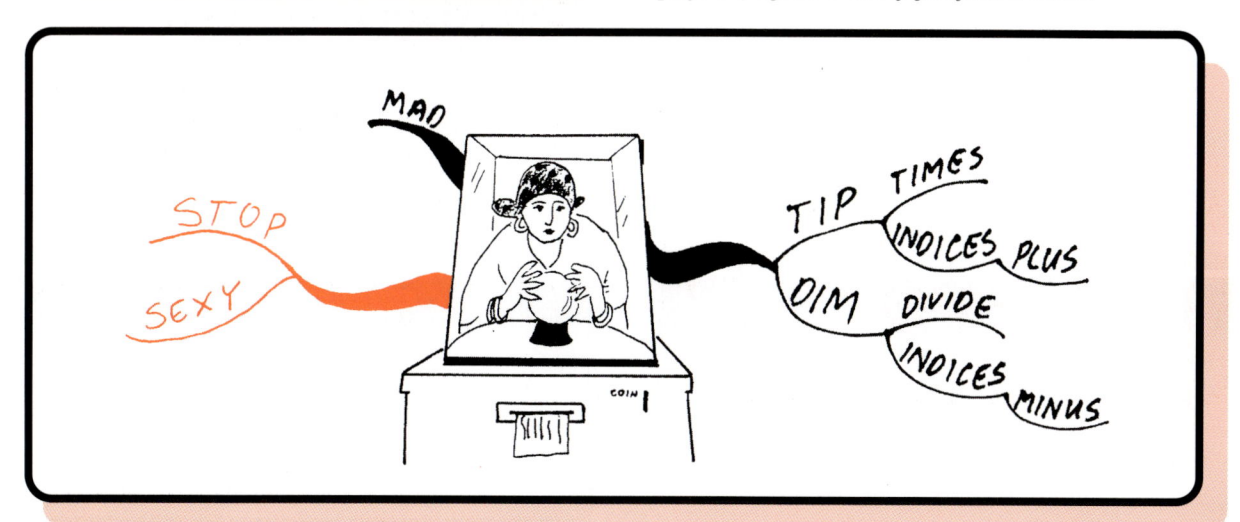

Algebra

Graphs in algebra

preview

By the end of this chapter you will be able to:

- match rates of flow in containers with their graphs
- solve simultaneous equations graphically
- interpret a straight-line graph involving two variables
- calculate and interpret the gradient of a straight-line graph
- calculate and interpret the y-intercept on a straight-line graph
- match simple graphs and their equations

Do these containers have you over a barrel?

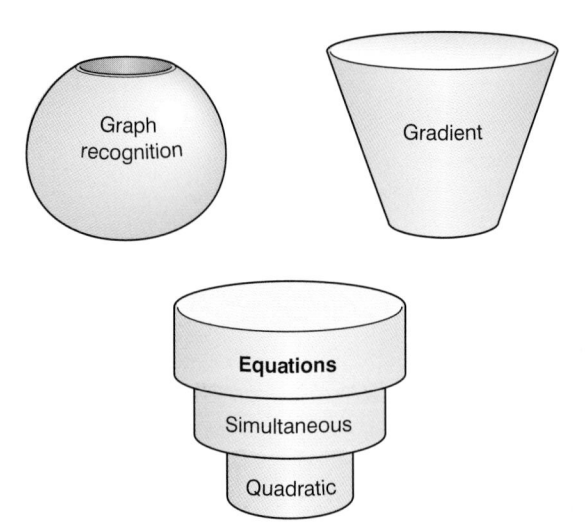

Graph recognition

Gradient

Equations
Simultaneous
Quadratic

How much do you know already?

Exercise 4.1

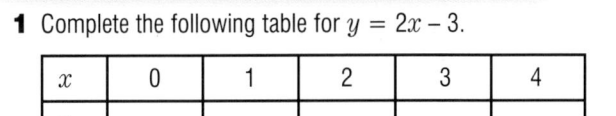

1 Complete the following table for $y = 2x - 3$.

x	0	1	2	3	4
y					

2 By adding a suitable line to this graph, solve the following simultaneous equations.

$y = 2x$
$x + y = 6$

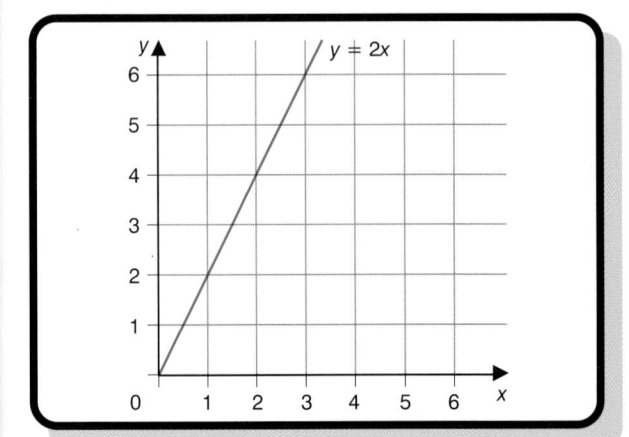

3 The graph below illustrates a family's telephone expenses.

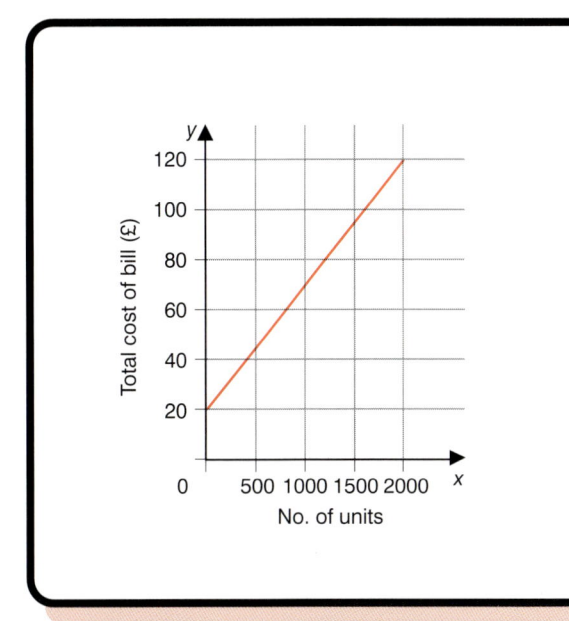

a) If the bill is £80.00, how many units were used?
b) Find the gradient of the graph.
c) What does this gradient represent?

4 From the graph below, solve $x^2 - 2x = 5$. Give your answers correct to 1 d.p.

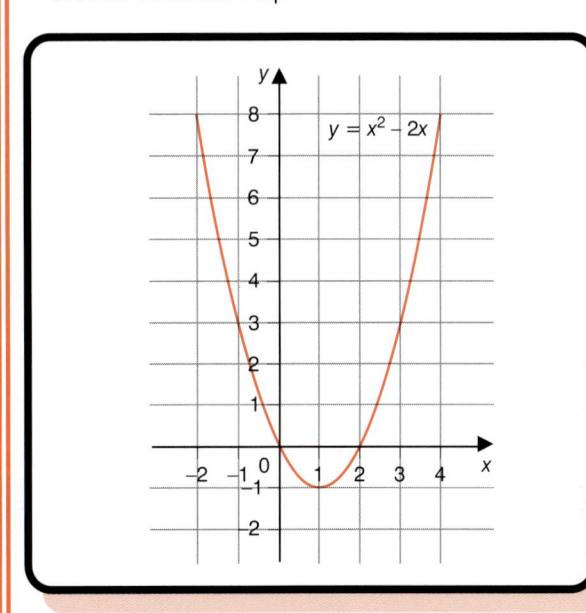

5 Find the equation of each of the straight lines below.

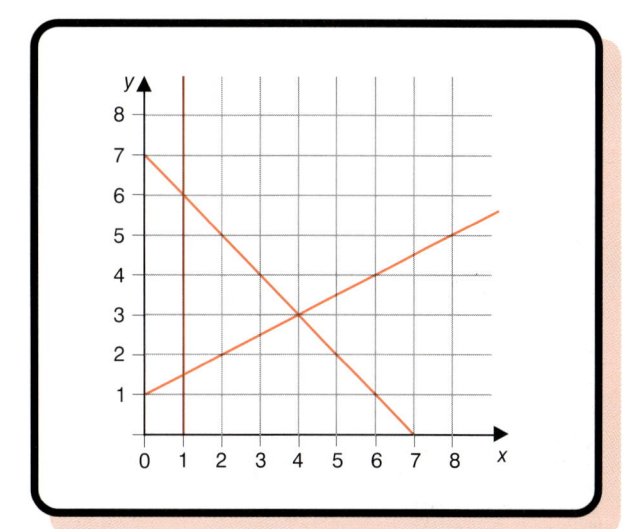

6 Match each equation to its graph.
a) $y = -x^2$
b) $y = x + 1$
c) $x + y = 3$
d) $y = x^3$

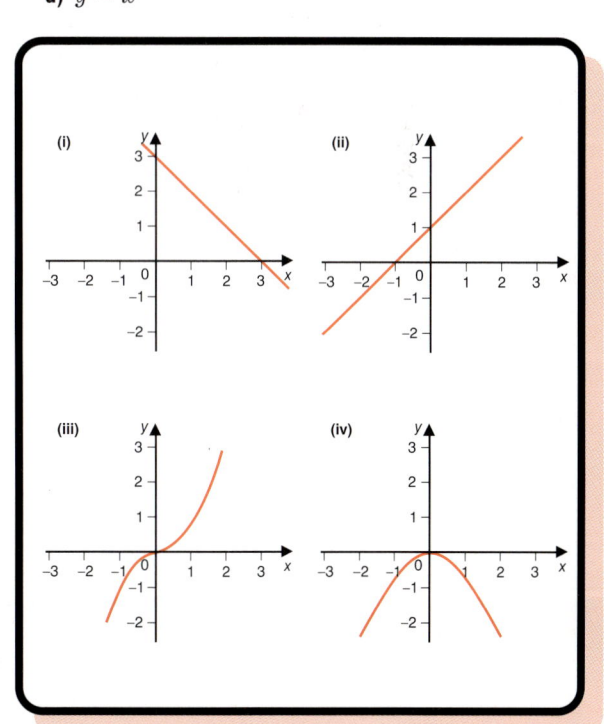

Revise Standard Grade and Intermediate Maths

7 Liquid flows into some containers at a constant rate.
Sketch the graph of the depth of liquid against time for the following containers.

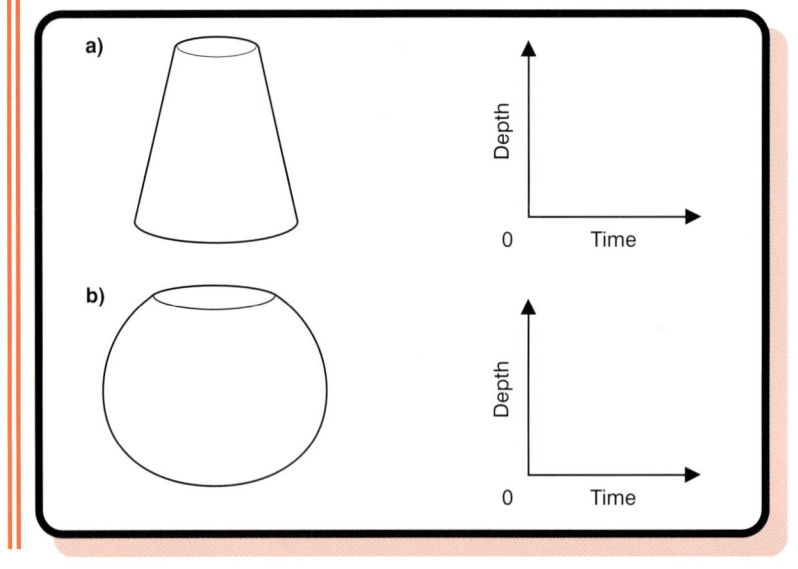

a)

b)

How did you get on?

All or most of them right?
Well done! You should be able to solve any question of the type shown above that you might find on your exam paper, but it's a good idea to flip through the rest of the exercises in this chapter just to make sure.

Half or more right?
It shouldn't take you long to fill in the gaps. Just work through the parts of the chapter which you need.

Don't even ask?
This is a short chapter and if you stay positive, you'll improve your score.

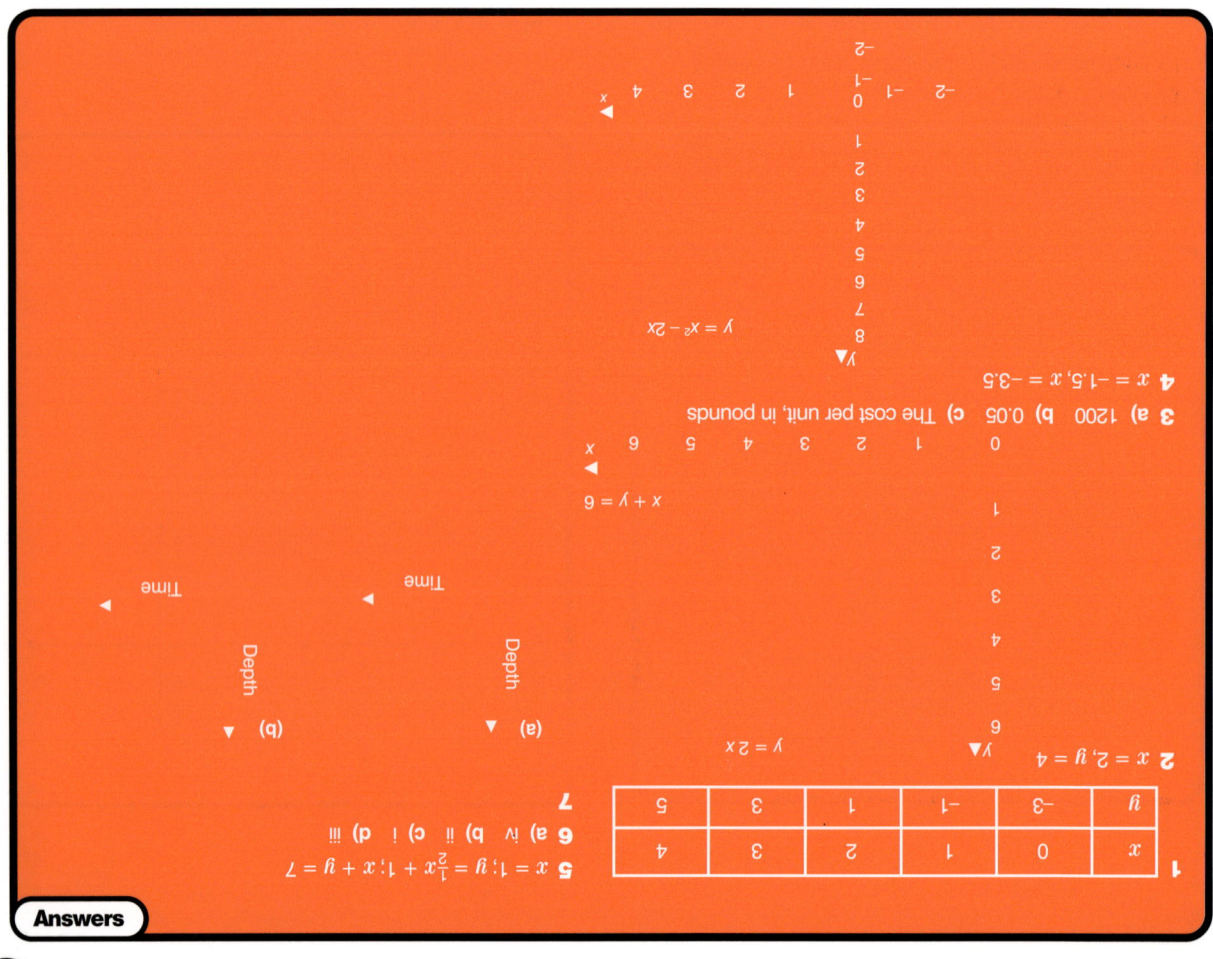

Answers

1

x	0	1	2	3	4
y	-3	-1	1	3	5

$y = 2x$

2 $x = 2, y = 4$

3 a) 1200 **b)** 0.05 **c)** The cost per unit, in pounds

4 $x = -1.5, x = -3.5$

$y = x^2 - 2x$

5 $x = 1; y = \frac{1}{2}x + 1; x + y = 7$

6 a) iv **b)** ii **c)** i **d)** iii

7

(a) Depth vs Time

(b) Depth vs Time

Graphs in algebra

Vases and vessels

In exams, you are sometimes asked to recognise or draw graphs which describe the depth of liquid in a container when it is filled at a constant rate. Occasionally you are given the graph and asked to identify the container.

The rate of increase of the height depends on the cross-sectional area. The wider the cross-sectional area, the slower the rate at which the height increases.

Cylinders

Cylinders have a constant cross-section. They stay the same width all the way up and do not get narrower or wider. Therefore the rate of increase in height is constant.

Other common shapes

Here are the shapes that often come up. Get to know their graphs.

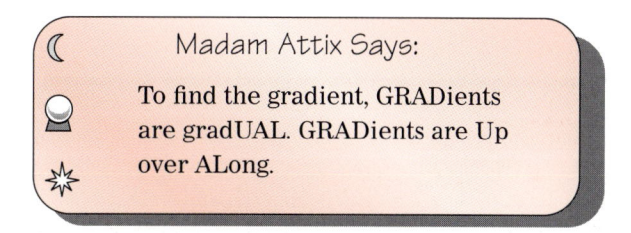

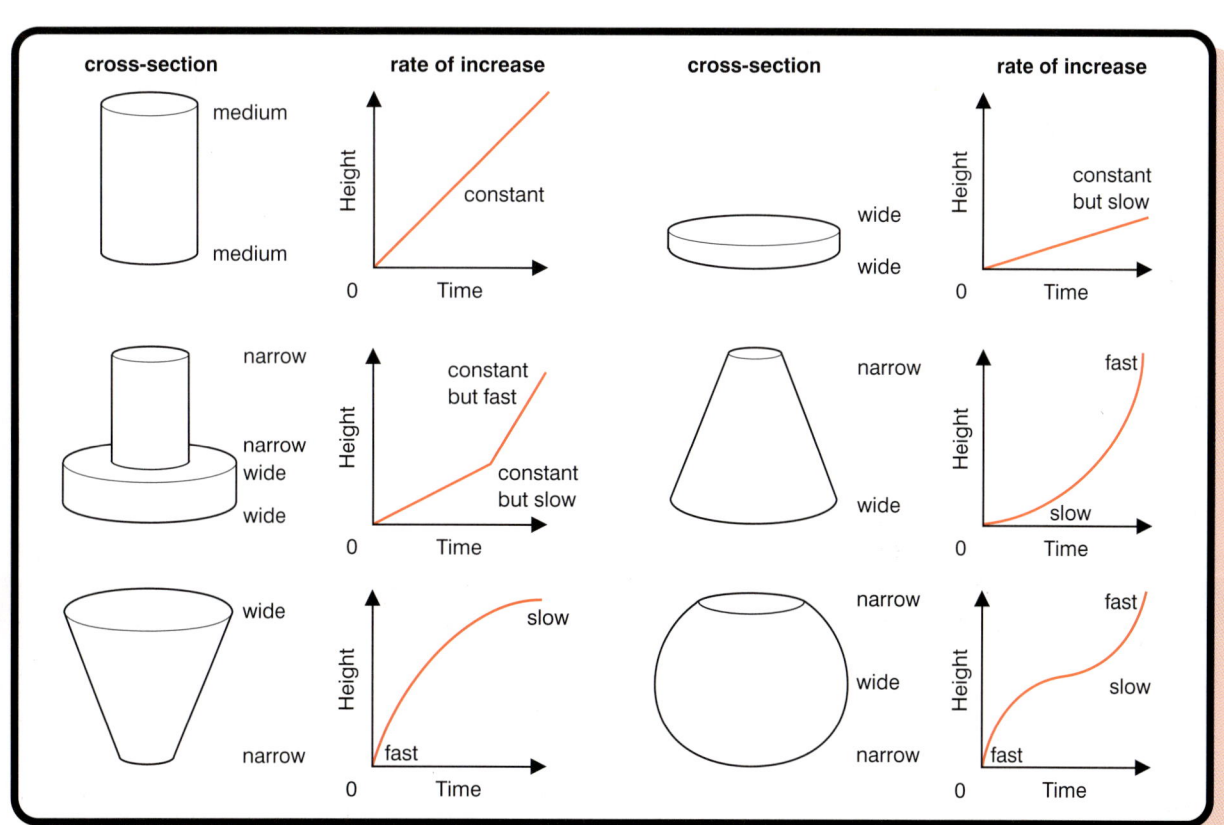

Gradients

The gradient of a line is also known as the **slope** of the line. If a line has a gradient of 2 units, then for every one unit you go along, you go up two.

Finding the gradient of a straight line

Two for the price of one, from Madam Attix!

Pick two points on the line, and construct a right-angled triangle.

> **Madam Attix Says:**
>
> To find the gradient, GRADients are gradUAL. GRADients are Up over ALong.

$$\text{GRADUAL GRADient} = \frac{\text{Up}}{\text{ALong}}$$

cross-section	rate of increase	cross-section	rate of increase
cylinder (medium / medium)	constant	wide / wide (shallow disc)	constant but slow
narrow / narrow wide / wide (stacked)	constant but fast, then constant but slow	narrow / wide (cone)	fast then slow
wide / narrow (inverted cone)	fast then slow	narrow / wide / narrow (sphere)	fast, slow, fast

Revise Standard Grade and Intermediate Maths

If you find this hard to remember, Madam Attix has another saying.

> **Madam Attix Says:**
> Gradients are GROTty, or Gradients are
> Rise (i.e. how much you go up or down)
> Over (divided by)
> Tread (how much you go along).

GROTty Gradient $= \dfrac{\text{Rise}}{\text{Tread}}$

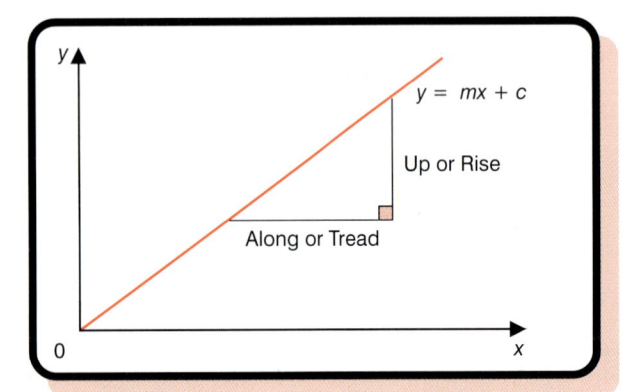

Remember: If the line slopes down, the gradient is negative.

Remember **N** for negative gradient.

The gradient and equation of a line

You may have seen the equation $y = mx + c$.

In this equation, m stands for the gradient and c is the y-intercept, or the point where the line crosses the y-axis.

The examiner may use different letters, e.g. $y = ax + b$. Do not be put off by this. The letter or number with the x always stands for the gradient and the letter or number on its own gives the y-intercept.

If lines are parallel, they have the same gradient.

Example 4.1

Find the gradient and the y-intercept of the line $y = 2x + 1$.

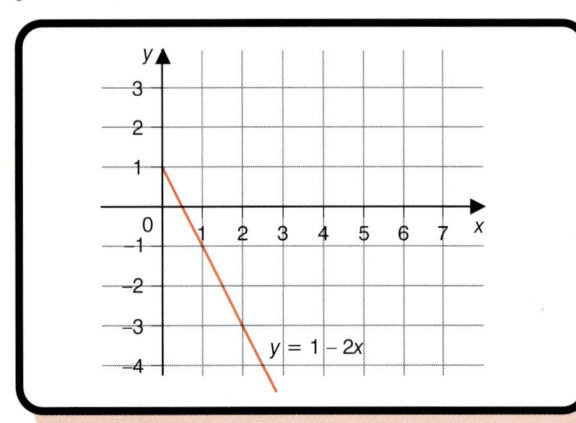

Solution

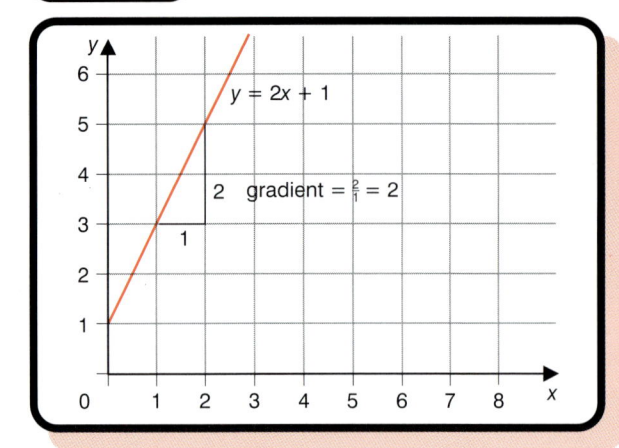

Compare the equation with $y = mx + c$.

The gradient is 2. The y-intercept is 1.

Example 4.2

Find the gradient and the y-intercept of the line $y = 1 - 2x$.

Solution

The gradient $= -2$. The y-intercept $= 1$.

Examples of this form are easier to solve if you turn them round i.e. $y = -2x + 1$.

Graphs in algebra

Exercise 4.2

1 For each of the following equations, find the gradient and the y-intercept.
 a) $y = 3x + 7$ b) $y = 0.5x + 2$
 c) $y = 4 - x$ d) $2x + y = 11$

2 Which of the following lines are parallel to $y = 2 - x$?
 a) $y + x = 3$ b) $y = x - 1$ c) $y = -x - 2$

Answers

1 a) gradient = 3, y-intercept = 7
 b) gradient = 0.5, y-intercept = 2
 c) gradient = −1, y-intercept = 4
 d) gradient = −2, y-intercept = 11

2 a) and **c)**

Solution

a) The gradient is $\frac{6}{2} = 3$

 The y intercept is at −1, so the equation is $y = 3x - 1$.

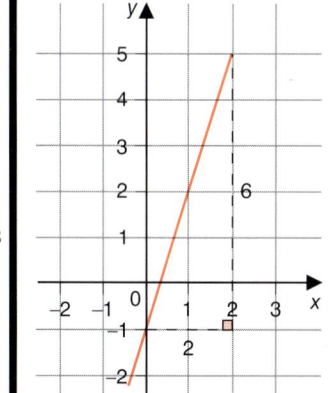

b) The gradient is $\frac{-4}{2} = -2$

 The intercept is at 1, so the equation is $y = 1 - 2x$, or $y = -2x + 1$.

Finding the equation of a line

Example 4.3

From the graphs below, find the equations of the lines.

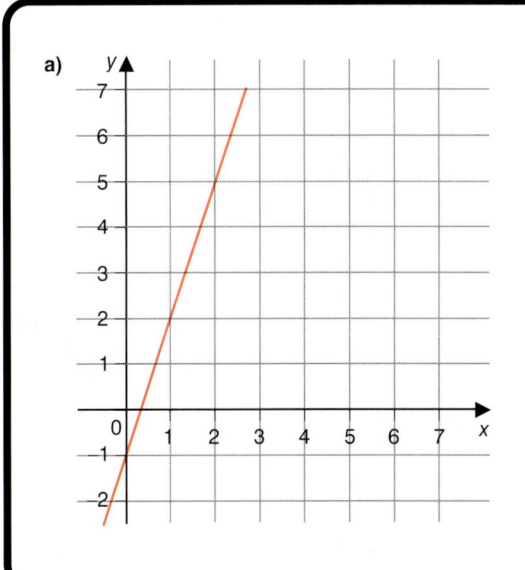

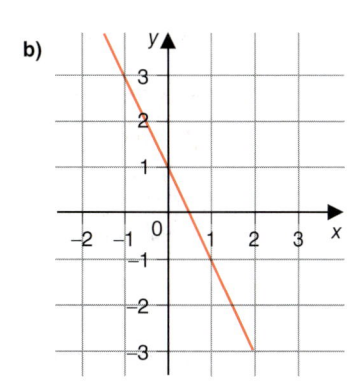

a)

b)

55

Interpreting the gradient and y-intercept

Sometimes you will be presented with a straight-line graph, and asked for the meaning of the gradient or the y-intercept.

Look at the labels on the axes, and insert the word 'per' between them as shown on the diagrams below.

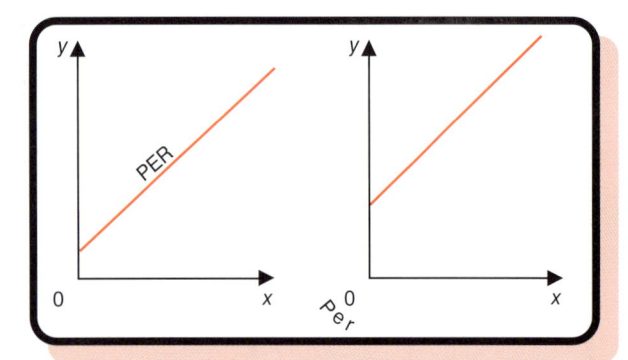

Graph 1 shows the number of pounds per dollar.

Graph 2 shows the cost in pounds (£) per unit.

Graph 3 shows the speed in km per hour.

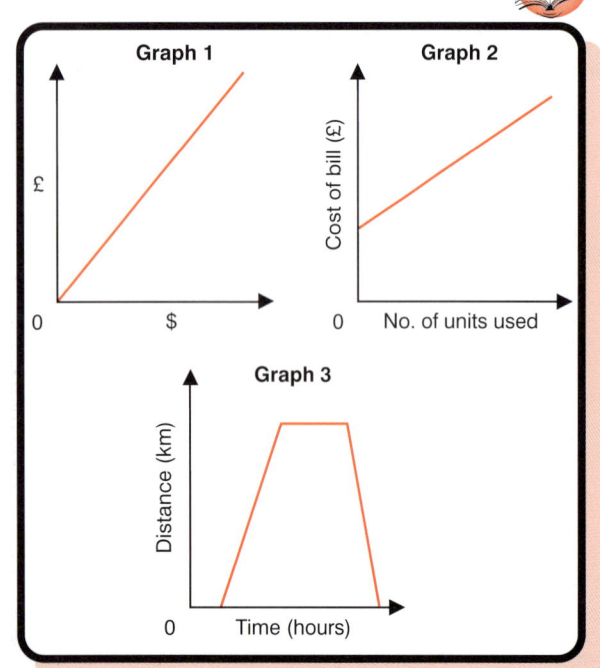

Gaynor Mark says Per means 'divided by' and it means the same as the gradient.

The y-intercept is the point where the graph crosses the y-axis. It is also the point where $x = 0$. It usually represents something like the fixed or standing charge that you have to pay, regardless of the quantity used. You generally need the y-intercept when calculating household bills, or hire charges.

> **Just to recap**
>
> The gradient of a line measures its slope.
>
> If the gradient is 0, the line is horizontal.
>
> The bigger the gradient, the steeper the line.
>
> If the line slopes down, the gradient is negative.

Do you get 'horizontal' and 'vertical' mixed up? Remember that the horizontal goes in the same direction as the horizon.

Graphical solutions to simultaneous equations

To solve simultaneous equations graphically, you simply need the values of x and y at the crossing points of the two graphs.

Sometimes the graphs are already drawn, and sometimes you need to construct them using a table of values. If there is no table given, you need to make your own. Take four values of x, such as $x = 0, 1, 2, 3$. Find the corresponding values of y.

Plot the resulting points on the given graph, and confirm that your graph is correct. If the points are not in a straight line, or a smooth curve, there is an error in either your calculations or plotting.

When drawing the line, extend it to the edge of the graph – don't just connect the first and last points.

Graphs in algebra

Example 4.4

Below is the graph of $2x + y = 6$.

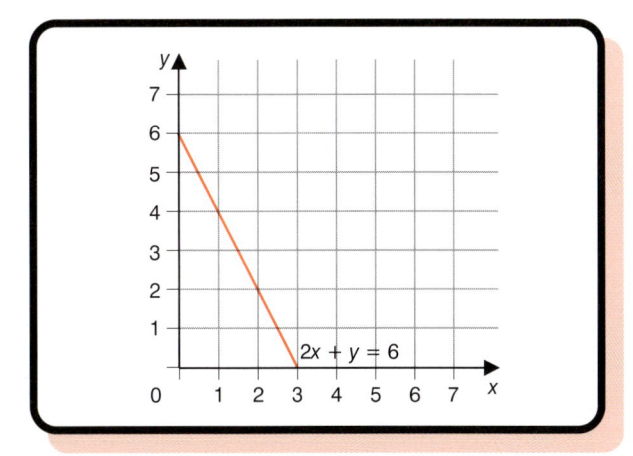

By adding a suitable line, solve the given simultaneous equations.

$2x + y = 6$

$y = 3x + 1$

Solution

Complete a table of values for $y = 3x + 1$ like this.

x	0	1	2	3
y	1	4	7	10

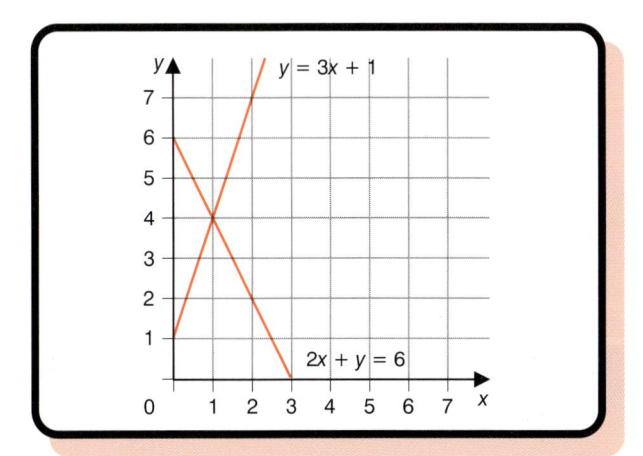

$x = 1, y = 4$

Remember: Simultaneous equations are SEXY, because you need to find both x and y.

Exercise 4.3

Below is a graph of $2x + y = 8$. By adding a suitable line, solve the given simultaneous equations.

$2x + y = 8$

$y = 2x + 2$

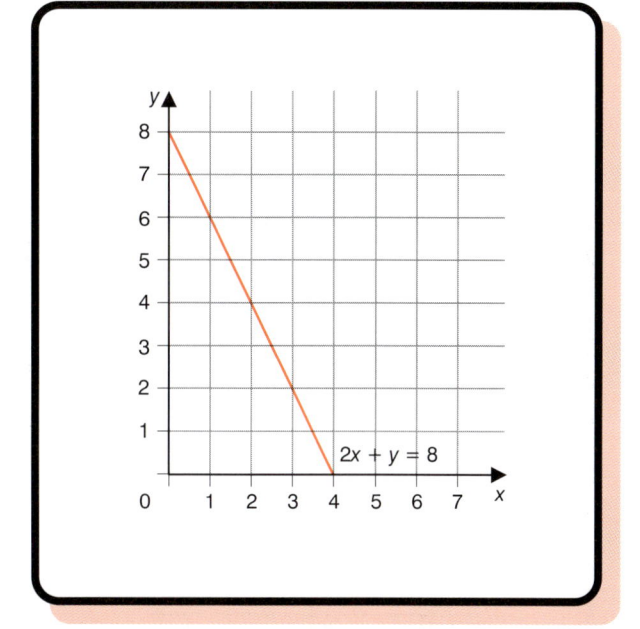

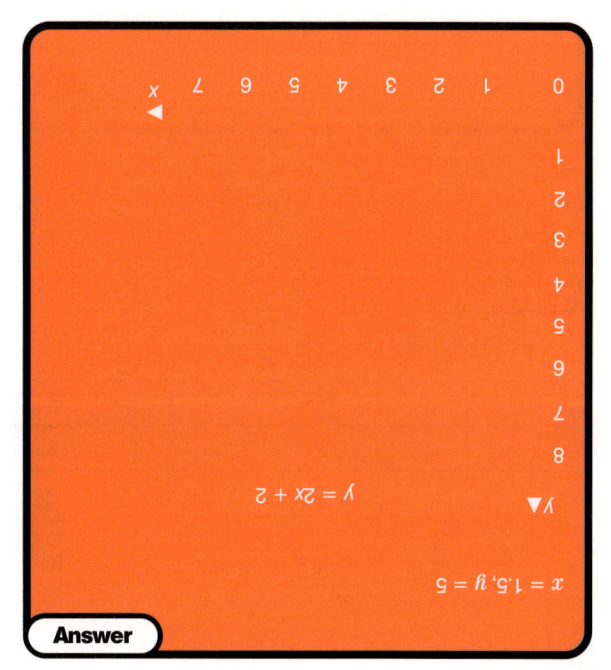

Answer

$x = 1.5, y = 5$

Curved graphs

Sketching quadratics

Example 4.5

a) Complete the table for $y = x^2 + x$.

x	−3	−2	−1	0	1	2	3
y		2		0			

b) Using the table, draw $y = x^2 + x$ on the graph below.

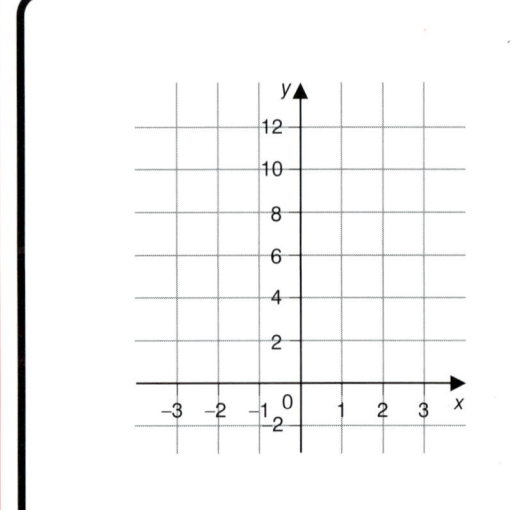

c) From your graph, find the values of x for which $x^2 + x = 3$, giving your answer correct to 1 d.p.

Solution

Complete the table of values.

x	−3	−2	−1	0	1	2	3
y	6	2	0	0	2	6	12

Note: The values at $x = -1$ and $x = 0$ are the same. To find out what happens between these points, find the y-value when $x = -0.5$.

If $x = 0.5$ then $y = (-0.5)^2 - 0.5 = 0.25 - 0.5 = -0.25$

Use the table to draw the graph.

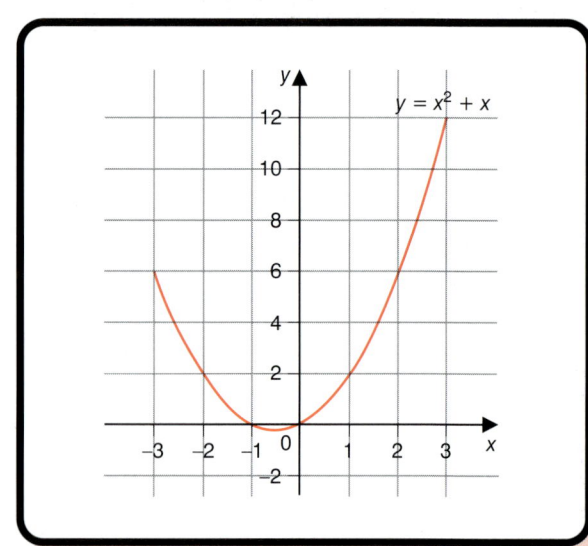

Now, to find the point where $x^2 + x = 3$, find where the graph of $y = x^2 + x$ cuts the graph of $y = 3$.

On the same graph as before, draw the line $y = 3$.

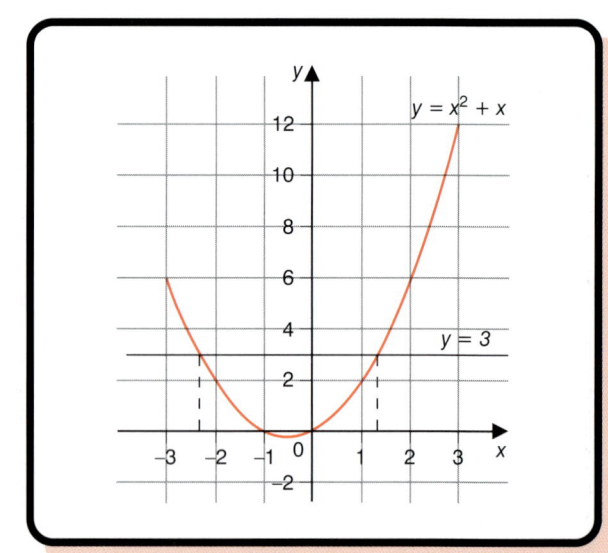

Remember: $y = 3$ is horizontal, $x = 3$ is vertical.

At the points where the two lines cross, $x = -2.3$, or $x = 1.3$.

Always join the points on a curved graph with a smooth line. Never join the points with a ruler.

Exercise 4.4

$y = x^2 - 5x + 3$

1 Complete the table of values.

x	−1	0	1	2	3	4	5	6
y		3		−3				9

2 Sketch the graph of $y = x^2 - 5x + 3$ on the graph below.

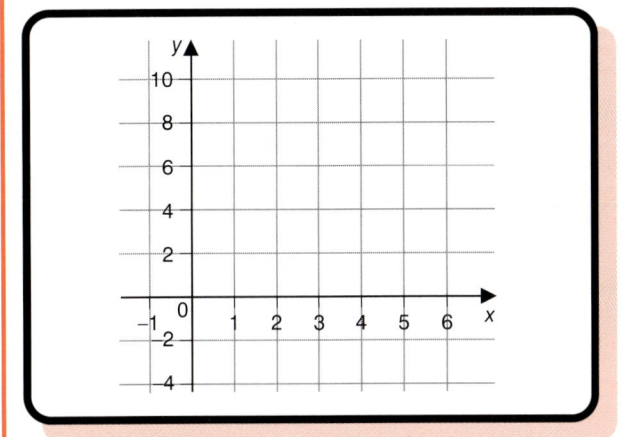

3 From your graph solve $x^2 - 5x + 3 = 0$, giving your answers correct to 1 d.p.

Answers

1.
x	−1	0	1	2	3	4	5	6
y	9	3	−1	−3	−3	−1	3	9

3. $x = 0.7, 4.3$

review
How much have you learnt?

Tick off each topic in the list when you are confident you can cope with it.

- Match rates of flow in containers with their graphs.
- Solve simultaneous equations graphically.
- Interpret a straight-line graph involving two variables.
- Calculate and interpret the gradient of a straight-line graph.
- Calculate and interpret the y-intercept on a straight-line graph.
- Match simple graphs and their equations.

If you feel the need, go back and try the questions at the beginning of the chapter. If you are feeling confident, try the Algebra review (page 61) next.

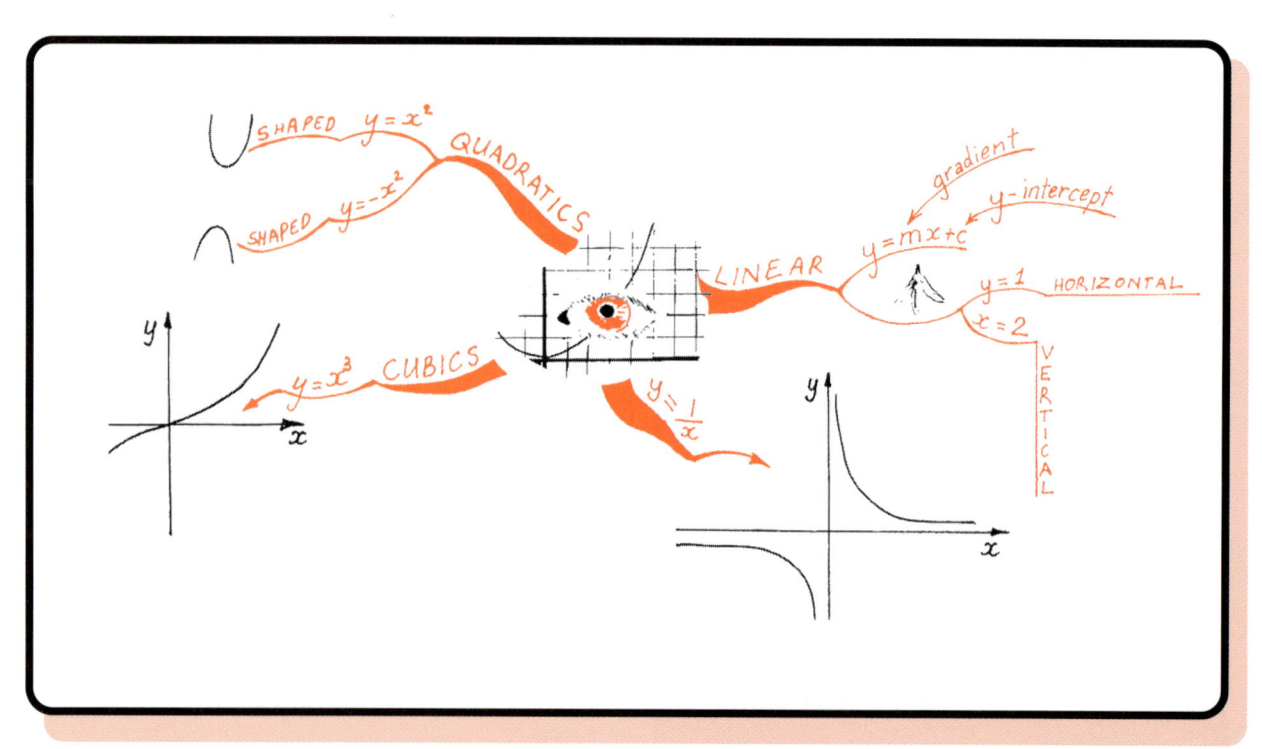

4

Revise Standard Grade and Intermediate Maths

Mind Map 1

- MAD
- STOP
- SEXY
- TIP
  - TIMES — INDICES PLUS
  - DIM — DIVIDE — INDICES MINUS
- GRADIENTS
  - GRADUAL
  - GROTTY

Mind Map 2

- QUADRATICS
  - U SHAPED $y = x^2$
  - ∩ SHAPED $y = -x^2$
- LINEAR $y = mx + c$
  - gradient
  - y-intercept
  - $y = 1$ HORIZONTAL
  - $x = 2$ VERTICAL
- CUBICS $y = x^3$
- $y = \dfrac{1}{x}$

Algebra review

1. Solve the following pair of simultaneous equations.
   $x + y = 6$
   $x + 2y = 8.5$

2. y varies directly as x^2 and $y = 72.4$ when $x = 5.1$
   a) Find y when $x = 2.8$.
   b) Find x when $y = 104.2$.
   Give both answers correct to 1 d.p.

3. Factorise these expressions completely.
   a) $3ab + 6b^2$ b) $10y^2 - 2y$ c) $16xy^2 + 7x^2y$

4. A boy's sister is three years older than he is, and his mother is three times as old as his sister.
   a) If his age is given as n years, write down in terms of n the ages of:
      i) his sister   ii) his mother.
   b) If the total of their ages is 67 years, form an equation in n, and simplify it.
   c) Solve the equation to find the ages of the three people.

5. y is inversely proportional to $\sqrt{x}$ and $y = 3.8$ when $x = 0.17$
   a) Find y when $x = 0.57$.
   b) Find x when $y = 8.7$.
   Give both answers correct to 1 d.p.

6. Find the equations of the four lines drawn on the graph below.

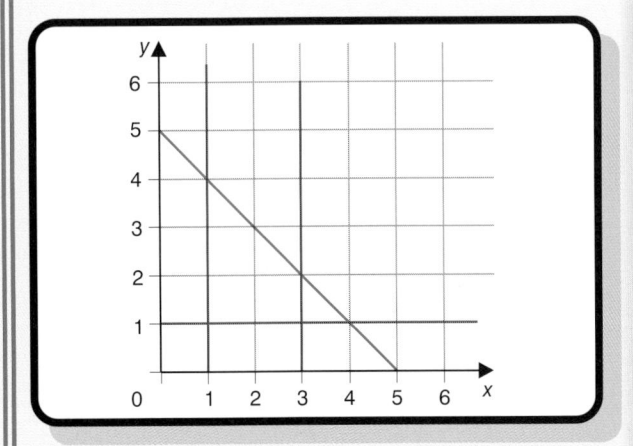

7 Write down the gradient and y-intercept of the graphs of the following equations.

   a) $y = -2x + 1$ **b)** $y + x = 3$ **c)** $y = \dfrac{x}{2} - 1$

8 The length of a rectangle is three times its width.
   a) If its width is x cm, write in terms of x:
      i) its length   **ii)** its area.
   b) If its area is 75 cm², write an equation in x and solve it to find x.

9 Solve the following quadratic equations.
   a) $x^2 + 7x + 10 = 0$ **b)** $x^2 + 4x - 5 = 0$
   c) $x^2 - 10x - 11 = 0$ **d)** $x^2 - 5x + 6 = 0$
   e) $x^2 - 5x - 6 = 0$

10 $c = a(m - v)^2$
   Find c when $a = 3$, $m = -2$ and $v = 4$.

11 $V = \frac{1}{3}\pi h^3$
   Rearrange the formula to give h in terms of V and π.

12 By drawing a suitable line on the graph below, solve the given simultaneous equations.
   $y = x + 1$
   $y = 5 - x$

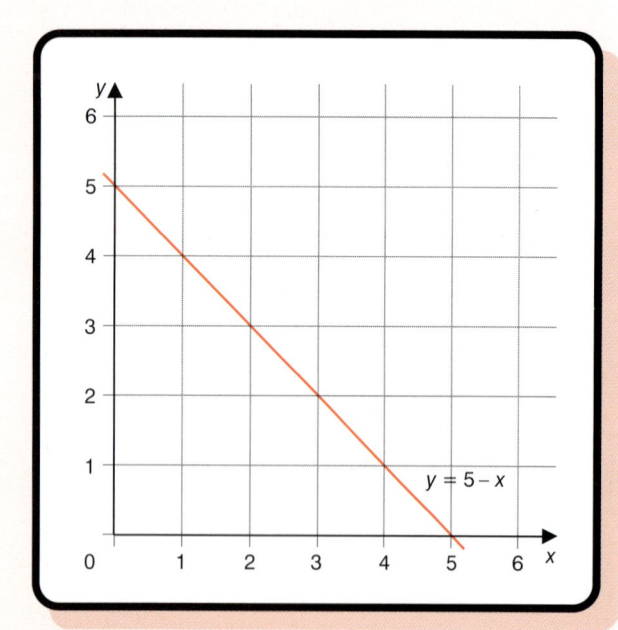

13 Factorise.
   a) $a^2 - b^2$ **b)** $4a^2 - 9b^2$

14 The graph below represents the daily hire charge for renting a car.

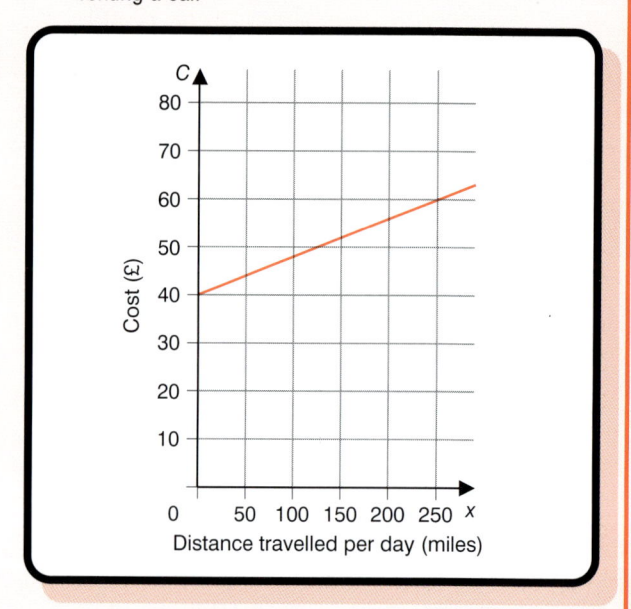

   a) What is the gradient of the line?
   b) What does the gradient represent?
   c) Express the equation of the line in the form $C = ax + b$.

15 Solve the following inequalities.
   a) $x + 2 < 9$
   b) $3x - 1 > 11$

16 Factorise the following expressions.
   a) $2x^2 + 7x + 3$
   b) $5x^2 + 9x - 2$

17 Match the following equations to the graphs below.

   a) $y = x^3$ **b)** $y = x + 1$ **c)** $y = \dfrac{1}{x}$ **d)** $y = x^2$

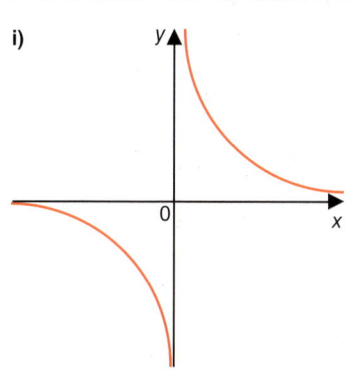

   i)

   ii)

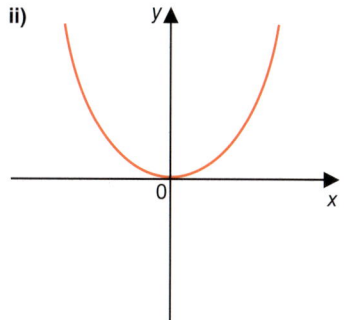

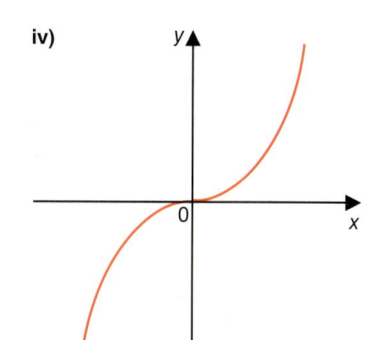

   iii)

   iv)

18 Complete the following table of values for $h = t^2 - 2t$.

t	−2	−1	0	1	2	3	4
h		3	0				8

Hence draw the graph of $h = t^2 - 2t$ on the axes on the right.

Use your graph to solve the equation $t^2 - 2t = 2$, giving your answer correct to 1 d.p.

19 The cost (c) of a function is given as £80 to hire the hall plus £22.50 per guest.
   a) If the number of guests is x, write an equation in c and x.
   b) Use your equation to find the cost of a function for 50 guests.
   c) Rearrange your equation to make x the subject.
   d) If a function cost £2105, how many guests were present?

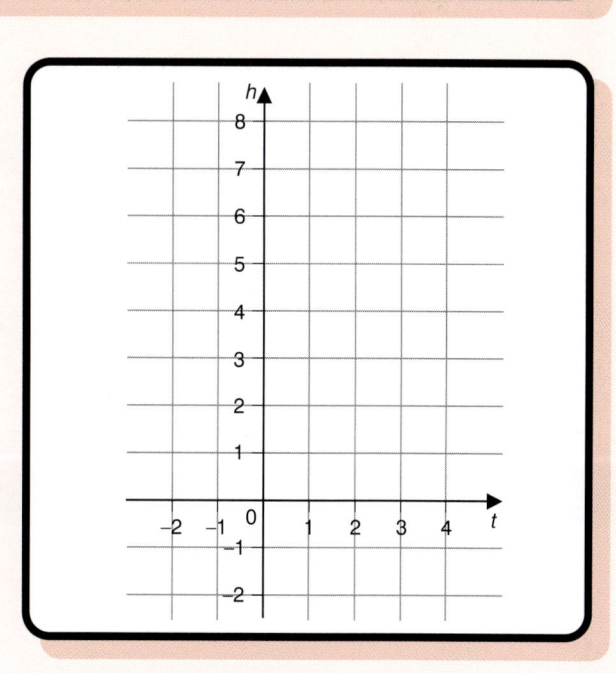

Revise Standard Grade and Intermediate Maths

Answers

1 $x = 3.5, y = 2.5$

2 $k = 72.4 \div 5.1^2 = 2.784$
 a) 21.8 b) $\sqrt{104.2 \div 2.784} = 6.1$

3 a) $3b(a + 2b)$ b) $2y(5y - 1)$ c) $xy(16y + 7x)$

4 a) i) $n + 3$ ii) $3(n + 3)$ or $3n + 9$, but not $3n + 3$
 b) $n + n + 3 + 3n + 9 = 5n + 12 = 67$
 c) $n = 11, n + 3 = 14, 3(n + 3) = 42$

5 $k = 3.8 \times \sqrt{0.17} = 1.57$

 a) 2.1
 b) 0.03

6 $x = 1; x = 3; x + y = 5; y = 1$

7 a) gradient = -2, y-intercept = 1
 b) gradient = -1, y-intercept = 3
 c) gradient = $\frac{1}{2}$, y-intercept = -1

8 a) i) $3x$ ii) $3x^2$ b) $3x^2 = 75, x^2 = 25, x = 5$

9 a) $(x + 5)(x + 2); x = -5, x = -2$
 b) $(x + 5)(x - 1); x = -5, x = 1$
 c) $(x - 11)(x + 1); x = 11, x = -1$
 d) $(x - 3)(x - 2); x = 3, x = 2$
 e) $(x - 6)(x + 1); x = 6, x = -1$

10 108

11 $h = \sqrt[3]{\frac{3V}{\pi}}$

12 $x = 2, y = 3$

▼ y

$y = x + 1$

6	
5	
4	
3	
2	
1	

$y = 5 - x$

◄
0 1 2 3 4 5 6 x

13 a) $(a - b)(a + b)$ b) $(2a - 3b)(2a + 3a)$

14 a) 0.08 b) The charge (in £) per mile
 c) $C = 0.08x + 40$

15 a) $x > 7$ b) $x < 4$

16 a) $(2x + 1)(x + 3)$ b) $(5x - 1)(x + 2)$

17 a) (iv) b) (iii) c) (i) d) (ii)

18

t	-2	-1	0	1	2	3	4
h	8	3	0	-1	0	3	8

$h = t^2 - 2t$

▼ h

8	
7	
6	
5	
4	
3	
2	
1	

$h = 2$

-2 -1 0 1 2 3 4 t
         -1
         -2
◄

$t = -0.7, t = 2.7$

19 a) $c = 22.5x + 80$ b) £1205 c) $x = \frac{c - 80}{22.5}$ d) 90

5 Pythagoras' theorem and trigonometry

Try your luck! Win the goldfish

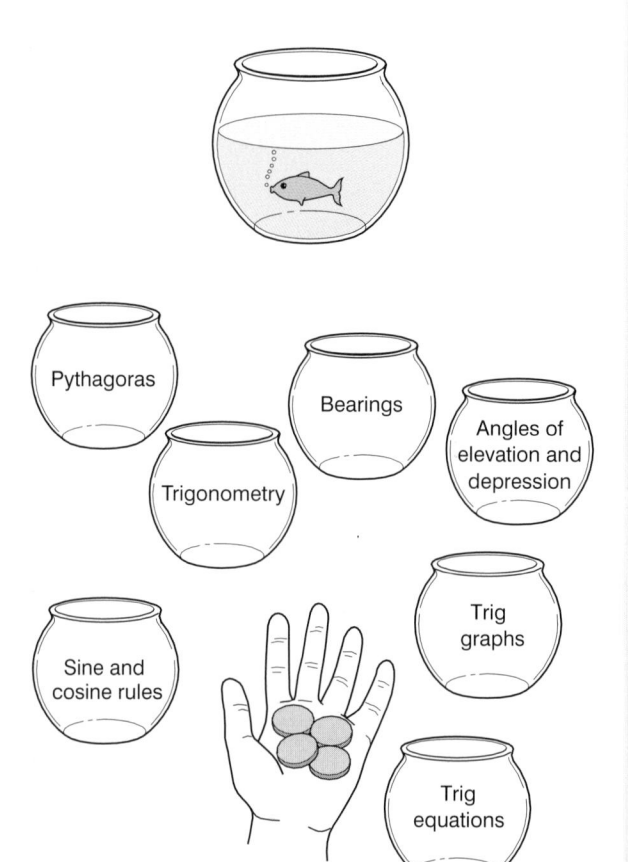

preview

By the end of this chapter you will be able to:

- use Pythagoras' theorem or trigonometry to calculate the side or angle of any right-angled triangle
- recognise when to use Pythagoras' theorem and when to use trigonometry
- calculate and use angles of elevation and depression
- understand and use bearings in conjunction with trigonometry or Pythagoras' theorem
- use the sine rule or cosine rule to solve non-right angled triangles
- draw and identify trigonometric graphs
- solve trigonometric equations

How much do you know already?

Questions in this section will often ask you to find lengths. If the question does not specify the number of **decimal places** or **significant figures** required in the answer, use the degree of accuracy that was used in the question. For example, if the question uses one decimal place, you should give your answer correct to one decimal place (1 d.p.).

If the question asks for an angle, you should give the answer to the nearest degree, unless the question asks otherwise.

Exercise 5.1

In questions 1–8, find the length of the side, or the size of the angle, marked x. Give all lengths to 1 decimal place and all angles to the nearest degree.

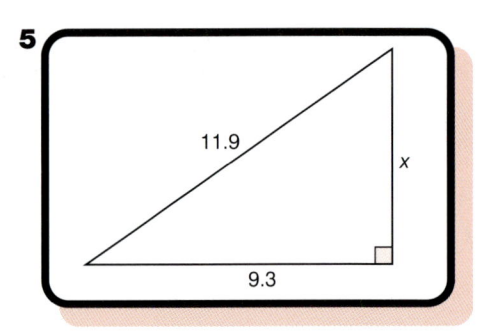

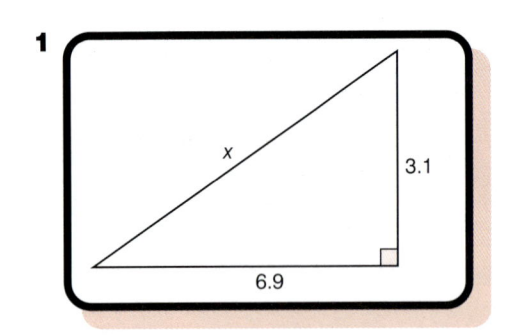

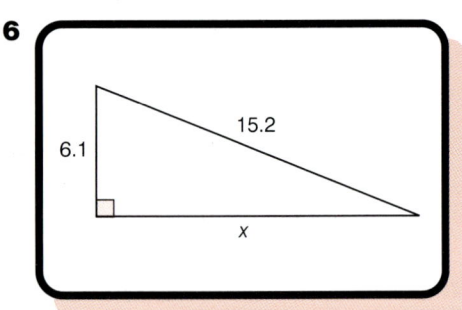

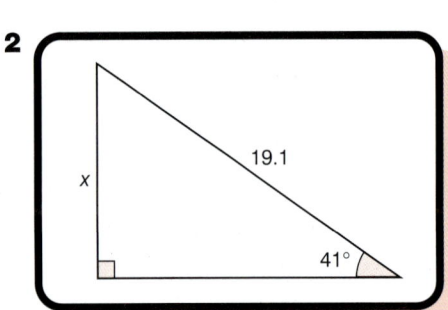

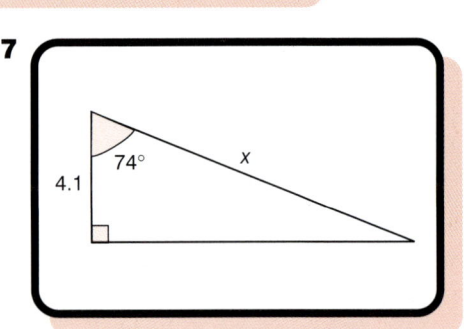

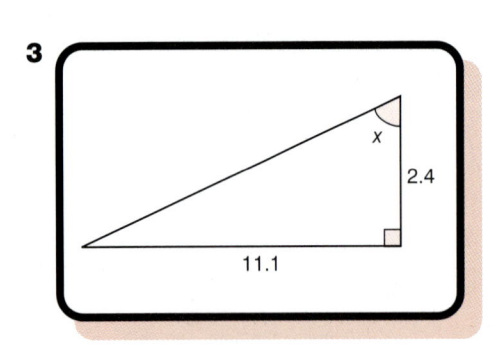

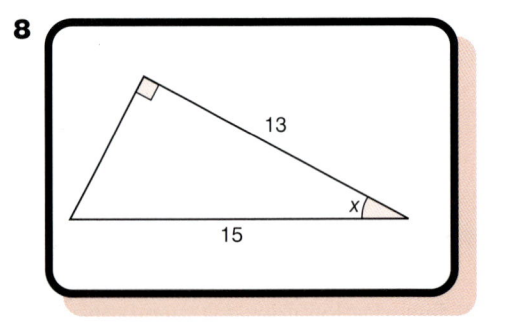

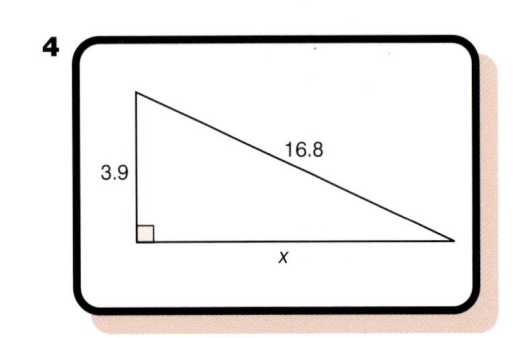

1 Triangle with sides 6.9 (base), 3.1 (right side), hypotenuse x, right angle at bottom-right.

2 Right-angled triangle with hypotenuse 19.1, angle 41° at bottom-right, side x on the left, right angle at bottom-left.

3 Right-angled triangle with base 11.1, right side 2.4, angle x at top, right angle at bottom-right.

4 Right-angled triangle with left side 3.9, hypotenuse 16.8, base x, right angle at bottom-left.

5 Right-angled triangle with hypotenuse 11.9, base 9.3, side x, right angle at bottom-right.

6 Right-angled triangle with left side 6.1, hypotenuse 15.2, base x, right angle at bottom-left.

7 Right-angled triangle with left side 4.1, angle 74° at top, side x, right angle at bottom-left.

8 Triangle with side 13, side 15, angle x at bottom-right, right angle at top-left.

9 Lou Kout has decided to give up lion-taming for the steadier job of stiltswalking. From a safe distance of 20 m his friend, Bea Ware, watches Lou Kout practising. If the angle of elevation of Lou from Bea is 10°, and she herself is 1.6 m tall, how high above the ground is the top of Lou Kout's head?

10 Oliver Transplant wants to live nearer the show ground. At present, he lives 8 km due south of the Big Top, but is moving to a house 3 km due east of it. What is the bearing of his new home from his old?

11 From a point 240 metres above sea level, a coastguard measures the angle of depression of two ships due east of him as 27° and 15°.
   a) Calculate the distance between the coastguard and ship 1.
   b) Calculate the distance between the ships.

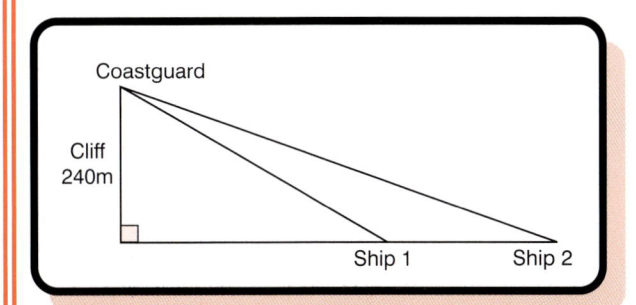

Pythagoras' theorem

The rule is $a^2 + b^2 = c^2$.

Identifying the hypotenuse

The **hypotenuse** is the name given to the longest side of a right-angled triangle. You will *always* find it opposite the right angle.

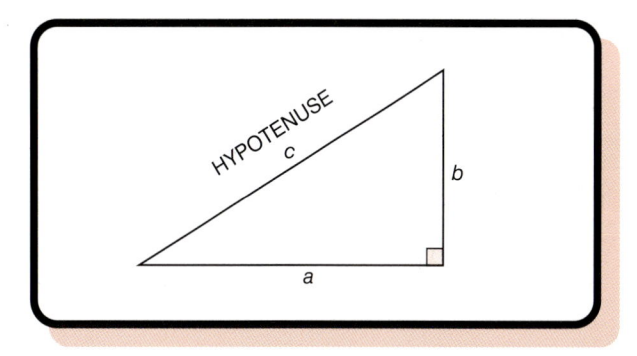

Sometimes they try to confuse you by turning the triangle round, but as long as you always **start by finding the right angle**, you can correctly identify the hypotenuse as being the side opposite it.

If you have an **isosceles** triangle (a triangle with two equal sides), you will probably not have a right angle. Don't worry! Karate Ken has the solution. Just turn it on to its odd side and chop downwards. (You're actually chopping down the perpendicular bisector.)

Answers

1. 7.6
2. 12.5
3. 78°
4. 16.3
5. 7.4
6. 13.9
7. 14.9
8. 30°
9. 5.1 m
10. 021°
11. a) 528.6 m b) 424.7 m

How did you get on?

All or most questions right?
Well done! You probably don't need to do the next few exercises. Turn to the examination-type questions in Exercise 5.9 on page 80 and see how you well you do. If you have any problems, turn back to the examples and exercises which you hoped to avoid, and work through some of them to sort out the difficulty.

Numbers 1, 4, 5, 6 right?
Fine! Pythagoras' theorem is no problem to you, but your trigonometry needs some help. Turn to page 76 where the juggling triplets will make everything clear.

Numbers 2, 3, 7, 8, 9, 10, 11 right?
You are brilliant at trigonometry, but somewhere along the line you have forgotten how to use Pythagoras' theorem. Don't worry! With a little help from Madam Attix, that's easily remedied.

Don't even ask?
Never mind. It's better to find out the worst now, because Madam Attix and the juggling triplets can easily help to sort out your problems.

Revise Standard Grade and Intermediate Maths

Calculating the hypotenuse

Once you have located the hypotenuse, it's plain sailing. Using your calculator, square the other two sides, add the results and then find the square root of the answer. Or, as Madam Attix so wisely says,

> **Madam Attix Says:**
> 'When finding the longest side, called the hypot,
> Add the squares of the sides, and square root the lot.'

So if c is the hypotenuse, then $c^2 = a^2 + b^2$ and $c = \sqrt{a^2 + b^2}$.

Example 5.1

In the triangle below, calculate the length of the side marked x. Give your answer correct to 1 d.p.

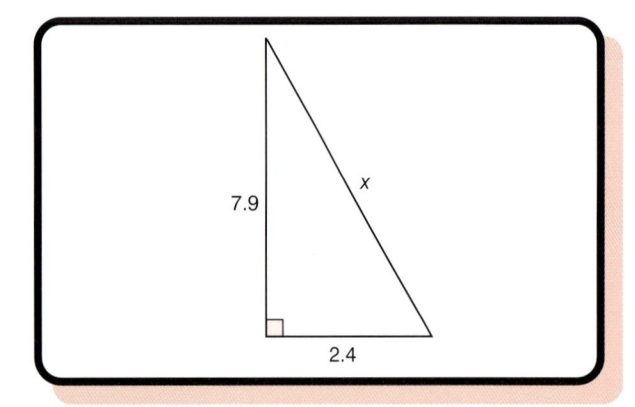

(Triangle with legs 7.9 and 2.4, hypotenuse x)

Solution

$7.9^2 + 2.4^2 = 68.17$

$\sqrt{68.17} = 8.3$ (1 d.p.)

You have to be careful not to get carried away and write all the calculations in one long string, e.g.

$7.9^2 + 2.4^2 = 68.17 = \sqrt{68.17} = 8.3$

because 68.17 cannot *possibly* equal $\sqrt{68.17}$, and it will not impress the examiners.

Exercise 5.2

In each triangle below, calculate the length of the side marked x. Give your answers correct to 1 d.p.

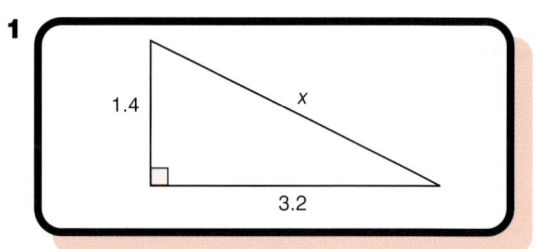

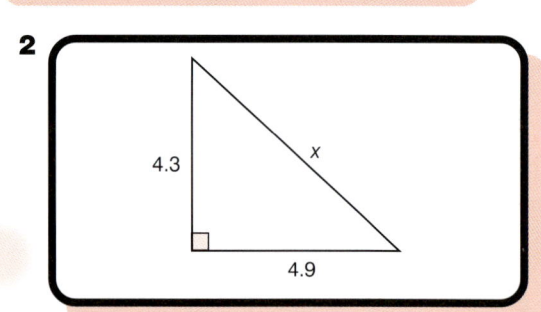

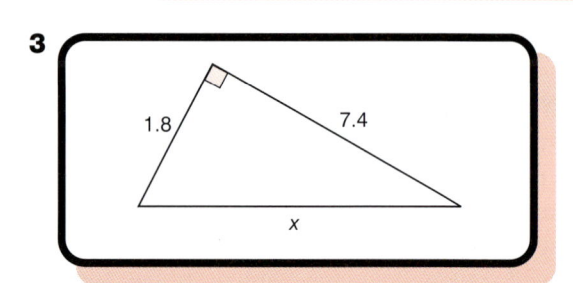

1 (Right triangle with legs 1.4 and 3.2, hypotenuse x)

2 (Right triangle with legs 4.3 and 4.9, hypotenuse x)

3 (Right triangle with legs 1.8 and 7.4, hypotenuse x)

Answers
1 3.5
2 6.5
3 7.6

TAKE A BREAK

If you were successful in that exercise, it's time to tackle the shorter sides. If you are still making mistakes, take a short break at this point and try again later.

Calculating a shorter side – i.e. one that is not the hypotenuse

$c^2 = a^2 + b^2 \Rightarrow c = \sqrt{a^2 + b^2}$

$a^2 = c^2 - b^2 \Rightarrow a = \sqrt{c^2 - b^2}$

$b^2 = c^2 - a^2 \Rightarrow b = \sqrt{c^2 - a^2}$

or simply remember,

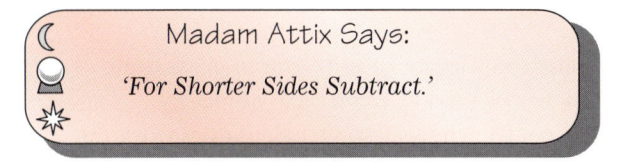

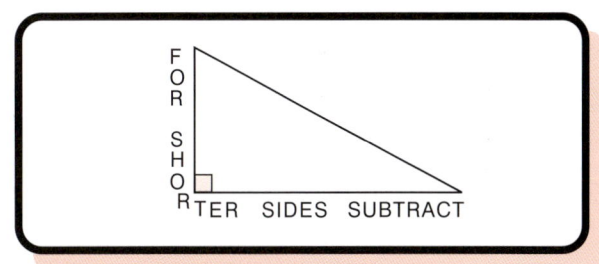

> **Madam Attix Says:**
>
> *'For Shorter Sides Subtract.'*

Example 5.2

In the triangle below, calculate the length of the side marked x. Give your answer correct to 1 d.p.

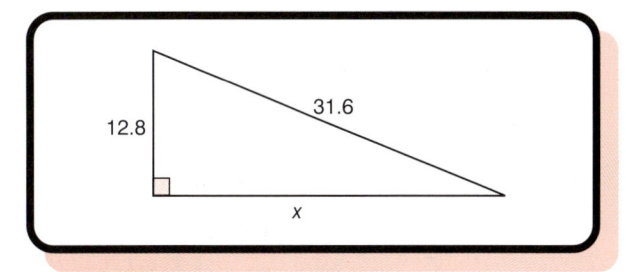

Solution

$31.6^2 - 12.8^2 = 834.72$

$\sqrt{834.72} = 28.9$ to 1 d.p.

When you are trying to find the length of a shorter side, you may sometimes find that your calculator shows the 'Error' or 'E' sign. This will happen if you start with the square of the shorter side and try to subtract the square of the hypotenuse. Your calculator will then have a negative number, for which it can't find the square root.

Safety first! Always start with the larger number.

Exercise 5.3

In each triangle below, calculate the length of the side marked x.

Give your answers correct to 1 d.p. where appropriate.

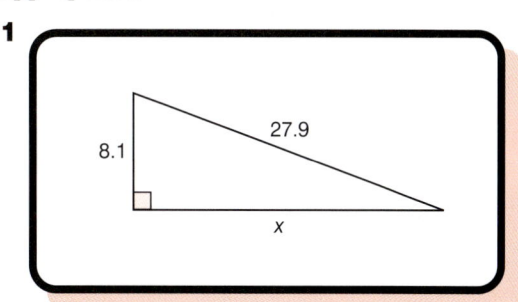

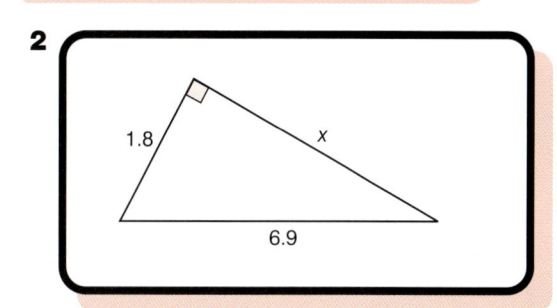

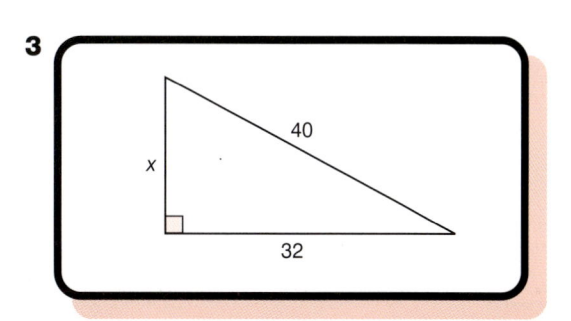

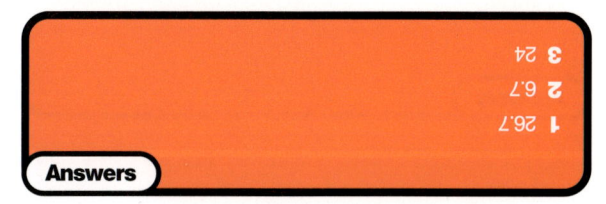

1

2

3

Answers

1 26.7
2 6.7
3 24

By now you should be feeling much more confident about using Pythagoras' theorem. The next exercise reinforces what you have just learnt, and gives you a chance to show off your new skill.

5

Revise Standard Grade and Intermediate Maths

Exercise 5.4

1 On the fairground, there is a chute for children. They slide down from the top, a height of 4 m, and land on cushions on the ground. If the cushions are at a distance of 7.2 m from the base of the chute, find the length of the chute.

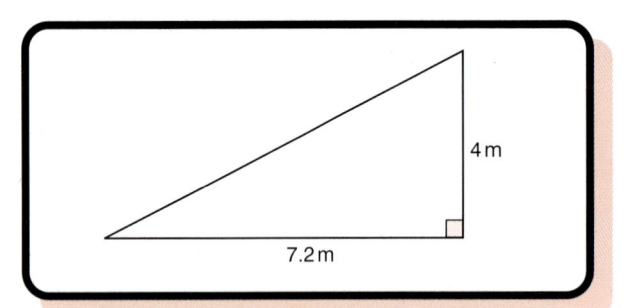

2 Two of the clowns do an act with a folding ladder. The ladder is 16 m long, and can be bent in half to form an upside-down V. The ladder extends to a width of 2.5 m when fully open. If a clown stands at the highest point, how high is he above the ground?

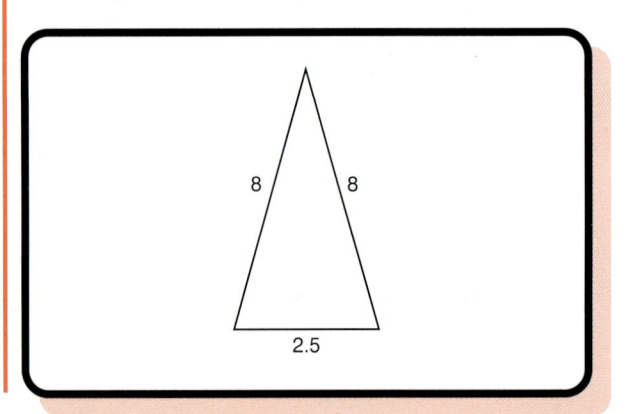

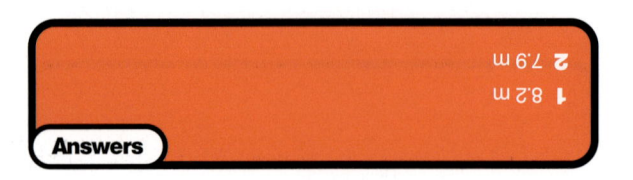

Answers
1 8.2 m
2 7.9 m

TAKE A BREAK

Now it's probably time for another short break before you and the juggling triplets tackle ...

Trigonometry

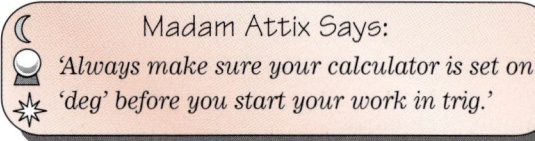

> **Madam Attix Says:**
> 'Always make sure your calculator is set on 'deg' before you start your work in trig.'

Some calculators require you to press the sin, cos or tan key before the number, e.g. sin 23, whereas some calculators work the other way round and would require 23 sin. Make sure you know how yours works.

Pythagoras' theorem or trigonometry?

Whereas Pythagoras' theorem gives a relationship between **three sides** of a right-angled triangle, trigonometry involves **two sides and an angle**.

You may have learnt the trigonometry rules by using SOH CAH TOA. If you find this hard to remember, say to yourself,

> **Madam Attix Says:**
> 'Some Old Hags Can't Always Hide Their Old Age.'

Pythagoras' theorem and trigonometry

To show you these formulae in action, here again are Willie Droppitt and his brothers Kenny and Noel. This time they are putting the *middle* letter at the top.

S: $\sin x = \dfrac{\text{opp}}{\text{hyp}}$
O: $\text{opp} = \sin x \times \text{hyp}$
H: $\text{hyp} = \dfrac{\text{opp}}{\sin x}$

C: $\cos x = \dfrac{\text{adj}}{\text{hyp}}$
A: $\text{adj} = \cos x \times \text{hyp}$
H: $\text{hyp} = \dfrac{\text{adj}}{\cos x}$

T: $\tan x = \dfrac{\text{opp}}{\text{adj}}$
O: $\text{opp} = \tan x \times \text{adj}$
A: $\text{adj} = \dfrac{\text{opp}}{\tan x}$

Just to recap
- The **hypotenuse** is the longest side of a right-angled triangle.
- The **opposite** is the side that is opposite (or does not touch) the angle you are using.
- The **adjacent** (which means 'next to') is the other side.

Using trigonometry to find sides

1. Write out the triplets for SOH CAH TOA, being very careful to put the *middle* letter at the top.

   O / S H   A / C H   O / T A

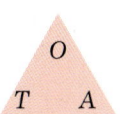

2. Look for the side which the question ignores, and cross out the triplets which contain it. The remaining triplet is the one to use.

3. Cover or cross out the letter representing the side or angle which you need to find. As usual, if the remaining letters are on the same level, you *multiply* them, and if one is on top of the other, you *divide* the top by the bottom.

Example 5.3

In the triangle below, calculate the length of the side marked x. Give your answer correct to 1 d.p.

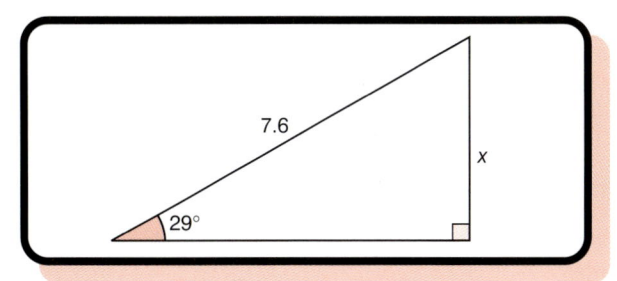

[Triangle: hypotenuse 7.6, angle 29°, side x opposite the right angle marker]

Method
1. Label the triangle in the usual way.
2. The side not mentioned is A, so cross out the triplets containing A and keep

   O / S H

3. You need to find O, so cover or cross it out, and you will be left with S H.

Solution
$\sin 29° \times 7.6 = 3.7$

Revise Standard Grade and Intermediate Maths

Example 5.4

In the triangle below, calculate the length of the side marked x. Give your answer correct to 1 d.p.

[Triangle with angle 23° at bottom left, right angle at bottom right, side 5.1 along the bottom, and x on the right vertical side.]

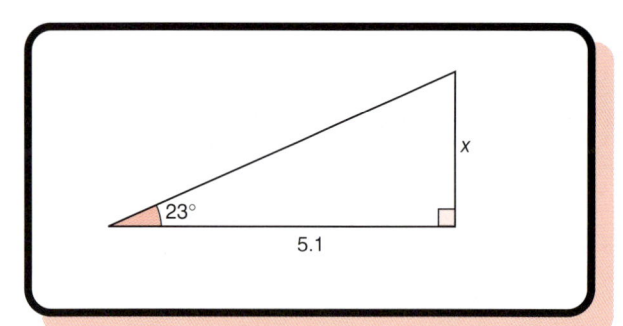

Method

1 Label the triangle in the usual way. This time the angle which you are using is at the bottom left of the triangle, so O will be the side marked x.

2 H is not mentioned, so cross out the two triplets containing it and you will be left with

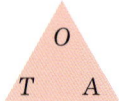

[Triangle labelled O at top, T and A at bottom]

3 You are looking for O so cover or cross it out. T and A are on the same level, so you multiply them.

Solution

$\tan 23° \times 5.1 = 2.2$ (1 d.p.)

Example 5.5

In the triangle below, calculate the length of the side marked x. Give your answer correct to 1 d.p.

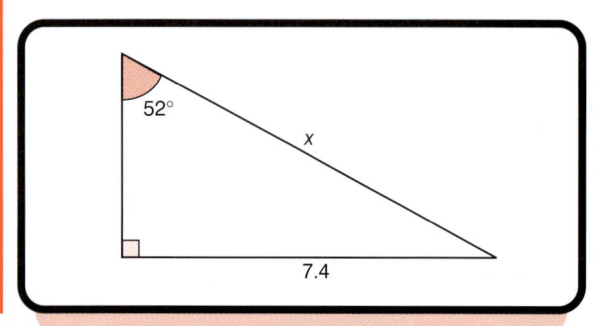

[Triangle with angle 52° at top, right angle at bottom left, side 7.4 along the bottom, and x on the hypotenuse.]

Method

When you have labelled the triangle, you should find that the unwanted side is A. Crossing out the unwanted triplets leaves

[Triangle labelled O at top, S and H at bottom]

This time, however, the required side is H, and covering or crossing this out leaves

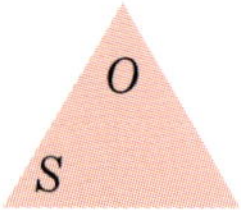

[Triangle labelled O at top, S at bottom left]

Solution

$7.4 \div \sin 52° = 9.4$

Check that you know how to get this answer on your calculator.

Example 5.6

In the triangle below, calculate the length of the side marked x. Give your answer correct to 1 d.p.

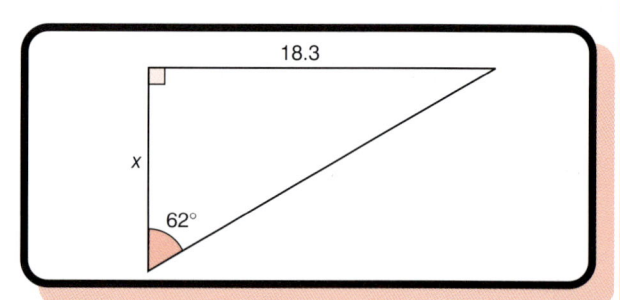

[Triangle with right angle at top left, 18.3 along the top, 62° at bottom, and x on the left vertical side.]

Method

When you have labelled the triangle, and crossed out the triplets in the usual way, you should have

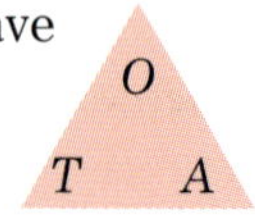

[Triangle labelled O at top, T and A at bottom]

As you are looking for A, you will have a division sum.

Solution

$18.3 \div \tan 62° = 9.7$ (1 d.p.)

Exercise 5.5

In each triangle below, calculate the length of the side marked x. Give your answers correct to 1 d.p.

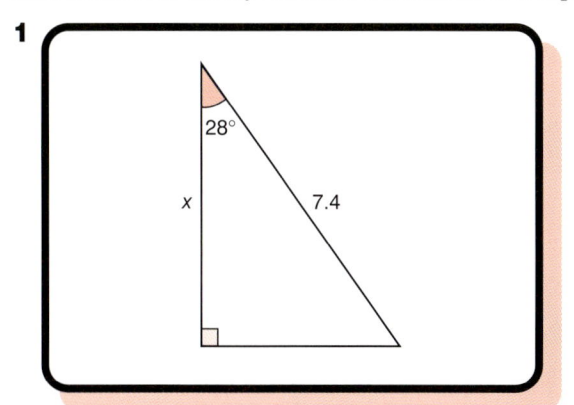

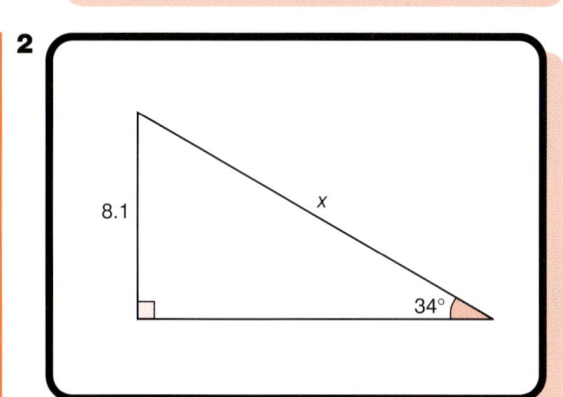

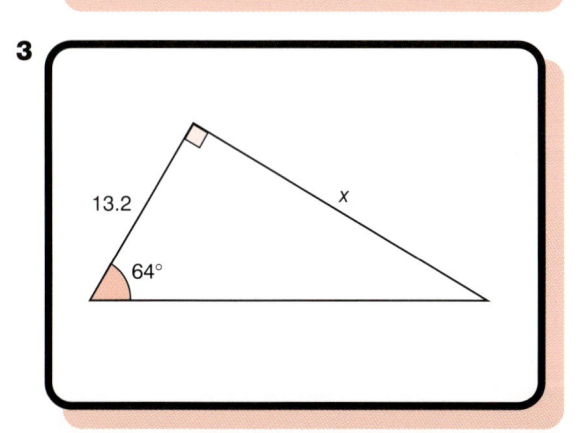

1 (triangle with 28° angle, side 7.4, side x)

2 (triangle with 8.1, x, 34°)

3 (triangle with 13.2, x, 64°)

Answers
1 6.5
2 14.5
3 27.1

Pythagoras' theorem and trigonometry

Using trigonometry to find angles

To find an angle, you must always start by finding its **inverse** sin, cos or tan, which some books write as **sin⁻¹**, **cos⁻¹** or **tan⁻¹**. To do this, you press the key which is probably in the top left-hand corner of your calculator, and labelled `inv`, `shift` or `2nd f`.

If you are getting an 'Error' or 'E' sign, or a ridiculous answer, you are probably not pressing `=` before you press `inv` `sin`, `cos` or `tan`. Also, some calculators require you to press `=` at the end, so it's a good idea to make sure how yours works, well ahead of the examination. If you still can't find where you went wrong, check that your calculator is set to degrees.

Example 5.7

In the following triangle, find, to the nearest degree, the angle marked x.

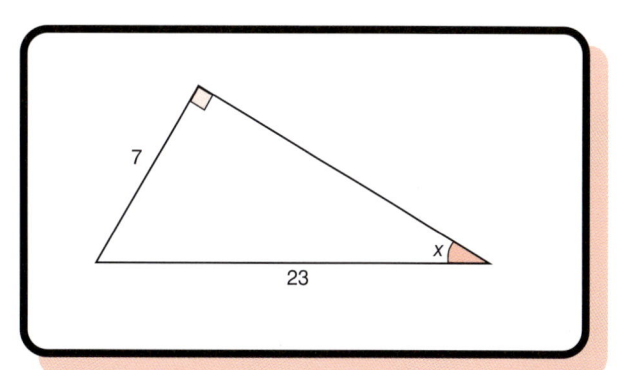

(triangle with sides 7 and 23, angle x)

Method
1 Label the triangle in the usual way.

2 You do not know anything about A, so cross out the two triangles containing this letter. You should have

$$\begin{array}{c} O \\ S \quad H \end{array}$$

Solution

$$\sin x = \frac{O}{H} = \frac{7}{23} = 0.304$$

Angle $x =$ `inv` `sin` $0.304 = 18°$ to the nearest degree.

73

Revise Standard Grade and Intermediate Maths

Example 5.8

In the following triangle find, to the nearest degree, the angle marked x.

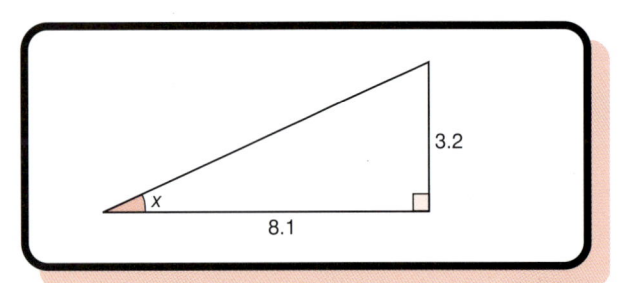

Labelling the triangle in the usual way should eliminate H.

Solution

$\tan x = \dfrac{O}{A} = \dfrac{3.2}{8.1} = 0.395$

Angle $x =$ [inv] [tan] $0.395 = 22°$

Example 5.9

In the following triangle find, to the nearest degree, the angle marked x.

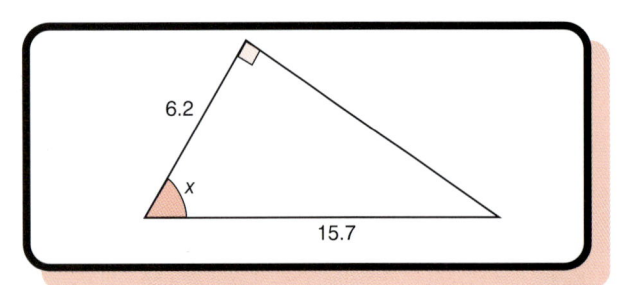

The required triplet this time is A C H

Solution

$\cos x = \dfrac{6.2}{15.7} = 0.3949$

Angle $x =$ [inv] [cos] $0.3949 = 67°$

Exercise 5.6

In each of the following triangles find, to the nearest degree, the angle marked x.

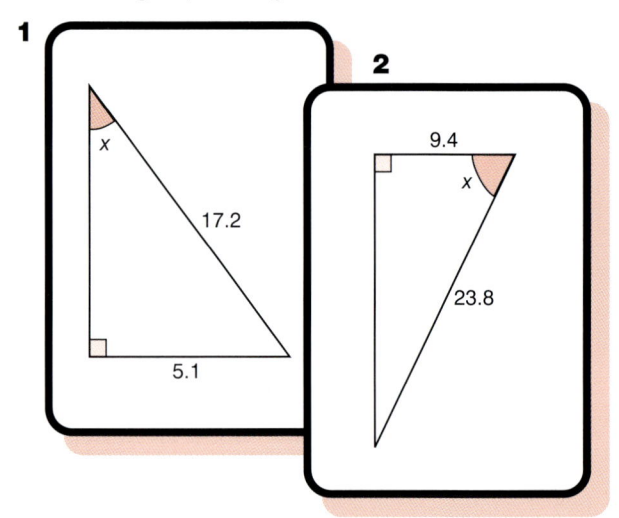

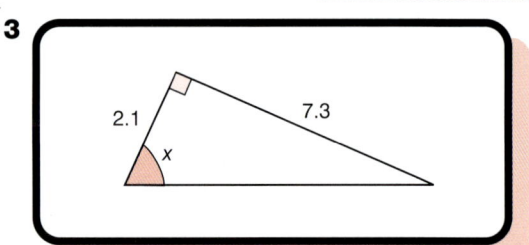

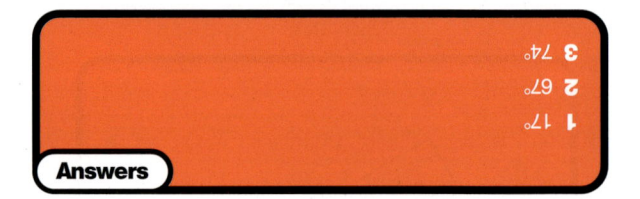

1

2

3

Answers

1 17°
2 67°
3 74°

TAKE A BREAK

Time for another break! Don't worry! There's not much more to do in this chapter, and you don't have to learn anything new to be able to deal with angles of elevation and depression, and bearings. They are merely further applications of trigonometry or Pythagoras' theorem, but they might come up in the examination.

74

Angles of elevation and depression

Angles of elevation and depression are always measured **from the horizontal**. Look at the horizon, and go **up for an angle of elevation** or **down for an angle of depression**.

Example 5.10

Eva Rupp is sitting at a horizontal distance of 3 m away from her friend and rival Honor Dyatt who is showing off – as usual – on the trampoline. Eva's eyes are level with the trampoline and the angle of elevation is 53°.

a) How high is Honor above the trampoline?

b) When Honor looks gloatingly down at Eva, what is the angle of depression?

Solution

a) Sketch a triangle of the situation, and label the triangle in the usual way.

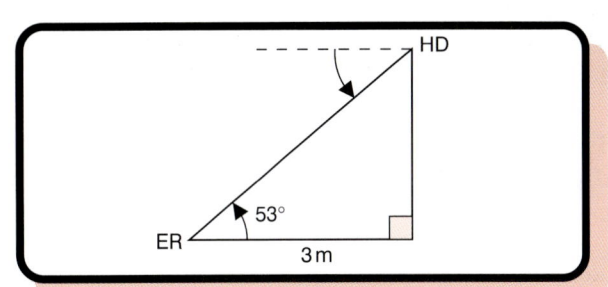

You are not interested in H, so the necessary calculation is

tan 53° × 3 = 3.98 m or 4 m

b) As you can see from the sketch, Eva's angle of elevation and Honor's angle of depression are the same.

Honor's angle of depression = 53°.

Bearings

Bearings are three-figure numbers which represent directions. They are measured as the **clockwise angle from the north**.

Bearings of 010°, 135° and 315° are shown below.

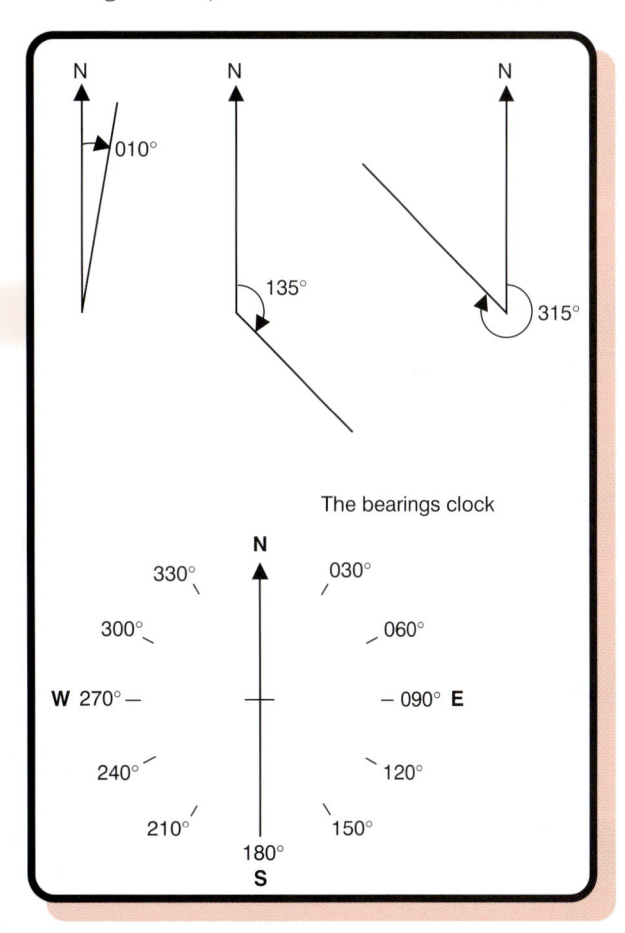

The bearings clock

Summary

- *Always use three figures.*
- *Always start from the north and go clockwise.*

Pythagoras' theorem and trigonometry

Revise Standard Grade and Intermediate Maths

Example 5.11

Everyone avoids Ivanitch when he is practising with his flea circus. If Bernie Stung is standing on a bearing of 024° from Ivanitch, what is the bearing of Ivanitch from Bernie Stung?

Solution

'From' gives the clue as to where you start.

Start by sketching the two men from the position of Ivanitch.

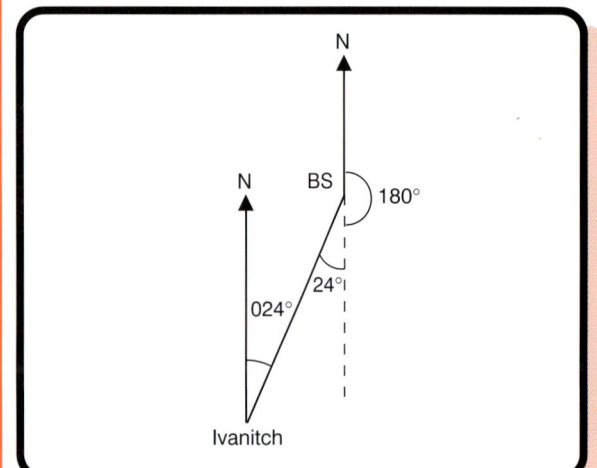

As you then have to calculate from Bernie Stung, draw a short line in the northerly direction and mark the required angle as indicated on the diagram. As both north lines are parallel, you have a pair of 'Z' or alternate angles. From north to south measures 180°, so the answer is

180° + 24° = 204°

Trigonometry or Pythagoras' theorem?

- You must have two sides to use Pythagoras' theorem.
- You must involve an angle for trigonometry.

Sometimes you can choose whichever you prefer, but remember:

TRig **IN**voles **A**ngles (TRINA).

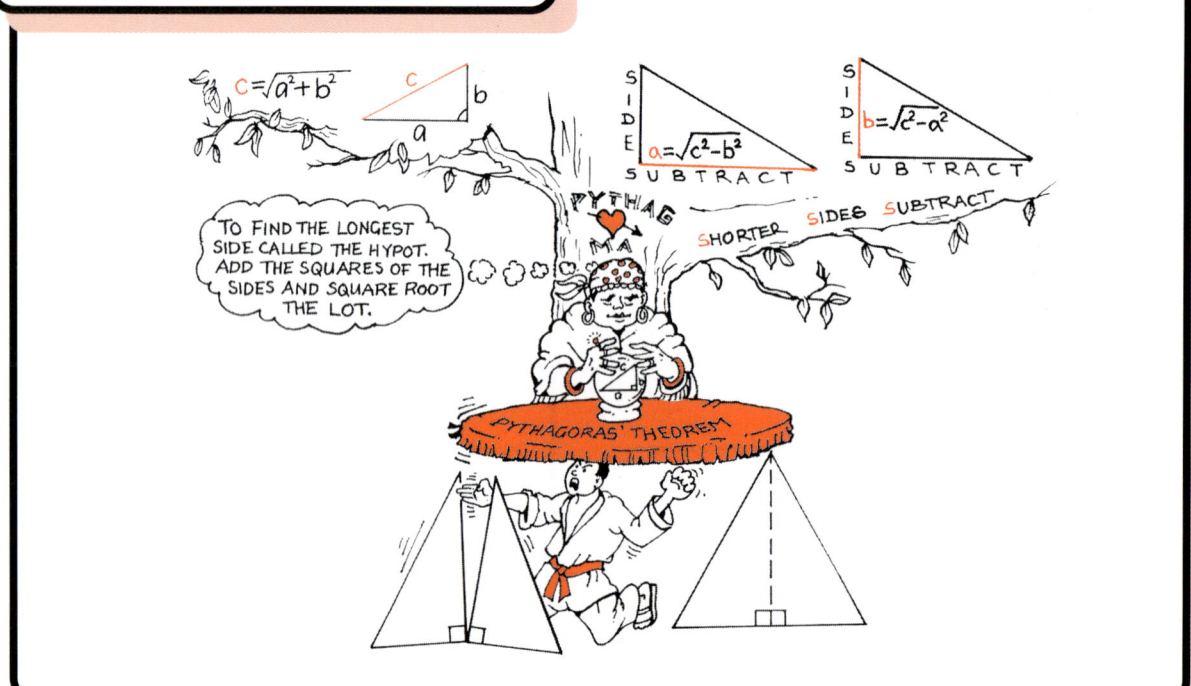

Exercise 5.7

1. A ship is at S, 5 km south of a lighthouse at L. It needs to sail to a port P which is due east of L. If the bearing of P from S is 035°, find the distance that it needs to travel.

2. From the top of a cliff Albert Ross sees a rock jutting up from the sea. If the angle of depression of the rock from the top of the cliff is 15°, and the rock is 76 m from the base of the cliff, how high is the cliff?

3. An isosceles triangle has a base of 10 cm and equal sides of 17 cm.
   a) Find its perpendicular height.
      (**Hint**: Remember Karate Ken.)
   b) Find its area.

4. Dilly Gent uses a ladder 8 m long to reach a window 6.5 m up from the ground.
   a) What is the furthest possible distance between the building and the base of the ladder?
   b) What angle would the ladder make with the building?

5. Use trigonometry or Pythagoras' theorem as appropriate.

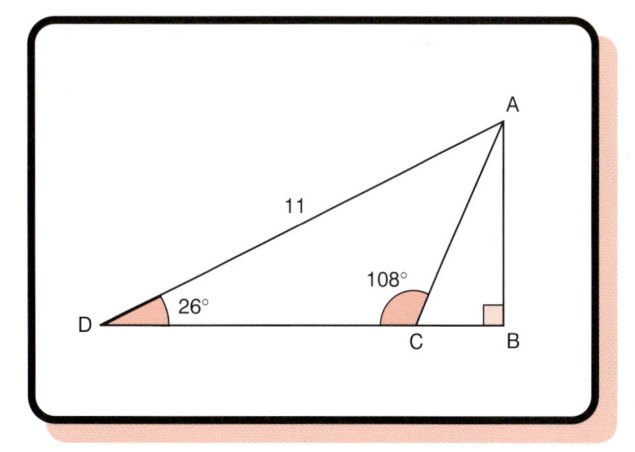

   a) Find AB.
   b) Find BD.
   c) Write down the size of angle ACB.
   d) Find AC.
   e) Find CD.

   (**Remember** that triangle ACD is not right-angled.)

Revise Standard Grade and Intermediate Maths

Answers

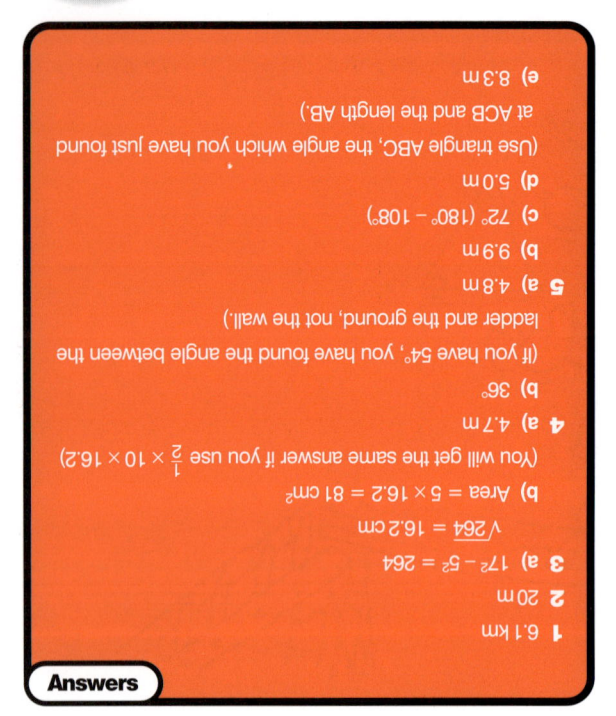

1. 6.1 km
2. 20 m
3. a) $17^2 - 5^2 = 264$
   $\sqrt{264} = 16.2$ cm
   b) Area $= 5 \times 16.2 = 81$ cm^2
   (You will get the same answer if you use $\frac{1}{2} \times 10 \times 16.2$.)
4. a) 4.7 m
   b) 36°
   (If you have 54°, you have found the angle between the ladder and the ground, not the wall.)
5. a) 4.8 m
   b) 9.9 m
   c) 72° (180° − 108°)
   d) 5.0 m
   (Use triangle ABC, the angle which you have just found at ACB and the length AB.)
   e) 8.3 m

Reasoning and enquiry/non-routine questions

Now try the following examples. Don't be put off if you can't spot the solution straight away. Ringo will give you the secret of solving problems so that you can cope confidently with anything that the examiners may throw at you.

Example 5.12

Morag Ressive needs to use a ladder to fix a TV dish to a wall of her house.

The ladder is 6 metres long and has to reach 5.7 metres up the vertical wall. She knows that a ladder is only safe when the angle between the ladder and the ground is between 71° and 76°. The ground is horizontal.

Can Morag use the ladder safely?

Solution

Although this looks tricky don't panic.

Read carefully all the information you are given. Try sketching a diagram

"The ground is horizontal" and the wall is vertical, so we have a right angle.

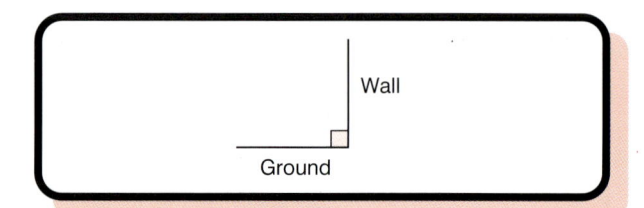

Right angled triangles often crop up in Pythagoras or trigonometry questions. You have to find an angle; so try trig.

Draw the ladder against the wall and write down the measurements.

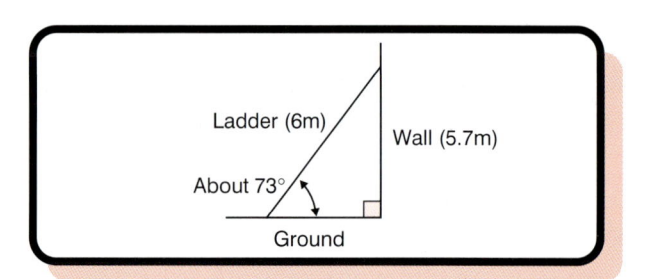

Ladder (6m) Wall (5.7m) About 73° Ground

The strategy seems to be "right angled trig", and as the angle is only approximate, let's use the two sides.

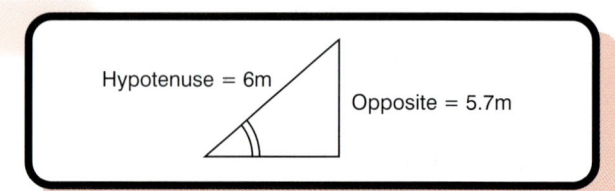

Hypotenuse = 6m, Opposite = 5.7m

Sin angle $= \dfrac{5.7}{6} = 0.95$

angle $= \sin^{-1}(0.95) = 71.8°$

71.8°, or 72° to the nearest degree, is between 71° and 76° so Morag can use the ladder safely.

Example 5.13

Doug McGarden wants to use a metal strip to strengthen a bookcase. The back of the bookcase is rectangular. It measures 75 cm by 190 cm.

He wants to put the metal strip along the diagonal of the back of the bookcase. He has a 2 m long strip. Is it long enough?

Solution

First of all interpret the information:

"The bookcase is rectangular", and the metal strip is to be placed diagonally; so we have a right angled triangle.

Then decide the strategy – as it does not involve angles, use Pythagoras' theorem.

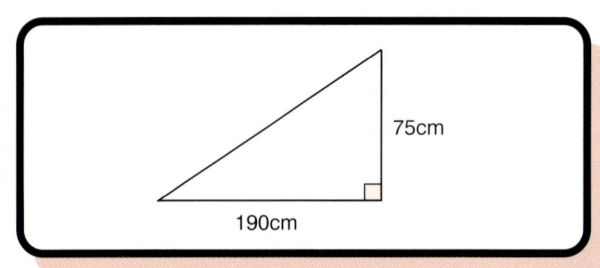

$190^2 + 75^2 = 41725$

$\sqrt{41725} = 204.27$

The diagonal is roughly 204 cm, so the 2 m strip will not be long enough.

Exercise 5.8

1. Isla Gree has bought a jigsaw puzzle. It says on the box that the jigsaw puzzle measures 28 inches by 22 inches and is rectangular in shape. Isla has a circular table with diameter 36 inches.

   Will she be able to fit the completed jigsaw on to the table?

2. Bruce Umtee wants to build a ramp up to his vertical door. The regulations state that the slope of the ramp should be 25° or less. The ramp has to reach up to the door at a height of 2.1 metres. He wants to start the ramp at a horizontal distance of 4.7 metres from the bottom of the door.

   Will the ramp meet the regulations?

Answers

1. Yes. Diagonal of rectangle = 35.6 inches, which is less than diameter of circle = 36 inches
2. Yes. Angle is 24.1°, which is less than 25°

Trigonometry for non-right angled scalene triangles

Scalene triangles have no sides equal. There are two rules for non-right angled scalene triangles: the sine and the cosine rules. These formulae are given in the *Formulae list* in the Credit and Intermediate 2 examination papers.

How do I know which rule to use?

If there is an angle and its opposite side given in the question, use the sine rule. Otherwise use the cosine rule.

The sine rule

This rule is used when the question involves two angles and two lengths.

This version of the formula is easier to use for finding angles:

$$\frac{\sin A}{a} = \frac{\sin B}{b} = \frac{\sin C}{c}$$

and this one is easier for finding lengths:

$$\frac{a}{\sin A} = \frac{b}{\sin B} = \frac{c}{\sin C}$$

The cosine rule

This rule applies when you are working with three lengths and one angle.

To find length a: $a^2 = b^2 + c^2 - 2bc \cos A$

To find angle A: $\cos A = \dfrac{b^2 + c^2 - a^2}{2bc}$

and use INV COS to find the angle.

Can you work out the formulae for sides b and c, and for angles B and C?

Exercise 5.9

1 In the triangle JKL, find:
 a) JL   b) KL

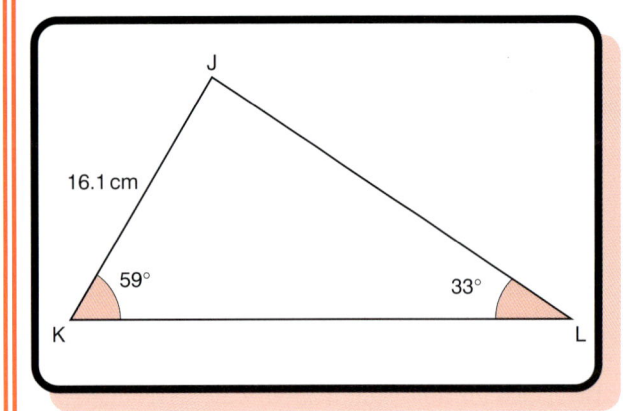

(Triangle JKL: angle K = 59°, angle L = 33°, JK = 16.1 cm)

2 A circus caravan, C, is at a bearing of 117° from a town, T, and a field, F, is at a bearing of 261° from the caravan and 197° from the town. The distance of the field from the town is 562 m. Find:
 a) angle TCF
 b) the distance of the field from the caravan.

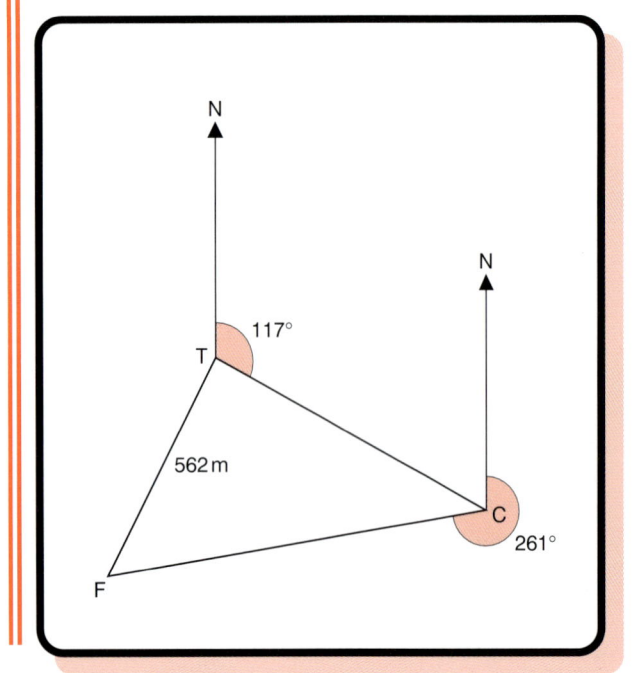

3 In the triangle ABC, calculate the length of BC.

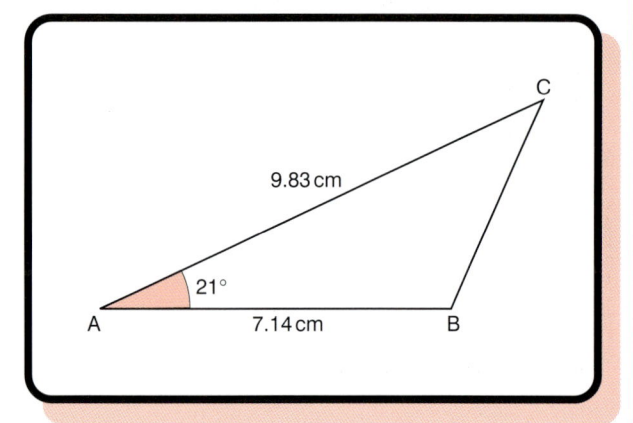

(Triangle ABC: angle A = 21°, AC = 9.83 cm, AB = 7.14 cm)

4 A triangular field, PQR, is shown below.

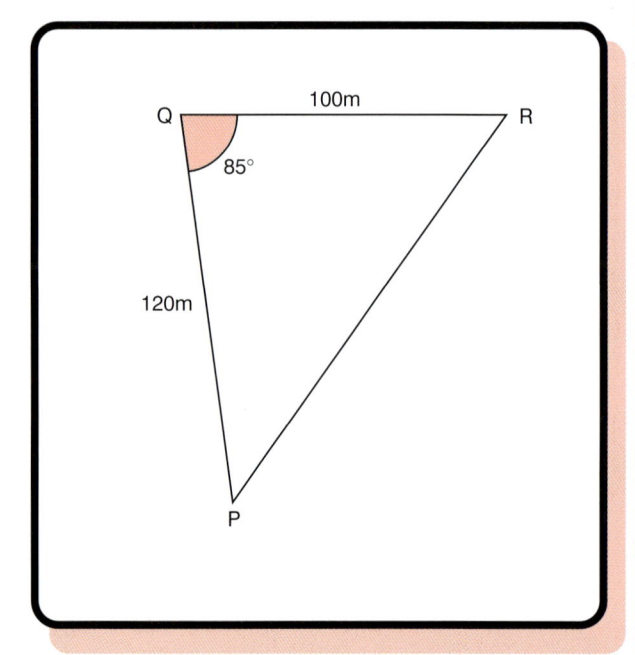

PQ = 120 metres, QR = 100 metres and angle PQR = 85°.

Calculate the length of PR. **Do not use a scale drawing.**

Pythagoras' theorem and trigonometry

5 Two spotlights, 120m apart on either side of a runway, pick up an aircraft coming in to land.

How far is the aircraft from spotlight A?

Do not use a scale drawing

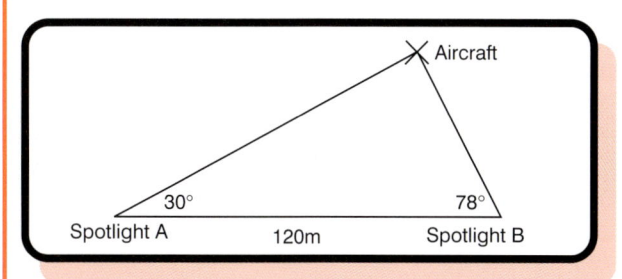

(Diagram: triangle with Spotlight A at left with 30° angle, Spotlight B at right with 78° angle, 120m base, Aircraft at top)

6 The diagram shows the position of three towns A, E and G.

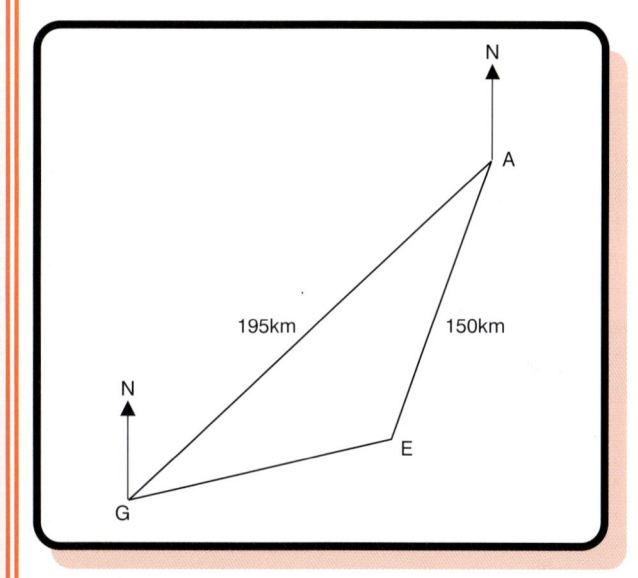

(Diagram: towns A, E, G with GA = 195km and AE = 150km, with North arrows at A and G)

G is 195 kilometres from A.

E is 150 kilometres from A.

From G the bearing of A is 050°.

From A the bearing of E is 215°.

How far apart are towns G and E?

Answers

1 a) 25.3 cm **b)** 29.5 cm
2 a) 36° **b)** 941.6 m
3 4.07 cm
4 149.4 m
5 123.4 m
6 $GE^2 = 195^2 + 150^2 - 2 \times 150 \times 195 \times \cos 15°$
GE = (63.39) 63.4 km

Sin, cos and tan graphs

Sine and cosine graphs have the same basic shape. The sine graph starts from the origin (remember original sin), but the cosine graph starts from 1 on the y-axis when $x = 0$ (the cosine graph).

$y = \sin x°$

$y = \cos x°$

$y = \tan x°$

Honor Dyatt loves Dr Tan's baked beans, but unfortunately for her fellow trapeze artist, they repeat every 180°.

DR TAN'S BAKED BEANS REPEAT EVERY 180°

DR TAN'S BAKED BEANS REPEAT EVERY 180°

DR TAN'S BAKED BEANS REPEAT EVERY 180°

Related trigonometric graphs

What does the graph of $y = \sin bx°$ or $y = \cos bx°$ look like?

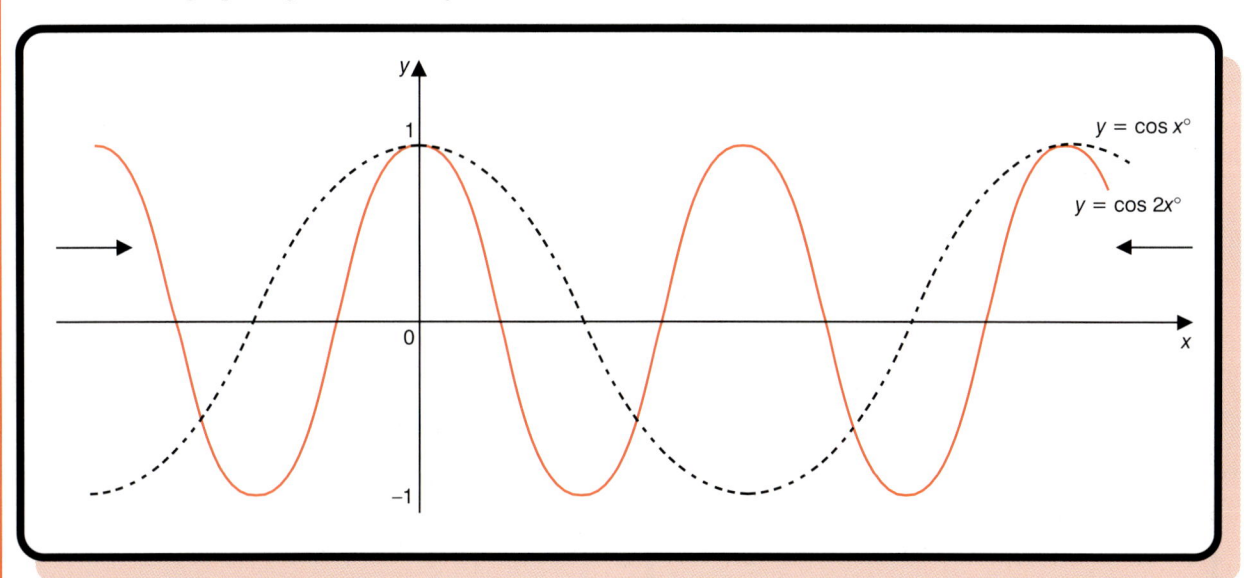

[Graph showing $y = \cos x°$ (dashed) and $y = \cos 2x°$ (solid) between -1 and 1]

With $\cos 2x°$, the fairground accordionist, Con Serteenar, squashes $\cos x°$ towards the y-axis to half its width.

With $\cos \frac{1}{2}x°$, he stretches it to twice its width.

Multiplying by a number greater than 1 squashes the line of $\cos x°$ towards the y-axis.

Dividing by a number greater than 1 (or multiplying by a fraction) stretches $\cos x°$ from the y-axis.

The same "squashing" and "stretching" happens with $\sin bx°$.

Times squashes → $\cos 2x°$

Divide stretches → $\cos \frac{1}{2}x°$

Revise Standard Grade and Intermediate Maths

What does the graph of $y = a \sin x°$ or $y = \sin x° + c$ look like?

Adding, subtracting, multiplying or dividing outside the $\sin x°$ or $\cos x°$ moves the graph in the positive or negative **vertical** direction as you would expect.

Adding to $\sin x°$ or $\cos x°$ moves the graph upwards.

Subtracting from $\sin x°$ or $\cos x°$ moves the graph downwards.

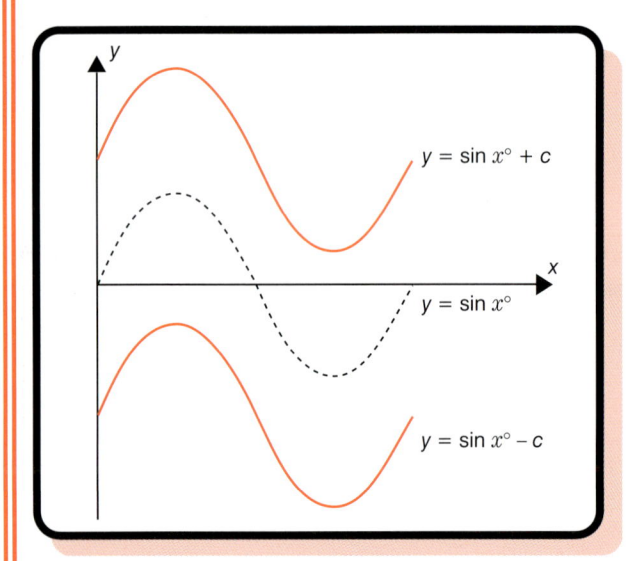

Multiplying $\sin x°$ or $\cos x°$ by a whole number stretches the graph from the x-axis.

Dividing $\sin x°$ or $\cos x°$ by a whole number (or multiplying by a fraction) squashes the graph towards the x-axis.

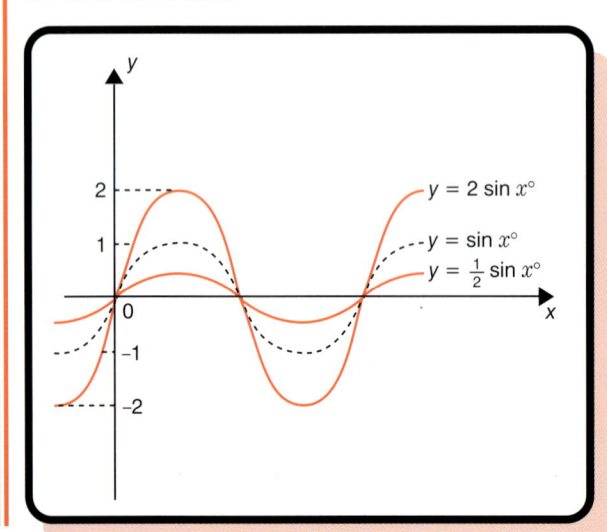

Exercise 5.10

1 The diagram below shows part of the graph of $y = \cos x°$ and the graph of a related function. Write down the equation of the related graph.

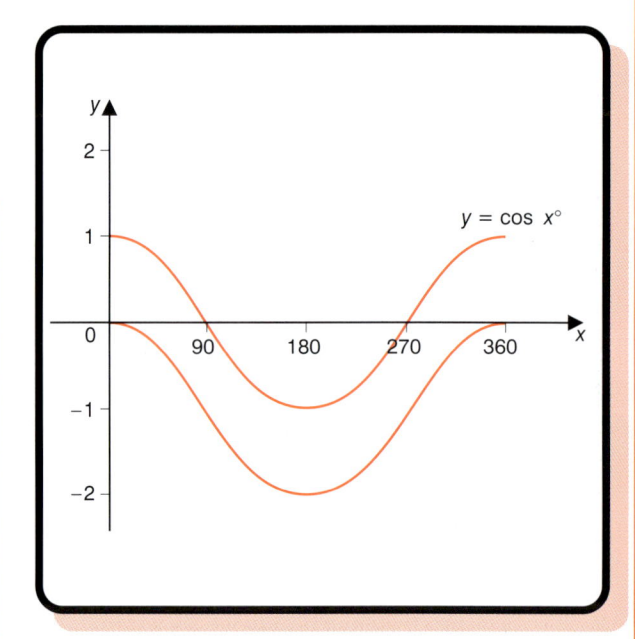

2 The diagram below shows part of the graph of $y = \sin x°$ and the graph of a related function (drawn as a broken line). Write down the equation of the related graph.

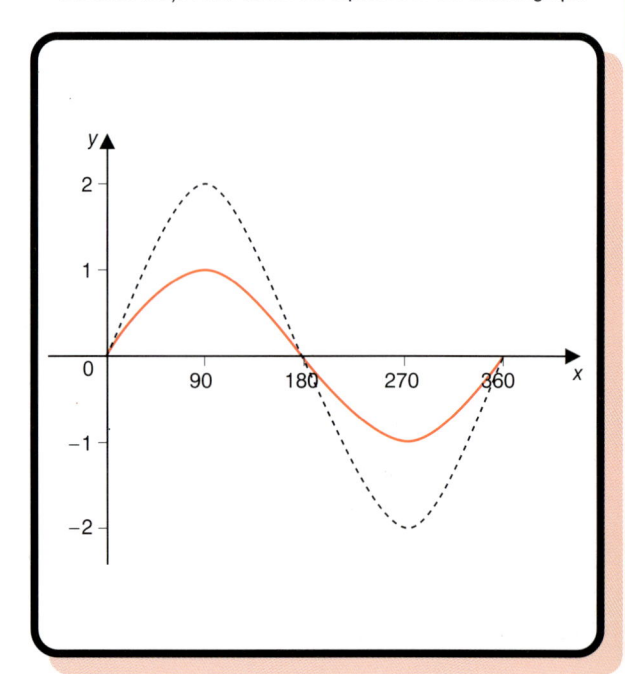

3 The diagram below shows part of the graph of $y = \sin x°$ and the graph of a related function. Write down the equation of the related graph.

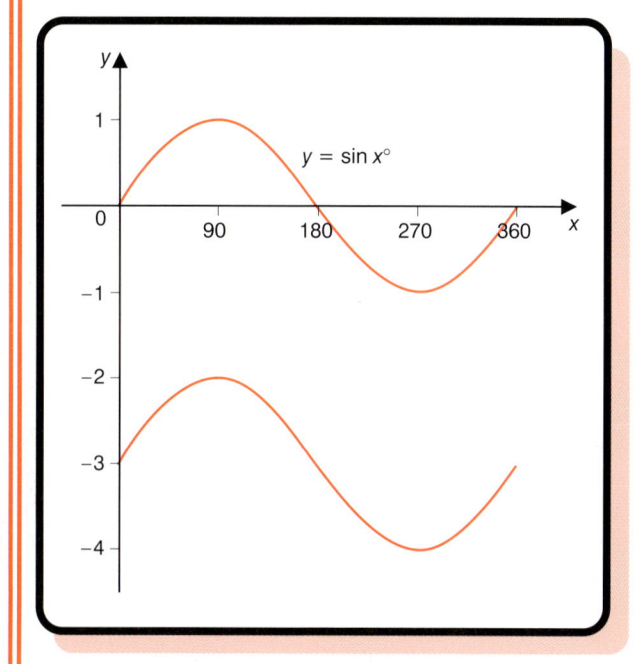

4 The diagram below shows part of the graph of $y = \cos x°$ (drawn as a broken line) and the graph of a related function. Write down the equation of the related graph.

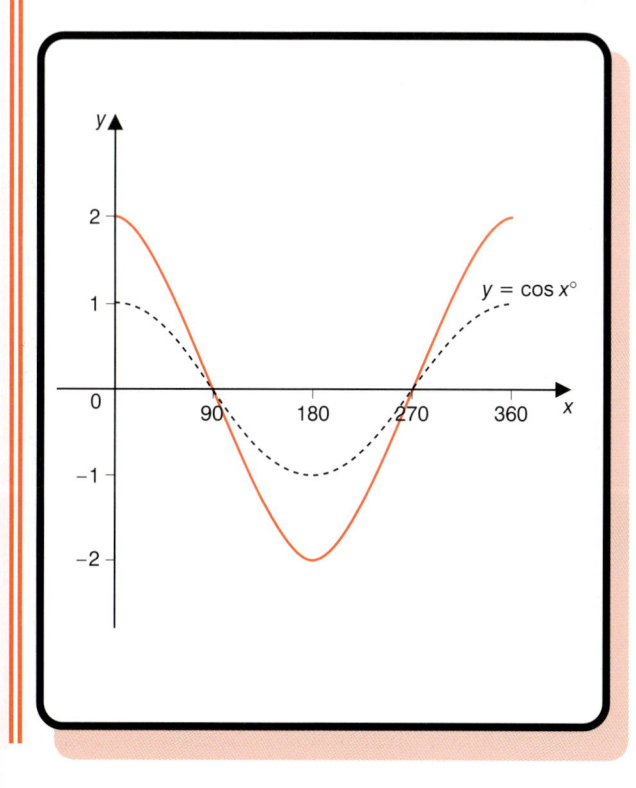

5 The diagram below shows part of the graph of $y = \cos x$ (drawn as a broken line) and the graph of a related function. Write down the equation of the related graph.

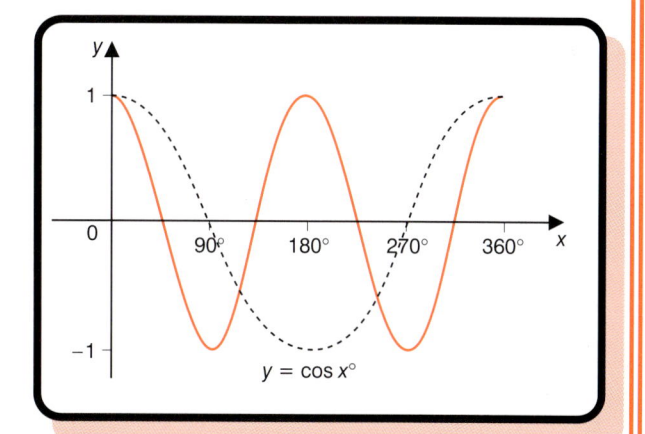

Answers

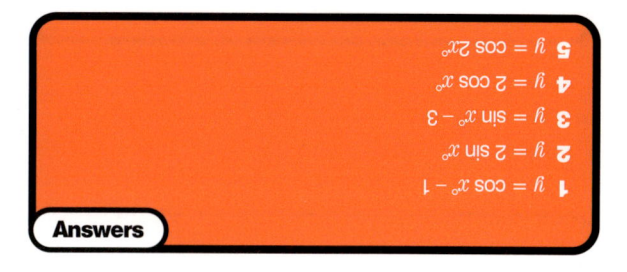

1. $y = \cos x° - 1$
2. $y = 2\sin x°$
3. $y = \sin x° - 3$
4. $y = 2\cos x°$
5. $y = \cos 2x°$

Solving trigonometric equations

Example 5.14

Find the solutions for x in the range $0 \leqslant x < 360$, which satisfy these equations.

a) $\sin x° = 0.5$
b) $\cos x° = 0.5$
c) $\cos x° = 0.61$
d) $\tan x° = -0.2$

Solution

a) Draw the graph of $y = \sin x°$, then draw a horizontal dotted line for $y = 0.5$. This crosses the $y = \sin x$ graph at two places. The solutions are where the line cuts the graph. Using your calculator for inverse sin (0.5) will give you one solution i.e. 30°.

85

Revise Standard Grade and Intermediate Maths

The other solution is found from the graph. It is $180° - 30°$ (or $90° + 60°$) or $150°$.

The solutions are $x = 30°, 150°$.

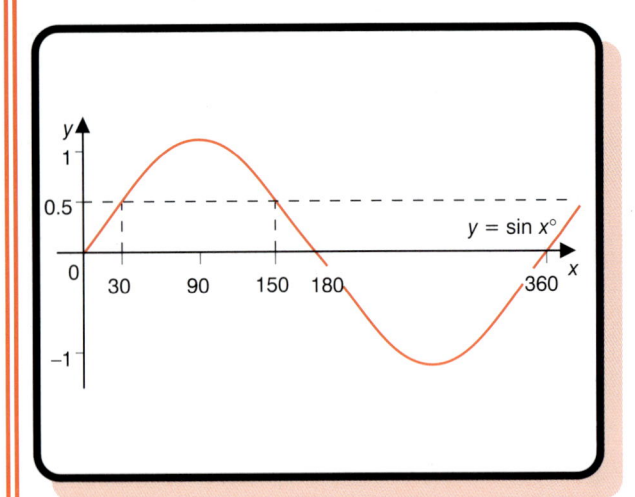

b) Draw the graph of $y = \cos x°$, then draw a horizontal dotted line for $y = 0.5$.

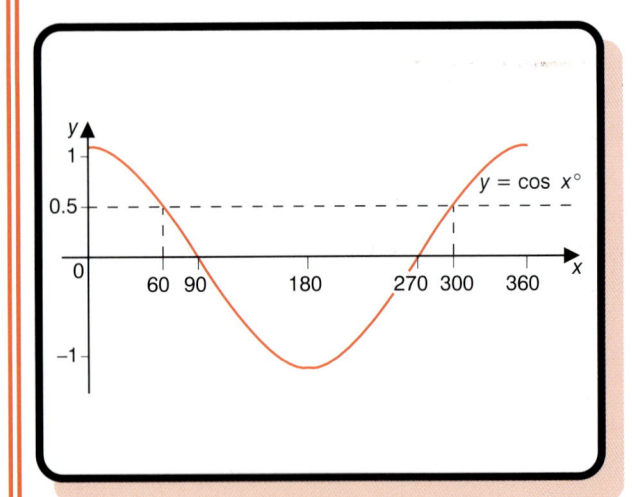

This crosses the $y = \cos x°$ graph at two places, giving the two solutions.

Using your calculator for inverse cos (0.5) will give you one solution i.e. $60°$. The other is the same distance from $360°$ so it is $360° - 60° = 300°$.

The solutions are $x = 60, 300$.

c) Again, draw the graph of $y = \cos x°$ and add a line at $y = 0.61$. The solutions are where the line cuts the graph. Your calculator will give you inverse cos (0.61) = $52.4°$. The other solution is at $360° - 52.4°$ (or $270° + 37.6°$).

The solutions are $x = 52.4°, 307.6°$.

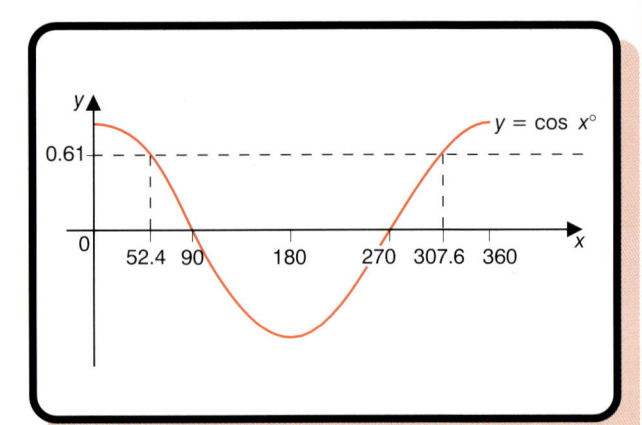

d) Draw the graph of $y = \tan x°$ and then draw a horizontal dotted line for $y = -0.2$. Where this line crosses the $y = \tan x°$ graph gives the solutions.

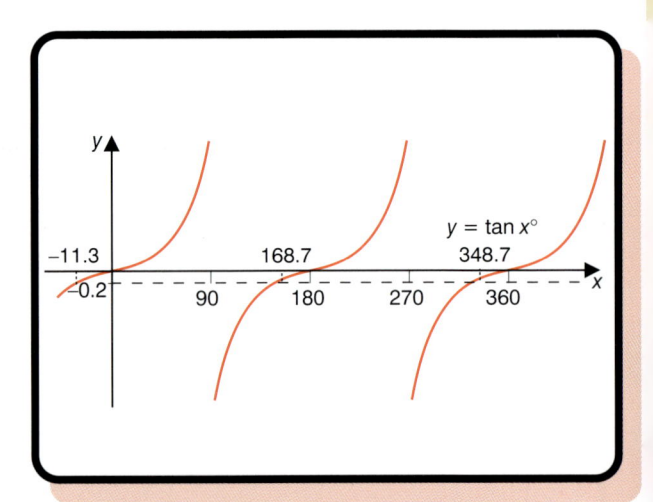

Using your calculator for inverse tan (–0.2) will give you $-11.3°$. This is a negative solution, and you want solutions between $0°$ and $360°$. Don't despair, just ask Dr Tan! Add $180°$ to $-11.3°$ to get $168.7°$, then add $180°$ again to find the second solution.

The solutions are $x = 168.7°, 348.7°$.

Pythagoras' theorem and trigonometry

You may have solved questions like these using the CAST diagram. If you are more at home with this method, stick with it.

S	A
T	C

Remember that you nearly always get more than one solution for this type of question.

Exercise 5.11

Sketch the sin, cos and tan graphs, then find all the solutions for x, correct to one decimal place, in the range $0° \leq x < 360°$ for the following equations.

1 $\sin x = 0.89$

2 $\tan x = -0.41$

3 $\cos x = 0.24$

4 $\sin x = -0.12$

5 $\cos x = 0.91$

6 $\tan x = \sqrt{3}$

Answers

1 $62.9°, 117.1°$
2 $157.7°, 337.7°$
3 $76.1°, 283.9°$
4 $186.9°, 353.1°$
5 $24.5°, 335.5°$
6 $60.0°, 240.0°$

TAKE A BREAK

All things being equal, this is a good time to take a break.

Revise Standard Grade and Intermediate Maths

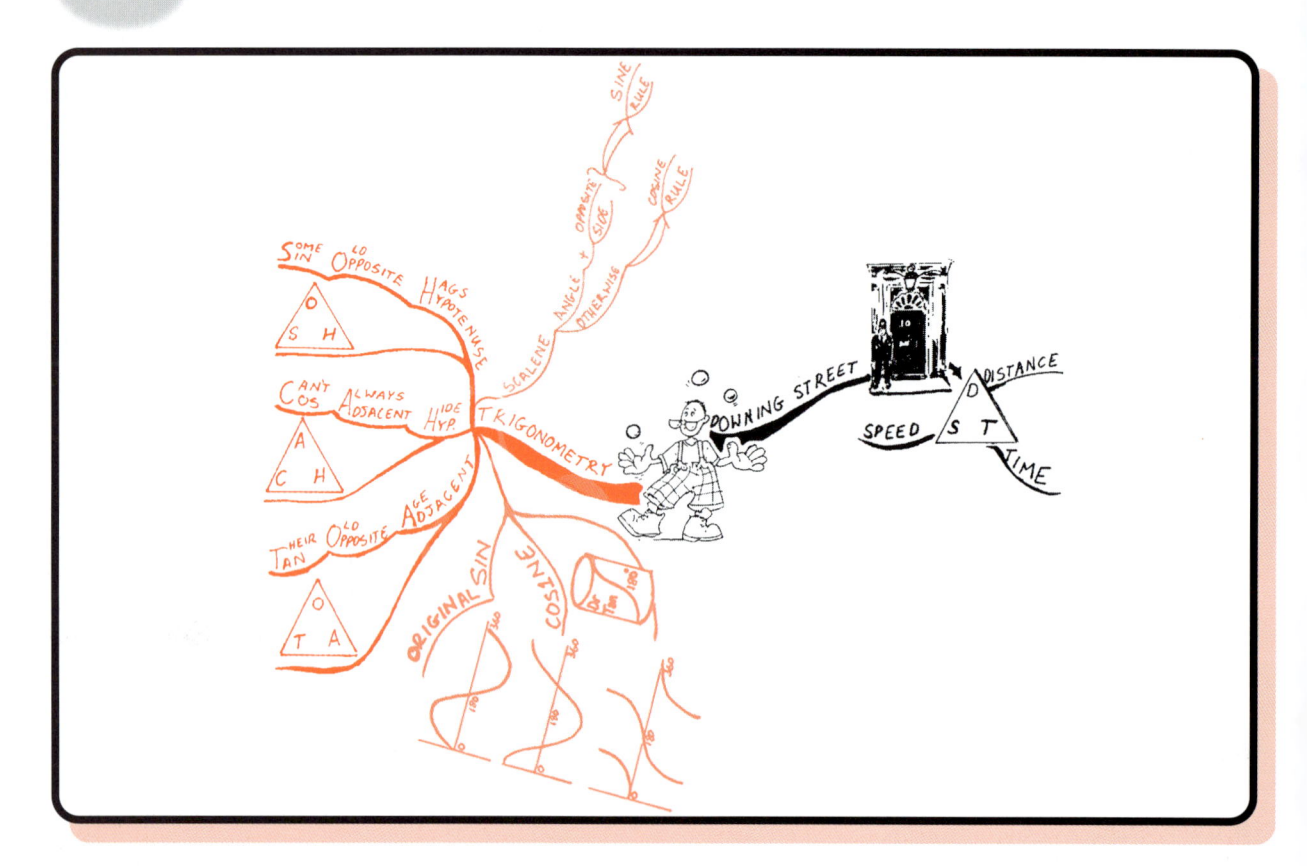

5

review
How much have you learnt?

Tick off each topic in the list when you are confident you can cope with it.

- Use Pythagoras' theorem to find the length of the hypotenuse.
- Use Pythagoras' theorem to find the length of a shorter side.
- Use trigonometry to calculate the side of any right-angled triangle.
- Use trigonometry to calculate the angle of any right-angled triangle.
- Recognise when to use Pythagoras' theorem and when to use trigonometry.
- Recognise angles of elevation and depression.
- Calculate and use angles of elevation and depression.
- Understand bearings.
- Use bearings in conjunction with trigonometry or Pythagoras' theorem.
- Use the sine rule or cosine rule to solve non-right angled triangles.
- Draw and identify trigonometric graphs.
- Solve trigonometric equations.

6 Length, area and volume

Can you see the point to all these?

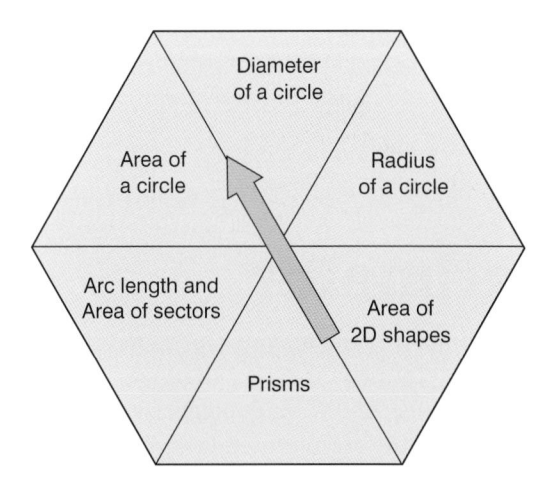

- Diameter of a circle
- Area of a circle
- Radius of a circle
- Arc length and Area of sectors
- Area of 2D shapes
- Prisms

preview

By the end of this chapter you will be able to:

- identify the centre, radius and circumference of a circle
- calculate the circumference and area of a circle, given the radius or diameter
- calculate the area of a rectangle, square, triangle, parallelogram
- calculate the surface area of a cuboid
- calculate areas of shapes made up of rectangles, triangles and semicircles
- find the area of a sector of a circle
- find the length of an arc of a circle
- find the area of a segment of a circle
- identify the cross-section of a prism and calculate its volume
- calculate base area of containers from their volume or capacity

How much do you know already?

Exercise 6.1

1. Find the area of a circle of radius 2.8 cm.

2. Find the volume of a cuboid 12 cm by 30 cm by 5 cm.

3. A circle has a diameter of 16.2 cm. What is its circumference?

4. A rectangle is twice as long as it is wide.
   a) If its width is x cm, state its length in terms of x.
   b) Give its perimeter in terms of x.
   c) What is its area in terms of x?
   d) If its area is 98 cm², write an equation in x and solve it to find the width of the rectangle.

5. Find the area of the following shape.

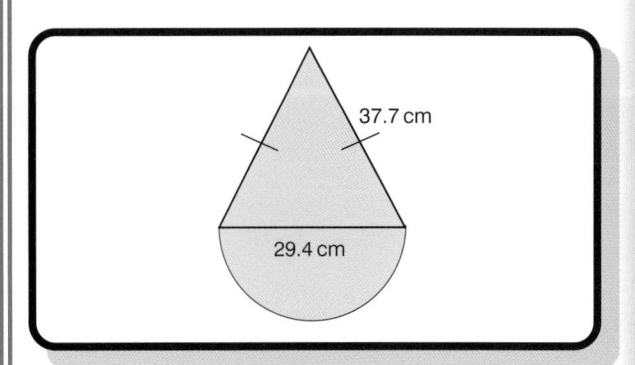

   37.7 cm
   29.4 cm

Revise Standard Grade and Intermediate Maths

6. A cylinder containing 2.25 litres of a mixture has a radius of 5.5 cm. How deep is the liquid? Give your answer to the nearest cm. (1 litre = 1000 cm^3)

7. Find the area of a circle radius 1.8 cm.

8. Find the area of the shape below.

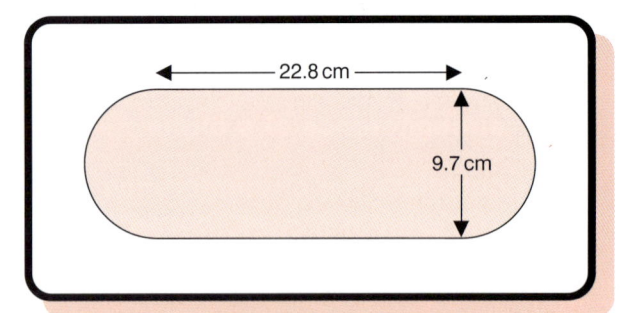

   ← 22.8 cm →

   9.7 cm

9. Compost is to be spread on a garden measuring 10 m by 6 m.

   If the depth of the compost is to be 10 cm, what will be the required volume of compost? Express your answer in m^3.

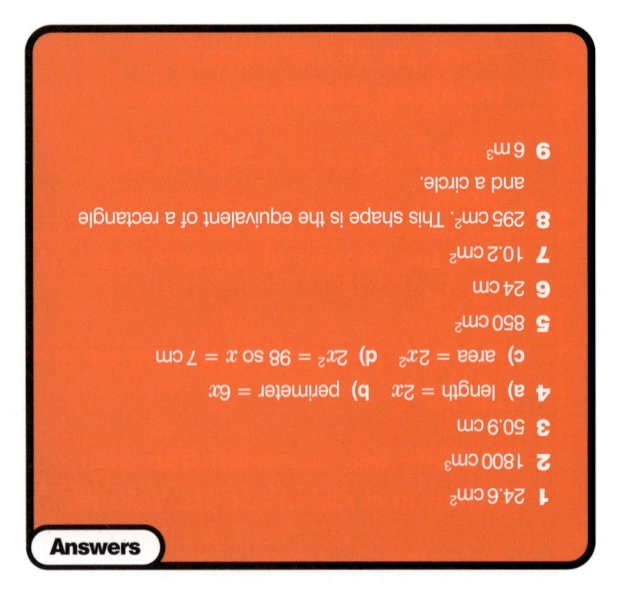

Answers

1. 24.6 cm^2
2. 1800 cm^3
3. 50.9 cm
4. a) length = 2x b) perimeter = 6x c) area = 2x^2 d) 2x^2 = 98 so x = 7 cm
5. 850 cm^2
6. 24 cm
7. 10.2 cm^2
8. 295 cm^2. This shape is the equivalent of a rectangle and a circle.
9. 6 m^3

How did you get on?

All or most of them right?
You only need to glance through this chapter to make sure there is nothing in it which will catch you out.

Six or more right?
Look on the bright side! Five or more right means that you already know at least half of this chapter.

Don't even ask?
Keep going, and you'll make it!

Perimeter

The perimeter is the distance all round a shape. The perimeter of a circle is called the **circumference**. You should memorise the formulae for the circumference and area of a circle. Many students muddle up the two formulae. The formulae are given as a reminder in the General and Intermediate 1 exam, but not at Credit or Intermediate 2.

Circles

These are the principal parts of a circle.

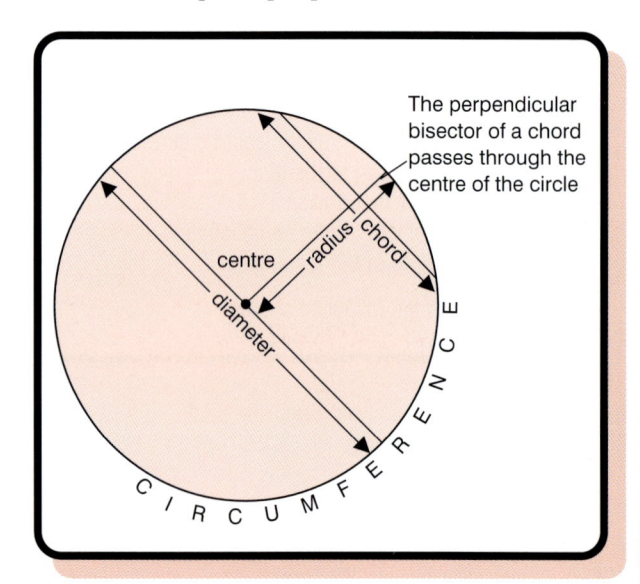

The perpendicular bisector of a chord passes through the centre of the circle

centre, radius, chord, diameter, CIRCUMFERENCE

90

Length, area and volume

The area and circumference of a circle

The area of a circle is $A = \pi r^2$.

The circumference of a circle is $C = 2\pi r$ or πd.

The formula for the area of a circle

> **Madam Attix Says:**
>
> πr squarea gives you the area.

This means the other formula must be for the circumference.

When calculating πr^2, it's safer to put r into your calculator, then square it, then multiply by π.

The formula for the circumference of a circle

From the formula for the area, πr^2, imagine the 2 running around the circumference to the front to give $2\pi r$. This is totally non-mathematical, but may help!

To remember the formula of the circumference, Willie Droppitt imagines a dog barking at a frightened cat on a table (π).

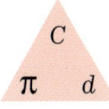

```
    C
  π   d
```

Thus $d = \dfrac{C}{\pi}$ or $C = \pi d$

This is sometimes useful if you are given the circumference and are asked for the diameter.

Example 6.1

A circle has a radius of 4.6 cm. Find:

a) its area

b) its circumference.

Solution

'πr squarea gives you the area.'

a) $\pi \times 4.6^2 = 66.5\,\text{cm}^2$ correct to 1 d.p.

b) If the radius is 4.6, the diameter $= 4.6 \times 2 = 9.2$.

$C = \pi d$ or $C = 2\pi r$

Circumference = 28.9 cm correct to 1 d.p.

Example 6.2 — Finding the radius when given the area

A circle has area 124.7 cm². Find its radius.

Solution

Use the formula.

$A = \pi r^2$

$124.7 = \pi r^2$

$r^2 = 124.7 \div \pi$

$r^2 = 39.7$

$r = \sqrt{39.7}$

$r = 6.3\,\text{cm}$

The area of a sector

If the area of a circle is πr^2 then:

- the area of a 1° sector is $\dfrac{\pi r^2}{360}$

- the area of a $\theta°$ sector is $\theta \times \dfrac{\pi r^2}{360}$

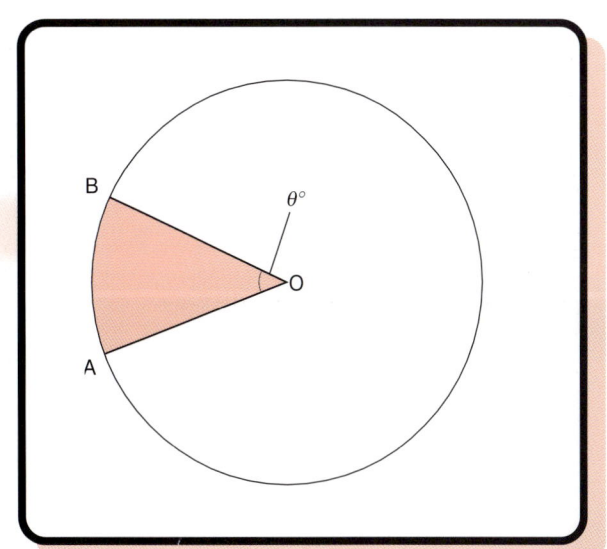

Arc length

If the circumference of a circle is $2\pi r$ then:

- an arc length which subtends an angle of $1°$ at the centre has length $\dfrac{2\pi r}{360}$

- an arc length which subtends an angle of $\theta°$ at the centre has length $\theta \times \dfrac{2\pi r}{360}$

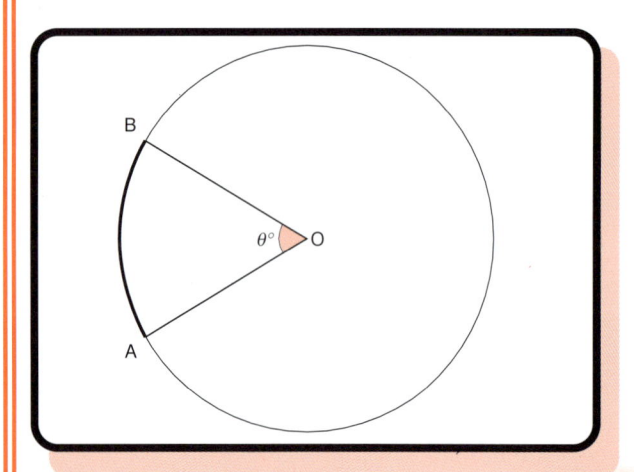

Area of a segment

area of a segment = area of the sector – area of triangle

It is easier to use the formula for the area of any triangle as $\frac{1}{2}ab\sin C$.

Example 6.3

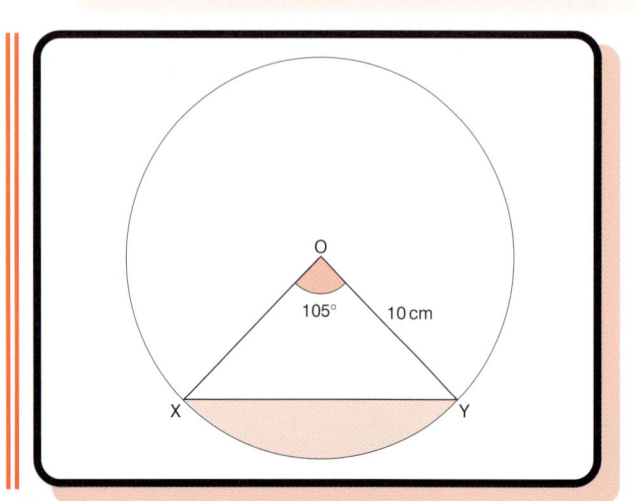

In the circle find:

a) the minor arc XY
b) the major arc XY
c) the area of sector OXY
d) the area of $\triangle$OXY
e) the area of the shaded segment.

Solution

a) Arc length = $\theta \times \dfrac{2\pi r}{360}$ = 18.3 cm

b) Major arc XY (this is the long way round from X to Y) = $\theta \times \dfrac{2\pi r}{360}$ = 44.5 cm

using $\theta = 360° - 105° = 255°$

c) Area of sector = $\theta \times \dfrac{\pi r^2}{360}$ = 91.6 cm²

d) Area of $\triangle$OXY = $\frac{1}{2}ab\sin C$ = 48.3 cm²

e) Area of shaded segment = 91.6 – 48.3 = 43.3 cm²

Exercise 6.2

1 Goldie Rings has a circular brooch of radius 27 mm. Calculate its area.

2 Rosa Chairz has a circular table with circumference of 408 cm.
 a) Find its radius to the nearest centimetre.
 b) Find its area correct to two significant figures.

3 DE is a chord of a circle centred at C, with a radius of 7.5 cm. Angle DCE = 124°. Find:
 a) the area of the sector CDE
 b) the area of triangle CDE
 c) the area of the shaded segment.

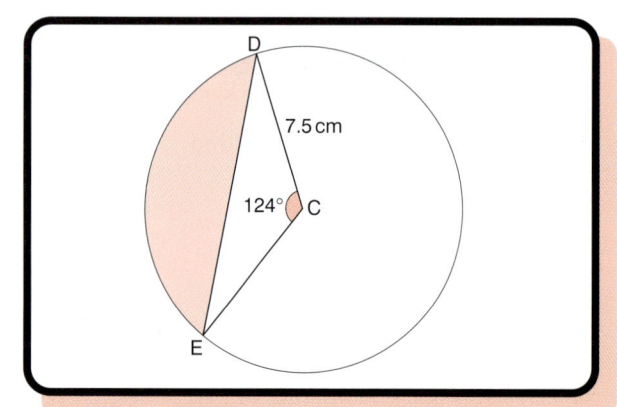

Length, area and volume

4 ABC is a sector of a circle centred at A, and with radius 18.4 mm. Find:
  a) the length of the minor arc BC
  b) the area of the sector.

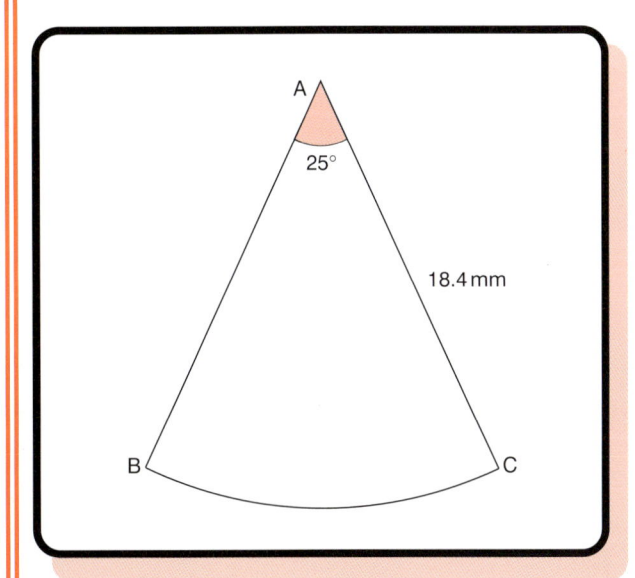

5 HJKL is a rectangle and HJ is a chord of a circle centred at M.
  a) Using the cosine rule, find the angle HMJ.
  b) Find the area of the sector HMJ.
  c) Find the area of triangle HMJ.
  d) Hence or otherwise, find the area of the whole shape.

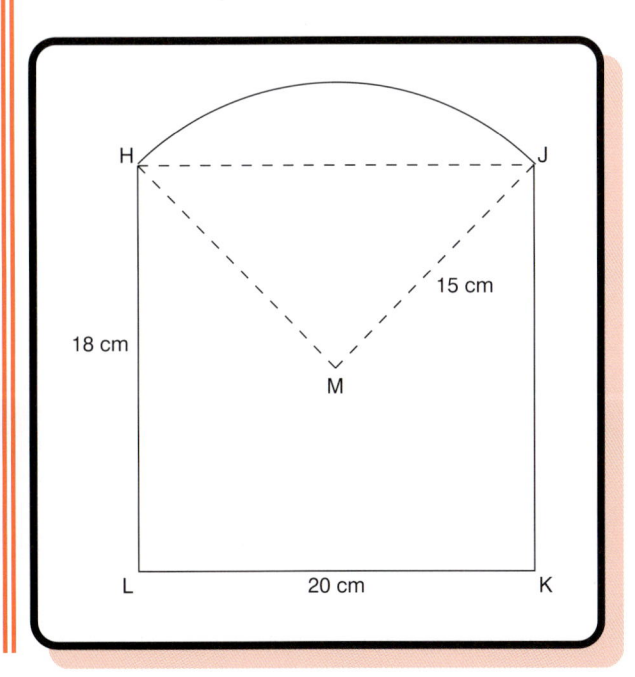

6 DEF is a sector of a circle centred at D. If the length of the minor arc EF is 4 cm, find θ to the nearest degree.

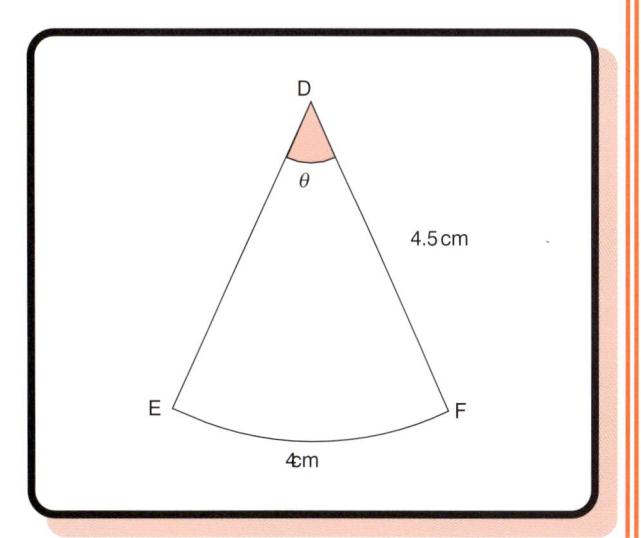

Answers
1 2290 mm^2
2 a) 65 cm   **b)** 13 000 cm^2
3 a) 60.9 cm^2 **b)** 23.3 cm^2 **c)** 37.6 cm^2
4 a) 8.0 mm   **b)** 73.9 mm^2
5 a) 83.6°   **b)** 164.2 cm^2 **c)** 111.8 cm^2 **d)** 412.4 cm^2
6 51°

Area of shapes other than circles

By now you probably know that the area of a rectangle is length × width. Since the length and width of a square are the same, you can find the area by multiplying one side by itself, or squaring it.

Sometimes, however, you are given the area and have to work back to find a side. If you are given the area of a square, you find the length of each side by finding the square root (√) of the area. If you start with a rectangle, you divide the area by the side which you are given.

If the area of a square is 100 cm², each side is $\sqrt{100} = 10$ cm.

If the area of a rectangle with a length of 6 cm is 18 cm², then the width is

$18 \div 6 = 3$ cm.

Area of a triangle

In a triangle, if you know the base and perpendicular height (or the equivalent turned around), you can use:

area of a triangle = $\frac{1}{2}$ × base × height

If not, use:

area = $\frac{1}{2}ab\sin C$

This will be on the *Formulae list* in the Credit and Intermediate 2 examination.

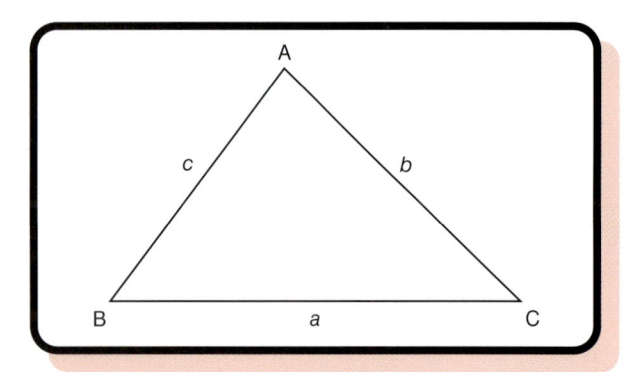

Area of a parallelogram

Area = base × perpendicular height.

Remember that the perpendicular height is the perpendicular from the base to the opposite side.

Areas of other shapes

You can usually split these up into rectangles, triangles, circles or semicircles. Then it is simply a matter of adding together all the separate parts.

Surface area of 3D shapes

Imagine your 3D shape opened out into a net, then describe the shape of each of the pieces. By finding the areas of these pieces and adding them, you will find the total surface area of the shape.

For example, a cylinder
= 2 circles + 1 rectangle = $2\pi r^2 + 2\pi rh$

Check if the cylinder or cuboid has a lid.

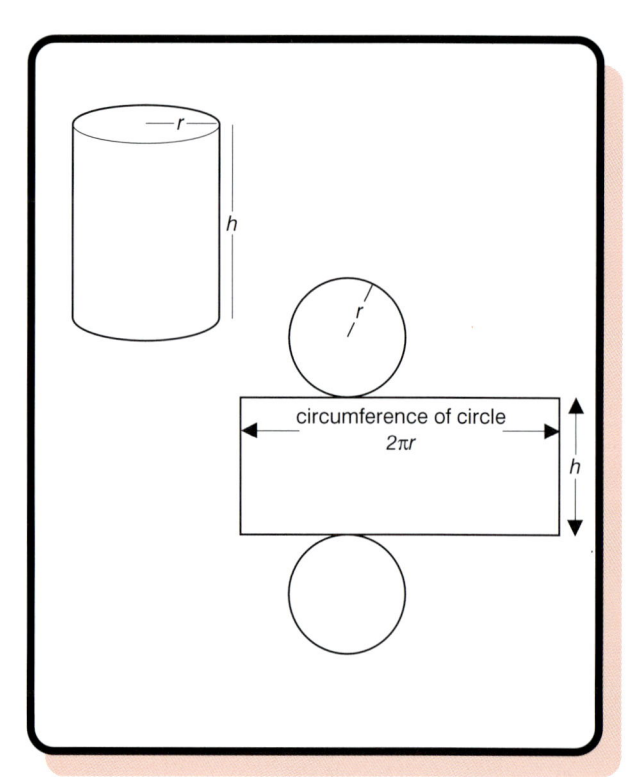

Volume of a prism

A prism is a 3D shape which can be cut into identical slices. For example, if you slice a cylinder, each piece is a circle. A prism with a rectangular 'slice' is called a cuboid.

The shape of each slice is called its **cross-section**.

The volume of a prism is found by multiplying its area of cross-section by its length.

Volume of a prism = area of cross-section × length

This is easy when the question involves an obvious length. Sometimes, however, the question asks for a depth or a thickness and you may not immediately spot that this is equivalent to asking for the length. If you recognise yourself in this situation, do not despair because Willie Droppitt has a method which just might work!

Length, area and volume

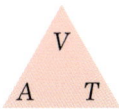

V
A T

V stands for volume.

A stands for the area of the cross-section.

T stands for The Other One. In place of T, you put the dimension you have not already used. This may be length, width, depth, height or thickness.

Example 6.4

a) Bart Ender makes a cocktail in a cylindrical glass of base radius 3.5 cm. If the glass is filled to a depth of 7.2 cm, find the volume of liquid in the glass.

b) Jean-Ann Tonnick does not like it and pours it into a vase in the shape of a cuboid with base dimensions 14.1 cm by 12.2 cm. How deep is the liquid?

c) Bart Ender pours the same-sized cocktail into a cylindrical glass of height 9.7 cm for Celia Fete. If the glass is completely filled, what is its radius?

Solution

a) Volume = $\pi r^2 h$ = 277 cm³

   or $V = A \times T$

b) $A = 14.1 \times 12.2 = 172.02$ cm²

   $T = V \div A = 277 \div 172.02 = 1.6$ cm

c) $\pi r^2 h = V$ or $A = \dfrac{V}{T} = \dfrac{277}{9.7}$

   $r^2 = \dfrac{V}{\pi h}$ $A = 28.6$

   $r^2 = \dfrac{277}{\pi \times 9.7} = 9.09$ $\pi r^2 = 28.6$

                            $r^2 = 9.09$

   $r = 3.0$ cm $r = 3.0$ cm

Exercise 6.3

1 The base of a cuboid measures 20 cm by 13.5 cm. If its volume is 1215 cm³, find its depth.

2 Find the volume of the triangular prism sketched below.

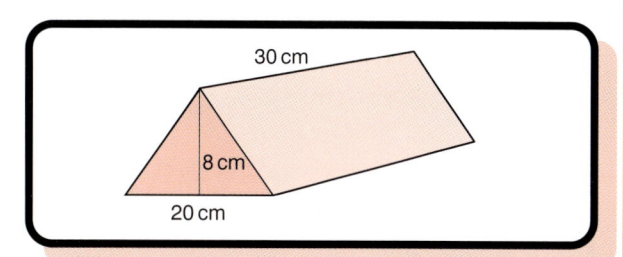

[Triangular prism: 30 cm long, triangular cross-section with base 20 cm and height 8 cm]

3 A cylinder holds 1 litre of water. If the radius of the cylinder is 4.5 cm, how deep is the water?

4 1 litre of fertiliser is to be spread to a depth of 4 cm. What area will it cover?

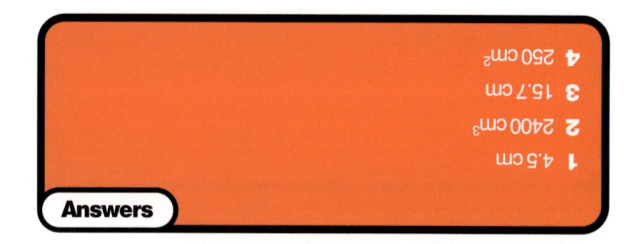

Answers

1   4.5 cm
2   2400 cm³
3   15.7 cm
4   250 cm²

TAKE A BREAK

This is a good point to take a short break.

Revise Standard Grade and Intermediate Maths

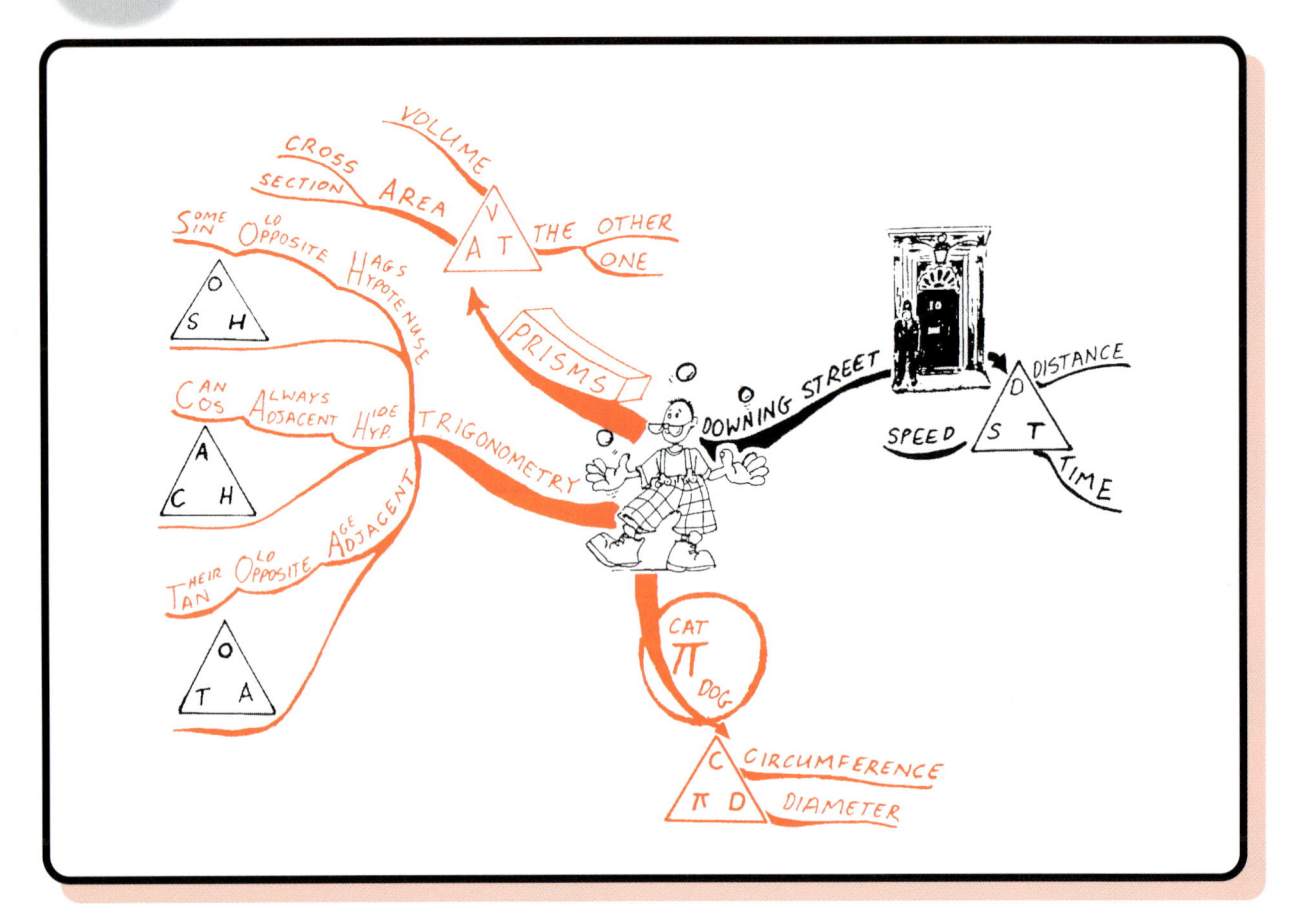

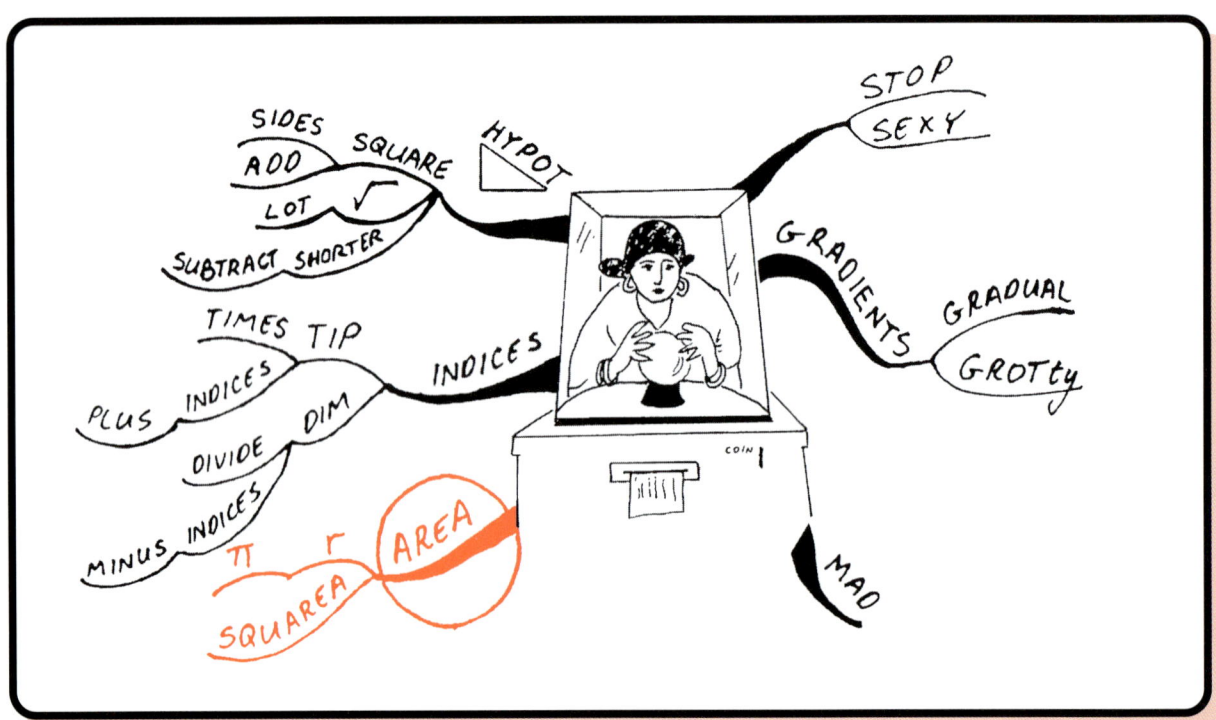

review
How much have you learnt?

Tick off each topic in the list when you are confident you can cope with it.

- ○ Calculate the circumference of a circle, given the radius or diameter.
- ○ Calculate the area of
  - a rectangle
  - a square
  - a triangle
  - a parallelogram.
- ○ Calculate the surface area of a cuboid.
- ○ Calculate areas of shapes made up of rectangles, triangles and semicircles.
- ○ Calculate the area of a circle, given its radius or diameter.
- ○ Find the area of a sector of a circle.
- ○ Find the length of an arc of a circle.
- ○ Find the area of a segment of a circle.
- ○ Identify the cross-section of a prism.
- ○ Calculate the volume of a prism.
- ○ Calculate base areas of containers from the volume of liquid in them.

Length, area and volume

Shapes

preview

By the end of this chapter you will be able to:

- name the different types of triangle (isosceles and equilateral)
- identify special angles formed by intersecting lines
- name and identify different types of quadrilaterals
- list the properties of different quadrilaterals
- recognise congruent shapes
- identify regular and irregular polygons
- draw a reflection in a line
- draw a rotation about a point

Do some of these panels get you into a flap?

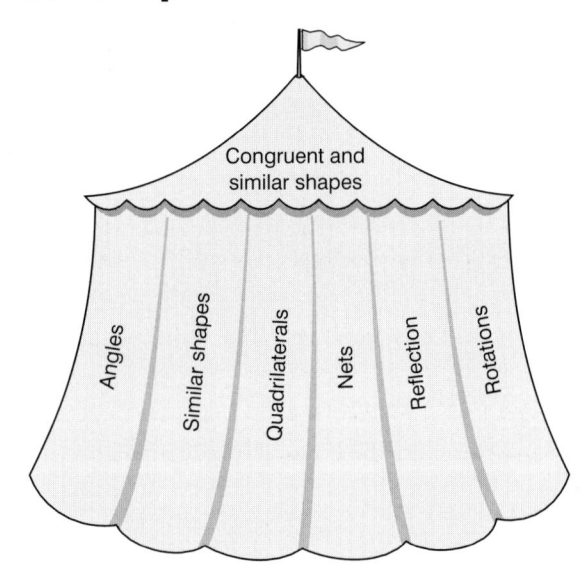

Congruent and similar shapes, Angles, Similar shapes, Quadrilaterals, Nets, Reflection, Rotations

Shapes

How much do you know already?

Exercise 7.1

1. What is the difference between isosceles and equilateral triangles?

2. Mark the angles in the diagram below which are equal to x. Give a reason in each case.

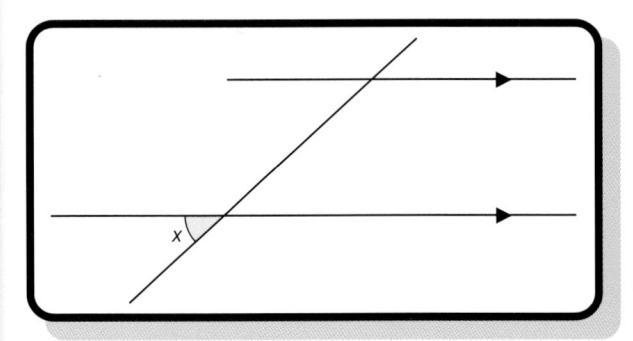

3. How many sides does a quadrilateral have?

Shapes

4 Mark angle AXD.

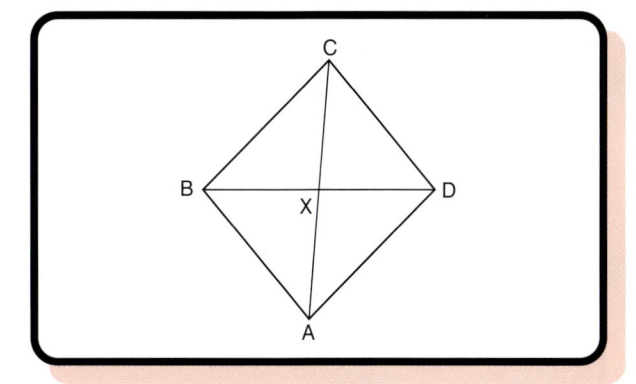

5 What is the difference between congruent and similar shapes?

6 Name the following shapes.

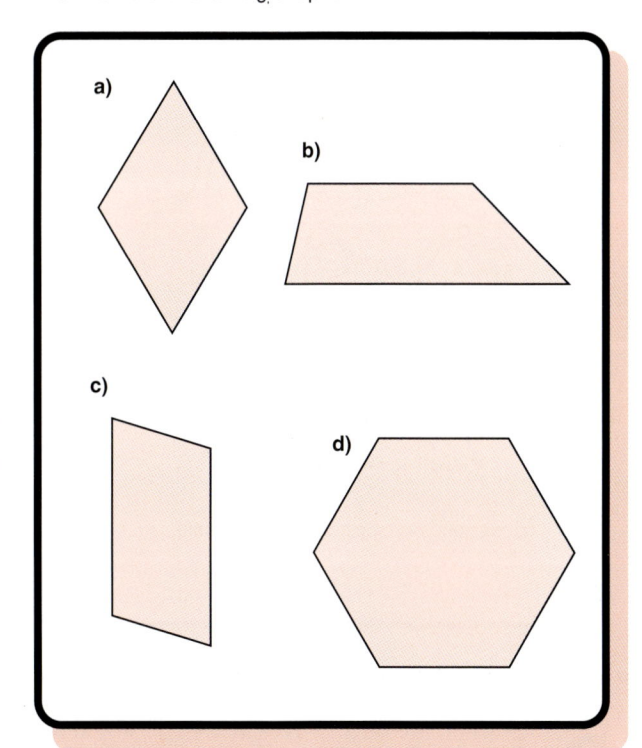

a)

b)

c)

d)

7 What is the difference between a polygon and a pentagon?

8 Name a capital letter of the alphabet with one axis of symmetry.

9 What is the difference between a regular and an irregular polygon?

10 Name a capital letter with rotational symmetry.

11 From the diagram below, calculate the angles labelled x, y and z.

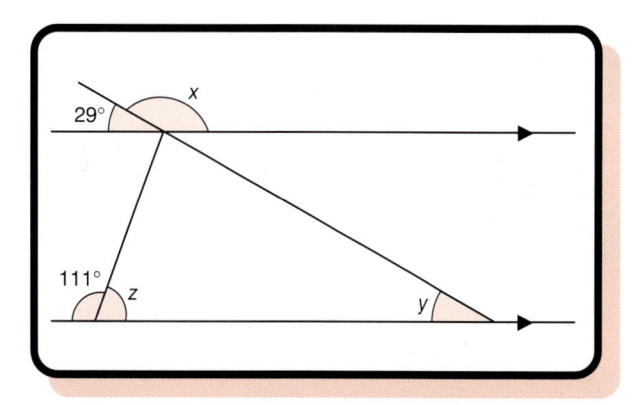

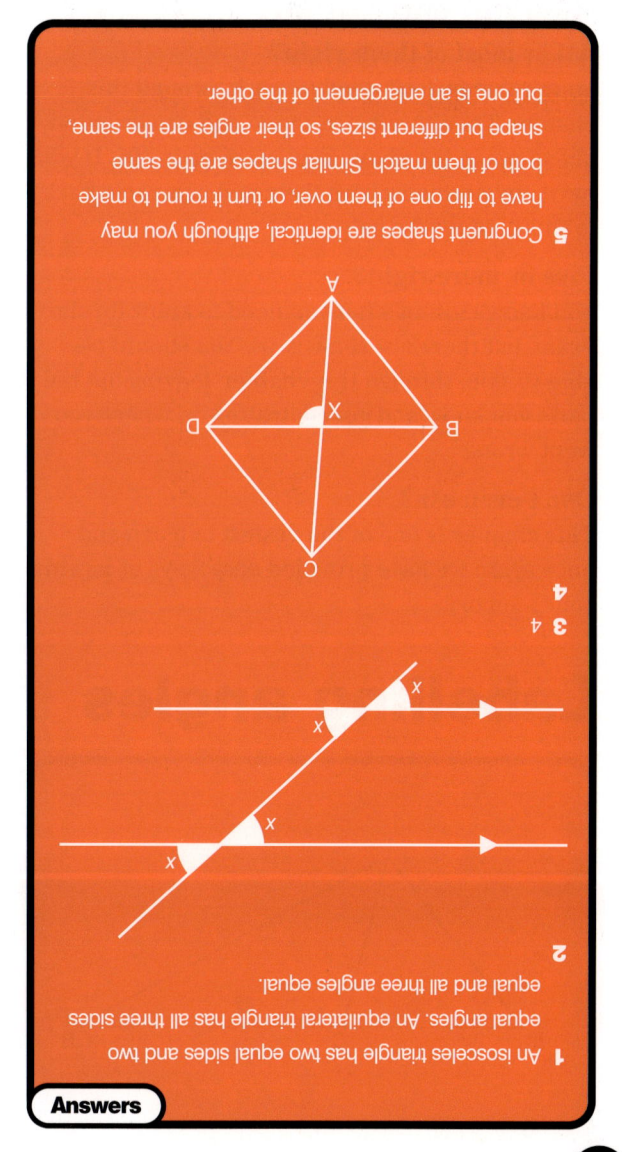

Answers

1 An isosceles triangle has two equal sides and two equal angles. An equilateral triangle has all three sides equal and all three angles equal.

2

3

4

5 Congruent shapes are identical, although you may have to flip one of them over, or turn it round to make both of them match. Similar shapes are the same shape but different sizes, so their angles are the same, but one is an enlargement of the other.

Revise Standard Grade and Intermediate Maths

Answers

6 a) rhombus b) trapezium c) parallelogram
   d) hexagon
7 A polygon is any two-dimensional (2D) straight-sided shape.
   A pentagon is a five-sided shape.
8 A, B, C, D, E, K, M, T, U, V, W or Y.
9 All the sides of a regular polygon are the same length, whereas the sides of an irregular polygon will be of different lengths.
10 H, I, N, O, S, X or Z
11 $x = 151°$, $y = 29°$, $z = 69°$.

How did you get on?

All or most of them right?

You probably don't need to work through this chapter. There are more shape and construction questions in the Shape review on page 106. If you have any problems with them you can come back to this chapter for help.

Five or more right?

You know most of what you need to know for the exam, but there are some gaps. You should be able to skim through this chapter, leaving out the parts you know and concentrating on where you went wrong.

Don't even ask?

This chapter is one of the easiest to learn and once again we have provided easy ways of jogging your memory.

Labelling angles

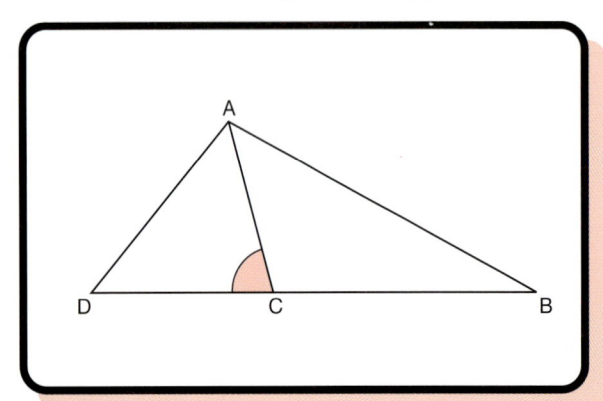

The angle marked at C may be called angle ACD or angle DCA. In some books this is written ∠ACD, ∠DCA, AĈD or DĈA.

The marked angle at C consists of two lines AC and CD. To name the angle, you would follow the line from A to C to D or vice versa. This is to avoid confusion with the other angle at C running from A to C to B, or vice versa – which is called ∠ACB or ∠BCA. The important letter is the middle one.

Just to recap

You need to know some special angles, and the angles formed by intersecting lines.

corresponding   opposite   alternate

Polygons

Similar shapes

Similar shapes have identical angles, but one is an enlargement of the other. Usually, if you are asked to find the length of a side, you can use X-Direct. However, if you are asked to find the scale factor of an enlargement between similar figures, remember Madam Attix's old saying.

> **Madam Attix Says:**
> To find the multiplier, you always put the **S**econd number **O**ver the **F**irs**T** – and you are SOFT in the head if you forget it!

Example 7.1

In the diagram below, BE and CD are vertical poles. Using the lengths given on the diagram, find AD.

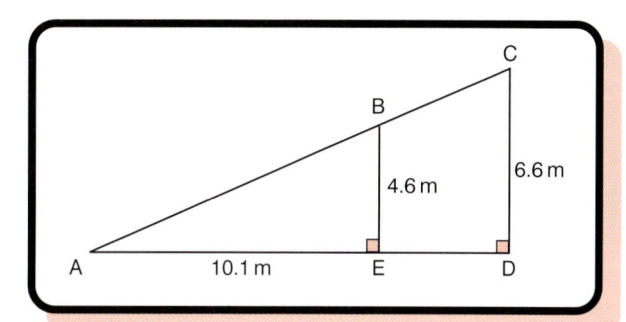

Solution

Triangles ABE and ACD are similar.

	ABE	ACD
Pole length	4.6	6.6
Horizontal distance	10.1	

$$\frac{10.1 \times 6.6}{4.6} = 14.5$$

The length of AD is 14.5 m.

In some questions like this you could use trigonometry, but this method is much quicker.

Example 7.2

Two pictures are similar. The smaller one has width 5.5 cm and length 7.4 cm. If the width of the larger one is 46.75 cm, find:

a) the scale factor of the enlargement

b) the length of the larger picture.

Solution

a) Using Second Over FirsT, the scale factor is
$$\frac{46.75}{5.5} = 8.5$$

b) The length of the larger picture is
$7.4 \times 8.5 = 62.9$ cm

Alternatively you can use X-Direct.

	Smaller	Larger
Width	5.5	46.75
Length	7.4	

Length of the larger picture = $\frac{7.4 \times 46.75}{5.5} = 62.9$

The length is 62.9 cm.

A polygon or a polyhedron?
A polygon is a 2D shape, such as a hexagon.
A polyhedron is a 3D shape, such as a pyramid.

Regular polygons are shapes with all sides the same and all angles the same.

Irregular polygons are shapes where the sides and angles are not all the same.

Congruent triangles
Congruent triangles are identical in size and shape, although you may have to flip one over or turn it around for the two to appear to match.

Note: The words 'congruent' and 'similar' can describe any group of shapes. However, 'congruent' is more usually applied to triangles.

7

Revise Standard Grade and Intermediate Maths

Quadrilaterals (i.e. four-sided shapes)

Square • 4 right angles • all sides are equal • opposite sides are parallel • diagonals cross at right angles	**Rhombus** (like a squashed square or a diamond) Like a square: • all sides are equal • opposite sides are parallel • diagonals cross at right angles • opposite angles are equal but angles are not right angles
Rectangle • 4 right angles • opposite sides equal and parallel	**Parallelogram** (like a squashed rectangle) Like a rectangle: • opposite sides are equal • diagonals do not cross at right angles • opposite angles are the same but angles are not right angles
Trapezium • one pair of sides parallel	**Kite** • 2 pairs of sides are equal • diagonals cross at right angles • 1 set of opposite angles are equal

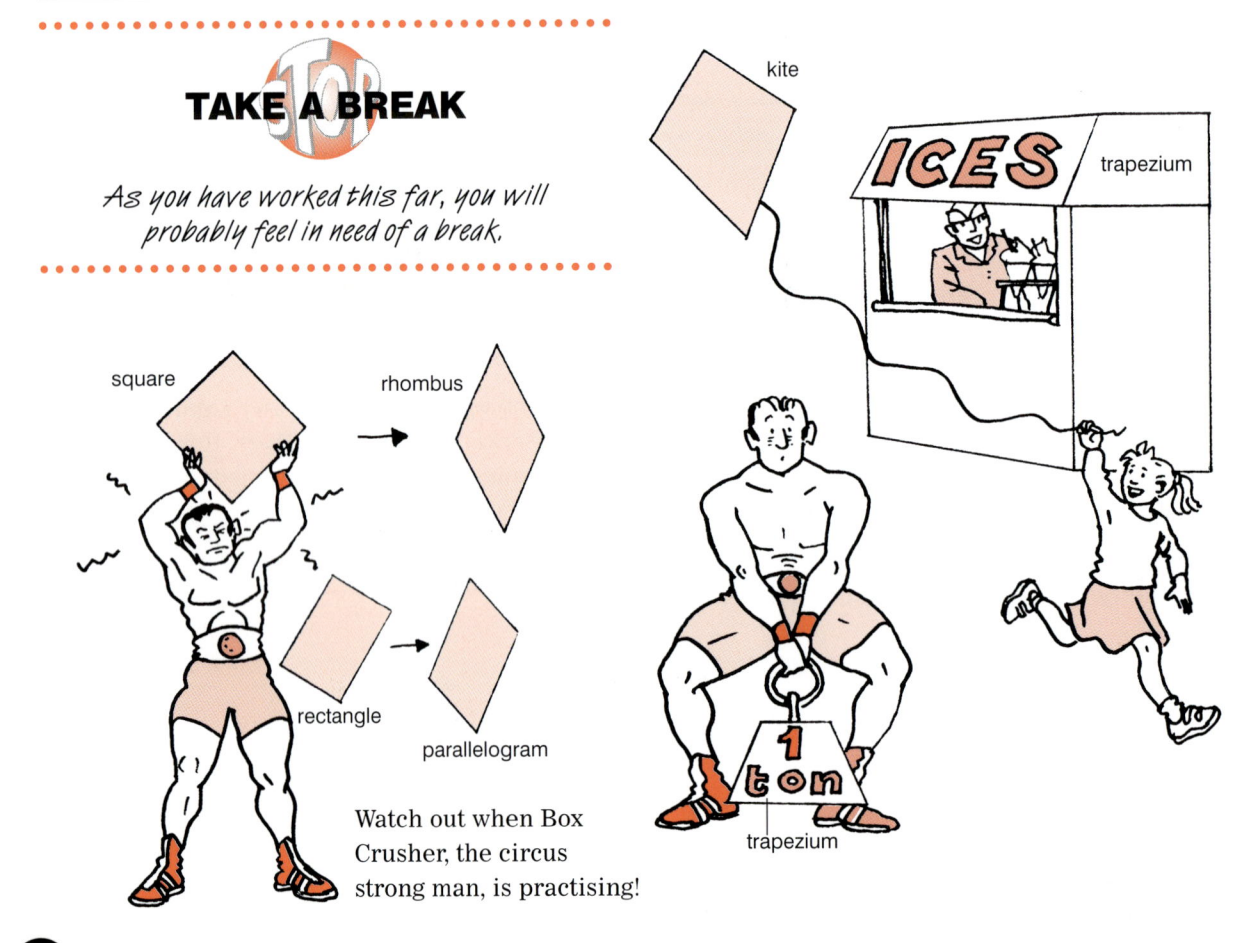

TAKE A BREAK

As you have worked this far, you will probably feel in need of a break.

Watch out when Box Crusher, the circus strong man, is practising!

Nets

Imagine the surfaces of a 3D shape, flattened and opened out.

Exercise 7.2

Sketch a net for each of the following closed objects.

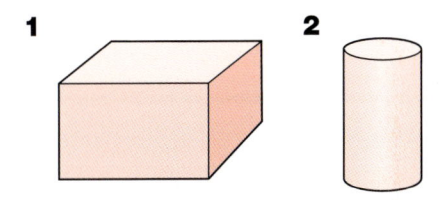

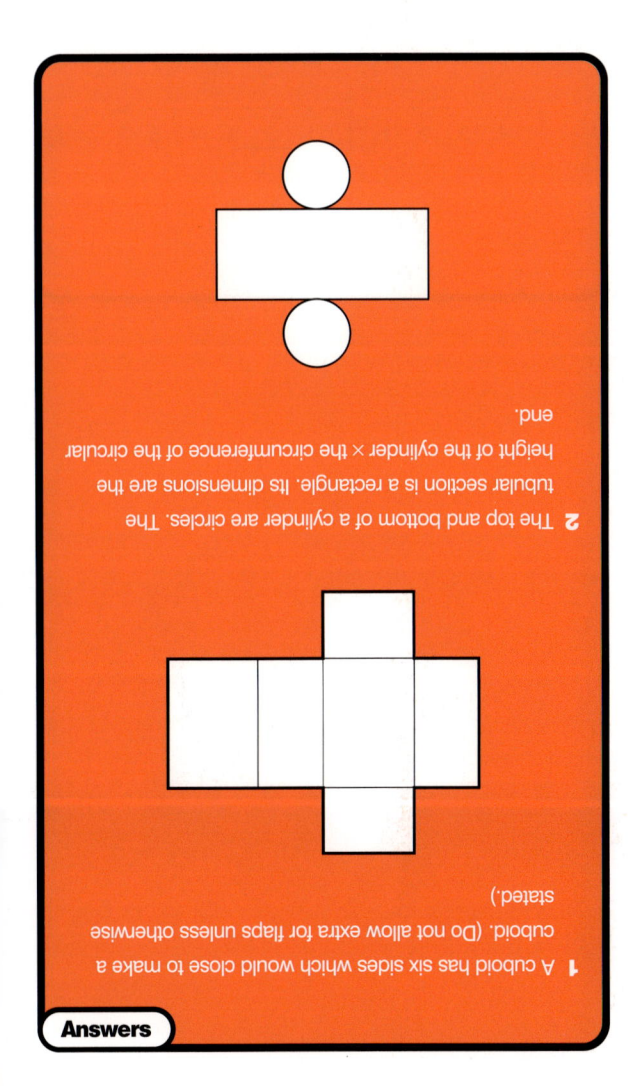

1.
2.

Read questions concerning cylinders and cuboids extra carefully, because sometimes they do not have a lid, e.g. waste paper bins, fish tanks, etc. There is often more than one right way of drawing the net. Always check at the end that the net you have chosen would fold up into the original shape.

Reflections

You need to identify the reflection or mirror line. This line is sometimes called the **axis of symmetry**.

It is usually easier to work out a reflection, if you get one in the exam, than to try to learn all the different combinations. To draw the image of a reflection in a line, you can use tracing paper and fold along the reflection.

Recognising reflections

These are usually obvious when the line of reflection is either the x-axis or y-axis. They are not always quite so obvious if the reflection line is $y = x$, or $y = -x$.

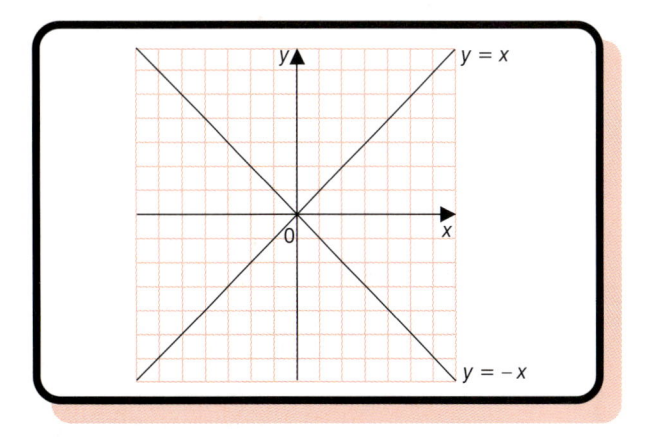

To test for reflection, take each point in turn, and count the squares or measure the distance at right angles to what you think may be the reflection line. If you are correct, the line and its image will be the same distance from the line, but on opposite sides. If the point is already on the line of reflection, it does not change.

Answers

1. A cuboid has six sides which would close to make a cuboid. (Do not allow extra for flaps unless otherwise stated.)

2. The top and bottom of a cylinder are circles. The tubular section is a rectangle. Its dimensions are the height of the cylinder × the circumference of the circular end.

7 Rotations

It is easier to draw a rotation if you use tracing paper.

1. Trace the object.
2. Put your pencil on the paper over the centre of rotation and move the tracing paper according to the question.
3. Draw heavily over your tracing to make the image.

An alternative approach

Imagine that the axes move and not the points. This sounds complicated, but is much easier to do than you might think.

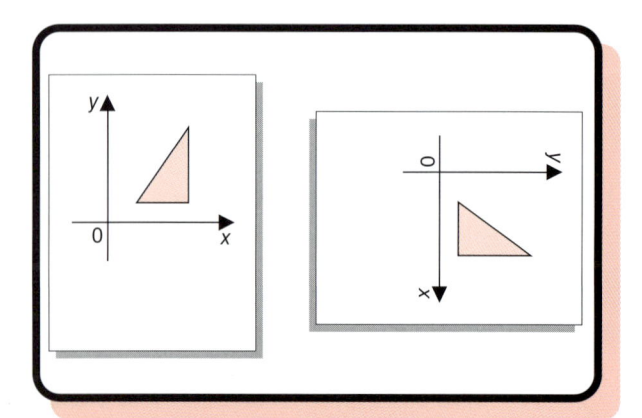

Example 7.3

On the diagram below, transform triangle T through a rotation of 90° clockwise, centred at (0, 0).

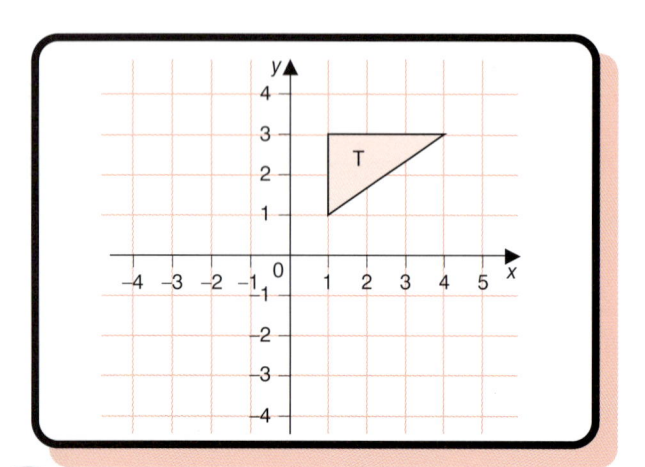

Solution

The triangle would move into the quadrant which is immediately below it.

Turn the page round so that the required quadrant is now at the top right-hand corner.

Now imagine your original triangle in exactly the same place as it was before.

Try looking at each original point and work out its new coordinates using left and right, and up and down.

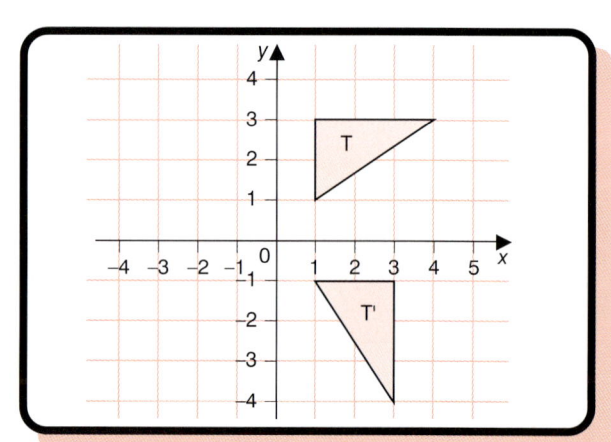

review
How much have you learnt?

Tick off each topic in the list when you are confident you can cope with it.

- ○ Name the different types of triangle (isosceles and equilateral).
- ○ Identify special angles formed by intersecting lines.
- ○ Name and identify different types of quadrilaterals.
- ○ List the properties of different quadrilaterals.
- ○ Recognise congruent shapes.
- ○ Identify regular and irregular polygons.
- ○ Draw a reflection in a line.
- ○ Draw a rotation about a point.

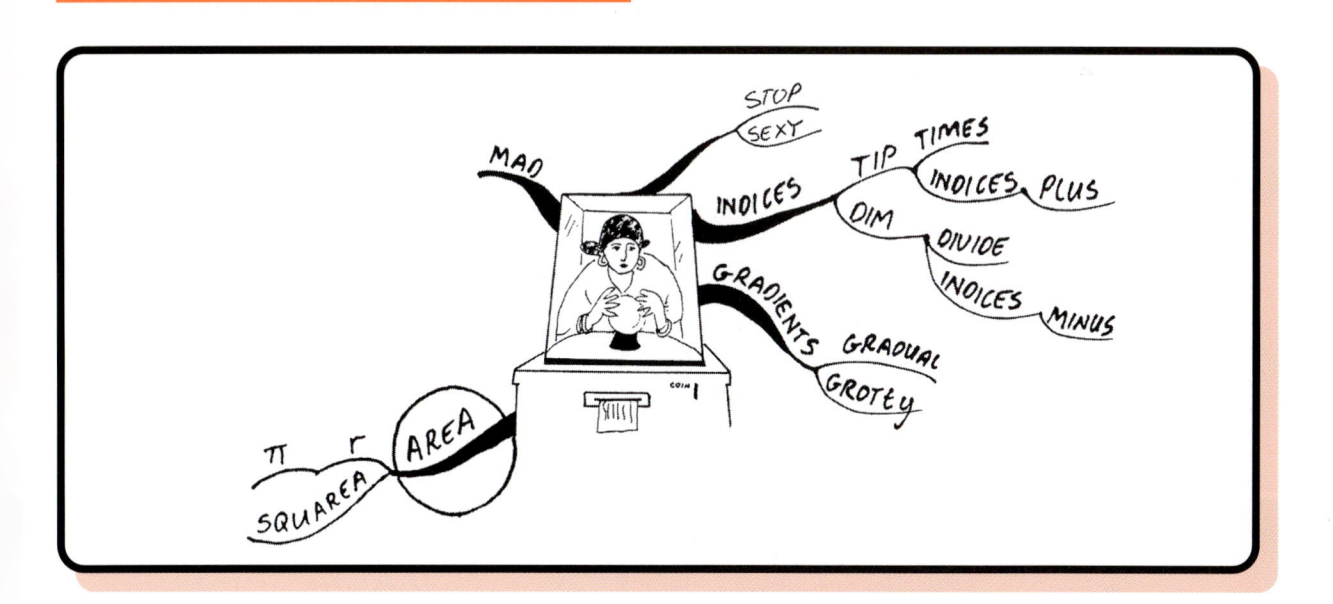

Shapes

Shapes review

1 A ladder 6m long leans against a wall, with its foot 2.6m away fro the wall.

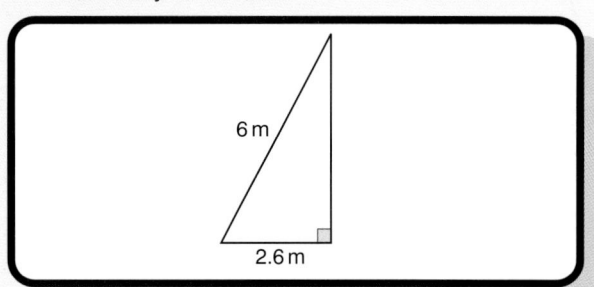

a) Use Pythagoras' theorem to find how far up the wall the ladder extends.
b) Find the angle between the ladder and the wall.

2 Circles of area 26 cm² are cut from card.

a) What is the radius of each circle?
b) If 24 circles are cut from a rectangle 25 cm by 30 cm, how much card is left?
c) Write this as a percentage of the original amount.

3 The library is on a bearing of 240° from the post office. What is the bearing of the post office from the library?

4 From a cliff top, the angle of depression of a rock out to sea is 27°. If the cliff is 45 m high, how far away is the rock from the top of the cliff?

5 What is the surface area of a solid cylinder of base radius 1.4 m and height 80 cm?
Give your answer in m² to 2 d·p· .

6 Triangle DEF is isosceles. DE = 8.4 m and EF = 8 m. X is the midpoint of EF.

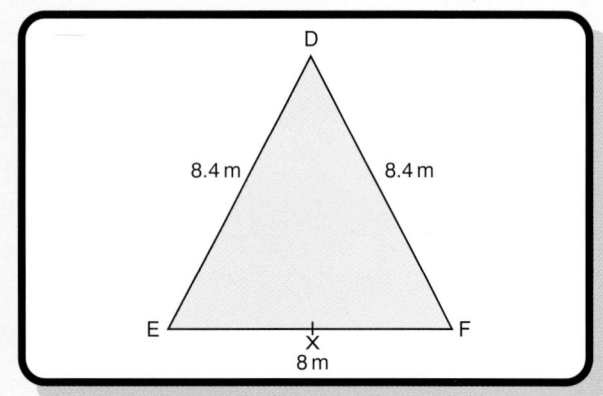

a) Find the length of DX.
b) Find angle DFE.
c) Find the area of triangle DEF.

7 a) In the diagram, BE is parallel to CD. How can you tell that triangle ABE and triangle ACD are similar?

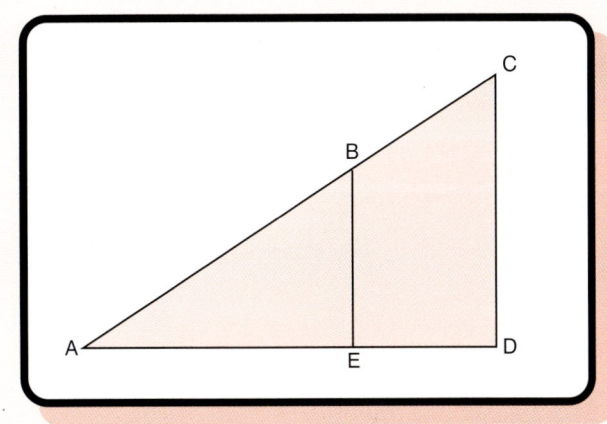

b) The length of AE = 71.1 cm, BE = 57.6 cm and CD = 80.7 cm. Using similar triangles, find AD.

8 a) Find the volume of water held by a full cylindrical glass of radius 3.1 cm and height 9.1 cm.
b) If this was poured into a cylindrical glass of radius 4.1 cm, how deep would the liquid be? Give your answer to 2 decimal places.

9 In the diagram below, what transformation maps:
a) P on to Q
b) Q on to R?
c) What single transformation maps P on to R?

Answers

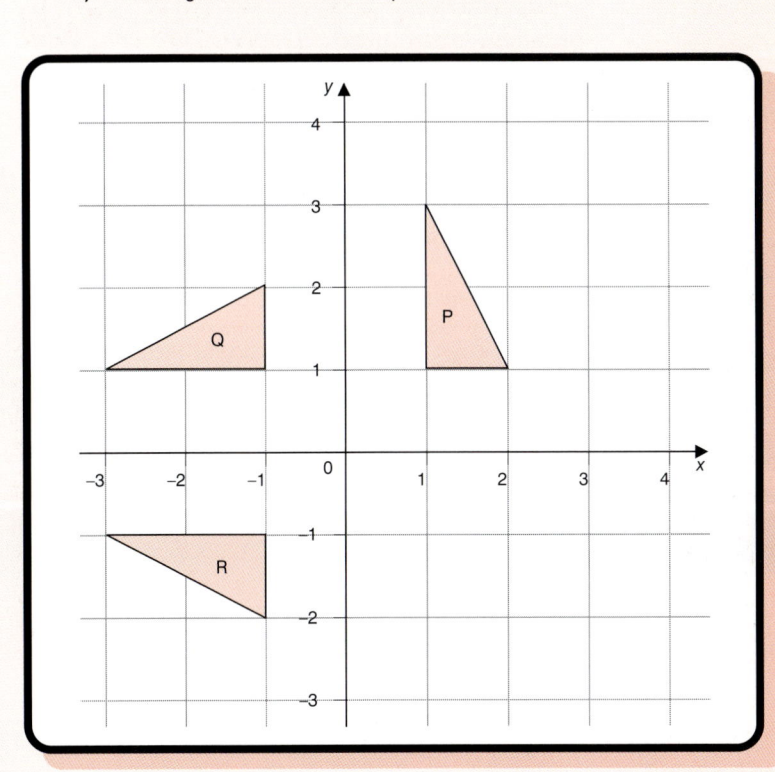

1 a) 5.4 m
b) 26°
If your answer was 64°, you found the angle between the ladder and the ground.
2 a) 2.9 cm **b)** 126 cm² **c)** 16.8% or 17%
3 060° Remember that bearings have 3 figures.
4 99 m. The angle of depression = 63° so you need to calculate 45 ÷ cos 63°.
Alternatively, you could use 45 ÷ sin 27°.
5 19.35 m²
6 a) 7.4 m **b)** 62° **c)** 30 m² (2 sig. figs.)
7 a) angle D = angle E and angle C = angle B (BE and CD are parallel.)
angle A is common to both. Therefore the triangles are similar.
b) AD = 99.6 cm
8 a) 274.7 cm³ **b)** 5.2 cm
9 a) Rotation of 90° anti-clockwise about origin
b) Reflection in the x-axis
c) Reflection in y = −x

Statistics

preview

By the end of this chapter you will be able to:

- find the mean, median and mode of a set of data
- find the range of a set of data
- draw a bar chart for a set of data
- draw a pie chart for a set of data
- draw up a cumulative frequency table
- find the interquartile range and semi-interquartile range of a set of data
- interpret scatter diagrams
- interpret and construct stem-and-leaf charts
- interpret and construct boxplots
- calculate, given the formula, the standard deviation of a set of data
- find the probability of a simple event

Are you a mean shot at statistics?

Averages: Mean, Median, Mode
Spread or dispersion: Range, Interquartile Range and semi-interquartile range, Standard deviation
Charts: Stem-and-leaf, Boxplots, Scatter Diagrams, Pie Charts, Bar Charts, Dotplots

How much do you know already?

Exercise 8.1

1 13, 7, 27, 12, 7, 10, 28, 7, 5, 11, 12, 8, 19, 12, 2.
Using the above numbers, find:
a) the mean
b) the median
c) the mode
d) the range.

2 The table below illustrates the distance between home and the town centre of a group of 75 students. The distances are rounded to the nearest kilometre.

Distance in km (d)	No. of students (frequency, f)
1	6
2	7
3	15
4	18
5	10
6	10
7	7
8	2

a) What is the mode?
b) Find the median distance from town centre to home.
c) Find the quartiles, interquartile range and semi-interquartile range for this set of data.

Statistics

3 Draw a boxplot for the set of data in question 2.

4 Draw a back-to-back stem-and-leaf chart for the following two sets of data.

Marks of 15 male pupils in a test.

38, 18, 20, 40, 24, 31, 26, 16, 33, 37, 24, 22, 14, 39, 28

Marks of 15 female pupils in the same test.

18, 9, 40, 35, 38, 29, 19, 18, 29, 38, 40, 40, 18, 36, 29

5 The results of a survey carried out on a sample of 450 people were displayed on a pie chart.
  a) How many people would 40° represent?
  b) How many degrees would represent 90 people?.

6 The results of a group of students who sat tests in French and Spanish are given below.

| French (x) | 20 | 12 | 64 | 50 | 68 | 37 | 38 | 25 | 31 | 83 |
| Spanish (y) | 36 | 28 | 60 | 50 | 48 | 75 | 38 | 30 | 41 | 64 |

  a) Display the results on a scatter diagram.
  b) Draw the line of best fit.
  c) One student scored 56 in French, but was absent for the Spanish test. What would a likely score have been? Show clearly how you reached your answer.

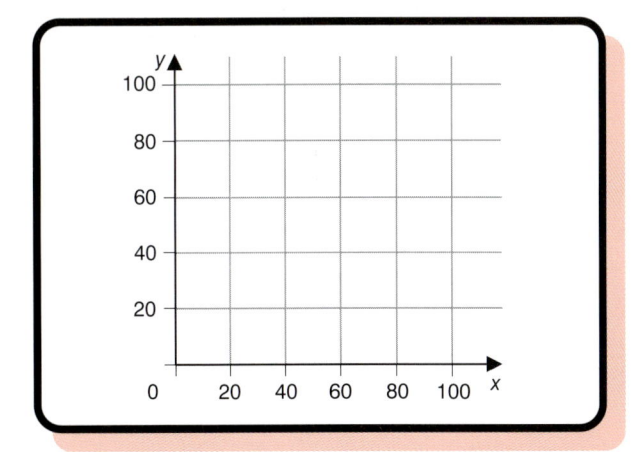

7 The National Lottery has balls numbered 1 to 49. What is the probability that a ball selected at random,

  a) is the number 27?
  b) is less than 20?

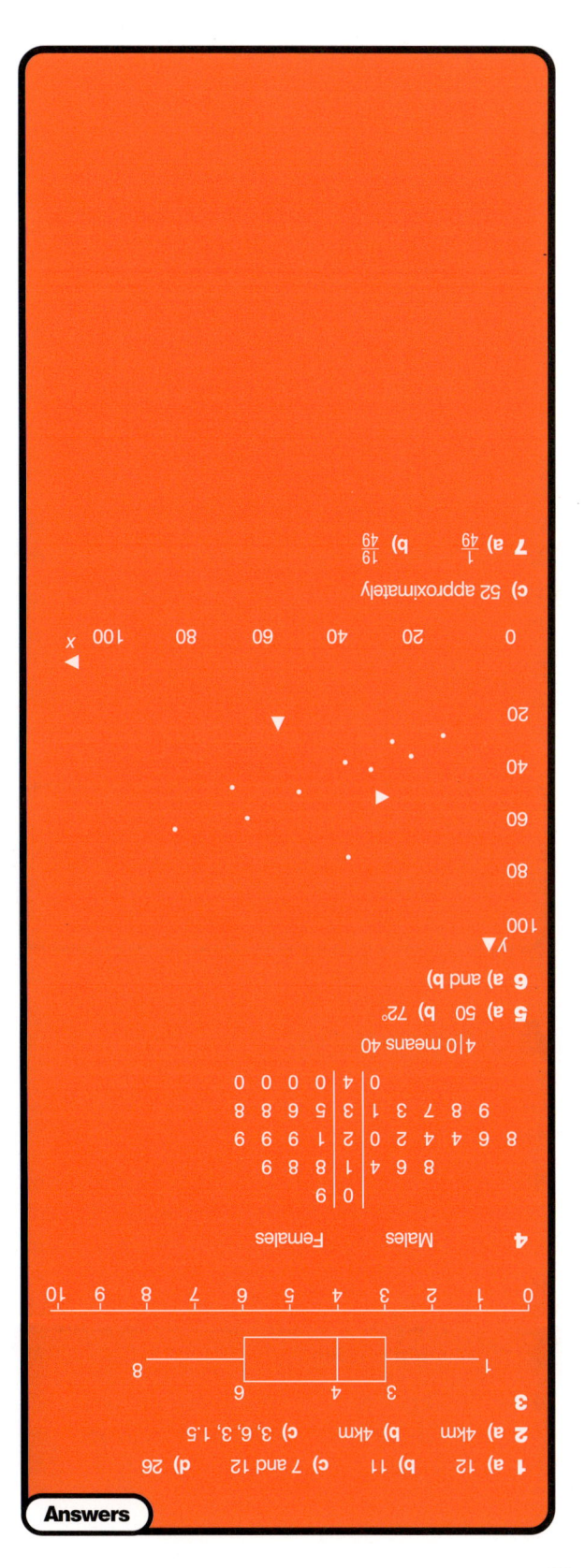

Answers

1 a) 12 **b)** 11 **c)** 7 and 12 **d)** 26
2 a) 4km **b)** 4km **c)** 3, 6, 3, 1.5
3

4 Males | Females
```
      9 | 0 |
  8 6 4 | 1 | 8 8 9
  9 4 2 0 | 2 | 9 9 9
  8 7 3 1 | 3 | 5 6 8 8
        0 | 4 | 0 0 0 0
```
4|0 means 40

5 a) 50 **b)** 72°
6 a) and b)

c) 52 approximately
7 a) $\frac{1}{49}$ **b)** $\frac{19}{49}$

How did you get on?
All or most of them right?
Lucky you – or was it just sheer hard work on your part? Either way it's good news because most exam papers are crammed with questions on this part of the syllabus and a good mark here will stand you in good stead. Look at the giant banana skin on page 113 and the Mind Map on page 117 to make sure that you won't slip up, no matter what question may be asked. If you made any mistakes, however trivial, it really is worth reading through the chapter to sort them out.

Don't even ask?
The material in this chapter carries about 15% of the total mark. Although there is a certain amount to remember, the questions are usually easy to understand.

This chapter will show you where most people lose marks in the questions on Statistics. Boxes like the one below will help you plan your work.

> **Question 1 wrong?**
> You need to brush up on averages. Otherwise go to Median and quartiles in the next column.

Averages

The mean, the median and the mode are three ways of expressing an average.

Mean   Add together all the values and divide by the number of values you have. (The mean is not necessarily a whole number.)

Median   Arrange the values in order from smallest to largest. The median is the middle value.

Mode   This is the most commonly occurring value. (There can be more than one mode.)

The pros and cons of using the mean, median and mode

	Pros	Cons
mean	• most commonly used • easy to calculate	• can be misleading, as if one term is much bigger or much smaller than the others it distorts the mean
median	• often gives a truer picture of the situation • not so affected by extreme values as the mean	• not used very often in the real world • takes longer to calculate because values must first be arranged in order
mode	• unaffected by extreme values • very appropriate when you need to find the most common result (e.g. if you were a buyer for shoes you would want to know the most commonly bought sizes.)	• there may be more than one mode • it ignores much of the information

> **Trouble with Question 2?**
> You need to revise median and quartiles.

Measures of spread

Range – the difference in value between the largest and the smallest values.

Interquartile and semi-interquartile range – the interquartile range requires the value at the **upper quartile** ($\frac{3}{4}$ way up the frequency) and the **lower quartile** ($\frac{1}{4}$ way up the frequency). The upper quartile minus the lower quartile gives the **interquartile range.**

$$\text{interquartile range} = \text{upper quartile} - \text{lower quartile}$$

Semi-interquartile range = $\frac{1}{2}$ (interquartile range).

Standard deviation – two versions of the formula are given in the Credit/Intermediate 2 formula test, but it is advisable to use the second of these.

$$s = \sqrt{\frac{\Sigma(x-\bar{x})^2}{n-1}} = \sqrt{\frac{\Sigma x^2 - (\Sigma x)^2/n}{n-1}},$$

where n is the sample size.

Note: Σ means the sum of the numbers in the sample. Σx^2 means that you must first of all square each of the numbers in the sample and then add up all these squares of numbers. $(\Sigma x)^2$ means that you first of all take the sum of all the numbers in the sample and then square this answer.

What does the interquartile range tell us?

The interquartile range shows how widely the central half of the sample is spread. A low interquartile range shows that the data is closely grouped together, whereas a higher figure would reflect wider differences between the data (also called a wider spread).

Example 8.1

What do these test results for classes A and B tell you?

| Interquartile range | Class A | 10 |
| Interquartile range | Class B | 25 |

Solution

The pattern of class A's results shows them to have a more similar ability level than class B – perhaps class A was streamed whereas class B was mixed ability.

Note that the interquartile range in the last example does not tell you which class had the better performance – one of the measures of the average would tell you this.

Median and quartiles

To find the median and quartiles of a set of data you should arrange the numbers in order first of all.

Example 8.2

Find the median and quartiles of the following data.

49, 8, 47, 23, 30, 17, 21, 36, 50, 31, 32.

Solution

median
=31

8, 17, 21, 23, 30   32, 36, 47, 49, 50

lower quartile   upper quartile

Note: the lower quartile is the median of the lower half of numbers. The upper quartile is the median of the upper half of numbers.

Trouble with question 3?
You need to revise boxplots. Otherwise go to Stem-and-leaf charts in the next column.

Boxplots

Boxplots are used to illustrate the range and central spread of a set of data. They are particularly useful when comparing two or more sets of data that have different spreads.

A boxplot shows the position of 5 values – the minimum, the lower quartile, the median, the upper quartile and the maximum.

Using the set of data in Example 8.2 the boxplot would look like this (see next page).

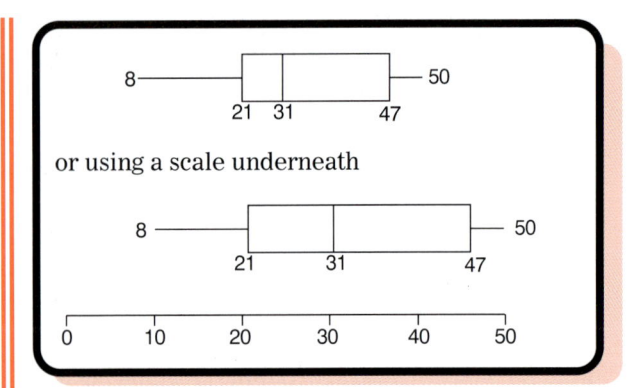

```
    8 ————————————— 50
       21   31    47

or using a scale underneath

    8 ————————————— 50
       21   31    47
    ├──┬──┬──┬──┬──┬──┤
    0  10 20 30 40 50
```

Question 4 wrong?
You need to revise stem-and-leaf charts.

Stem-and-leaf charts

Drawing a stem-and-leaf chart will help you to find the median and quartiles of a set of data.

Example 8.3

Draw a stem-and-leaf chart for the set of data below and find the median and quartiles.

107, 129, 145, 102, 141, 150, 149, 130, 114, 129, 150.

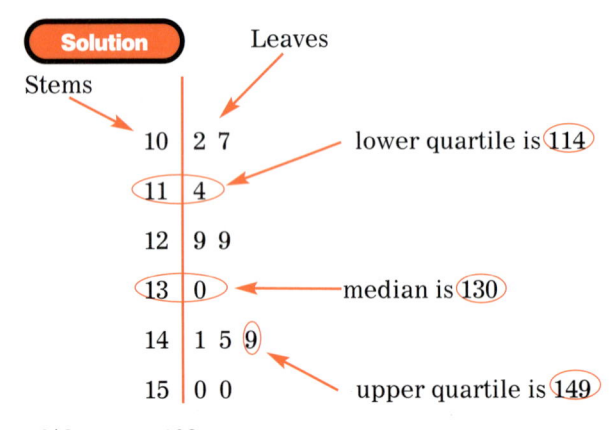

Solution

```
Stems    Leaves
  10 | 2 7          lower quartile is 114
  11 | 4
  12 | 9 9
  13 | 0            median is 130
  14 | 1 5 9
  15 | 0 0          upper quartile is 149
```

10|2 means 102

Question 5 wrong?
Just brush up on X-Direct. It's the easiest way to solve pie chart questions.

Questions on pie charts

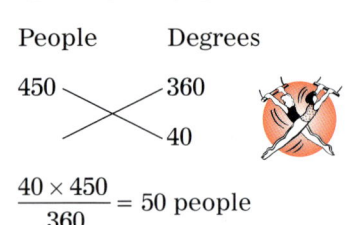

People   Degrees
450 ╲   ╱ 360
     ╳
      ╲ 40

$\dfrac{40 \times 450}{360} = 50$ people

The angle of 40° represents 50 people.

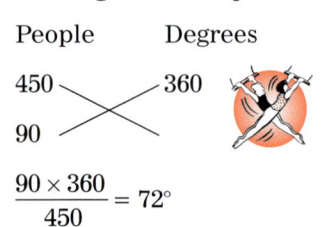

People   Degrees
450 ╲   ╱ 360
90 ╱   ╲

$\dfrac{90 \times 360}{450} = 72°$

The angle for 90 people is 72°.

Statistical Banana Skins

1 Mean
- This may be a decimal fraction, and may seem a ridiculous answer. For instance, the mean number of children per family is often stated as 2.4.

- If one or two values are either much bigger or much smaller than the rest, then they will alter the mean significantly.

2 Median
- If you are given some values and asked to find the median, you must first arrange them in order of size, starting with the smallest. To find the median of 7, 2, 6, 5, 4, firstly arrange them in order of size.
2, 4, 5, 6, 7
The median is then clearly seen as 5. Some people would have obtained the wrong answer

by taking the middle number before they had been rearranged, i.e. 6.

- To find the position of the median value, add 1 to the number of values, and divide this by 2.
  For example, the middle number of 7 items is the 4th, and the middle number of eight items is halfway between the 4th and 5th.
- If you have an even number of values, the median is still the midpoint.
  For example, take the numbers 3, 7, 8, 10, 13, 19. The midpoint between 8 and 10 is 9.
- Finding the median from a table of values can trip you up.

No. of people in a car	1	2	3	4	5
No. of cars	6	4	3	1	1

The answer is not 3, which is merely the middle group. There are 15 cars in total, and if they were all lined up in order with the least full cars first, the middle car would be the eighth ($\frac{15+1}{2} = 8$). The eighth car would have two passengers.

Always find the median from the frequency.

3 Mode

- You may be asked a question in which you have to compare two graphs. For instance, which of the graphs below has the higher mode?

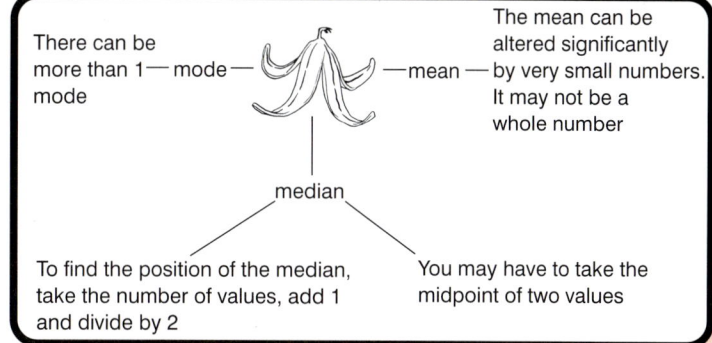

> There can be more than 1 mode — **mode**
>
> The mean can be altered significantly by very small numbers. It may not be a whole number — **mean**
>
> **median**
>
> To find the position of the median, take the number of values, add 1 and divide by 2
>
> You may have to take the midpoint of two values

The mode of the Saturday traffic is 3 and that of Sunday is 5. Therefore, Sunday has the higher mode.

You have now completed a lot of the work on Statistics. This is a good point to make sure that you are clear about the material so far covered in this chapter.

Just to recap
1. Can you now distinguish between mean, the median and the mode?
2. Can you now use boxplots, stem-and-leaf charts and pie charts?

TAKE A BREAK

If you answered 'Yes' to the above questions, you deserve a break.

If you answered 'No', you probably need one anyway!

Question 6 wrong?
You just need to look at correlation and scatter diagrams.

Make sure that you understand the meaning of the words used.

Revise Standard Grade and Intermediate Maths

Scatter diagrams

Two sets of data can be plotted on a set of axes. The scatter diagram shows how the data relate to each other. The **line of best fit** is a line that passes through – or close to – most of the points.

Correlation shows a link between the variables on both axes.

Positive correlation – if one variable rises the other is expected to rise.

Strong positive correlation

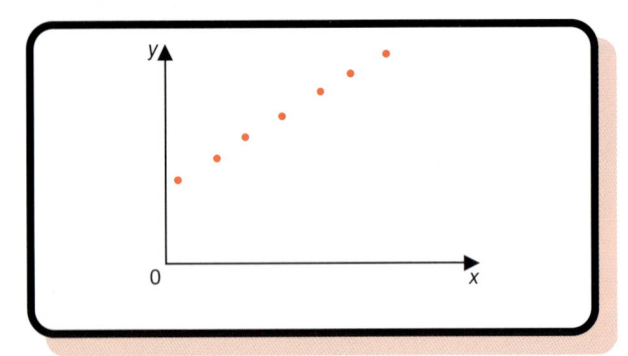

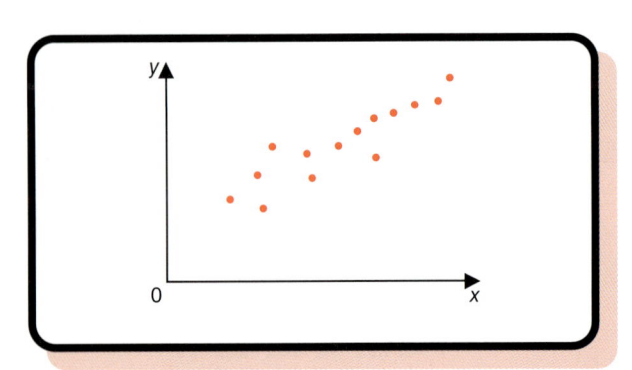

Strong negative correlation

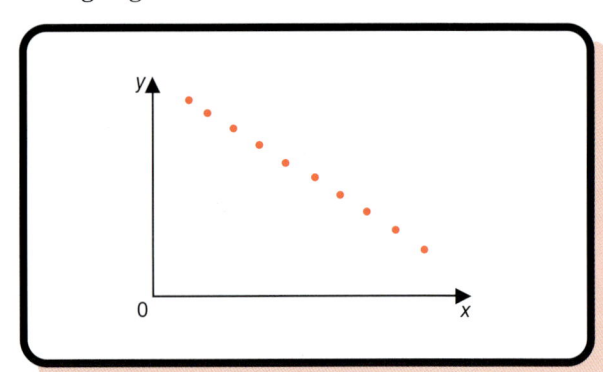

Moderate positive correlation

Moderate negative correlation

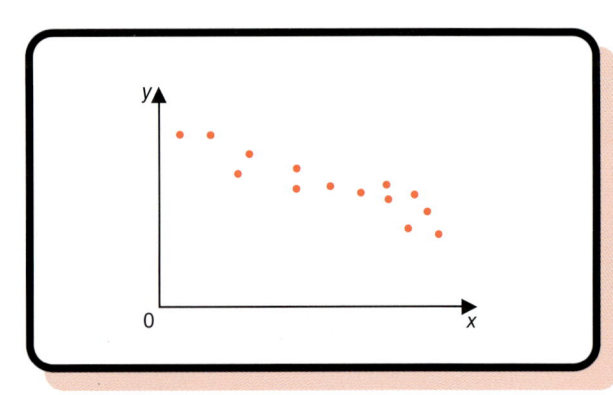

Negative correlation – if one variable goes up, the other will probably fall.

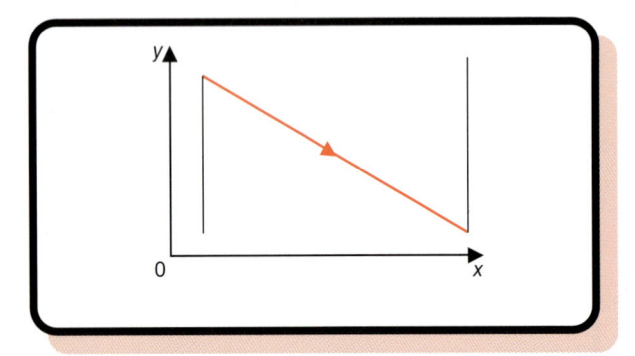

No correlation – there is no link between the two variables.

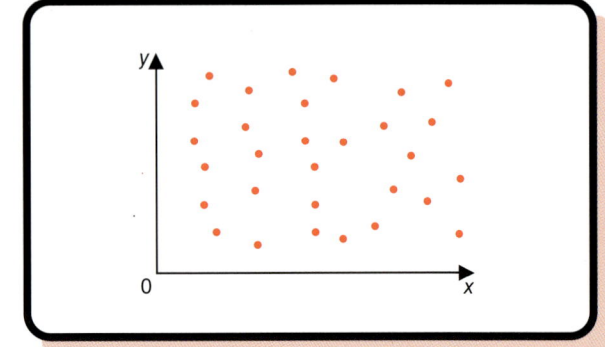

Remember **N** for negative correlation.

Statistics

The grand parade

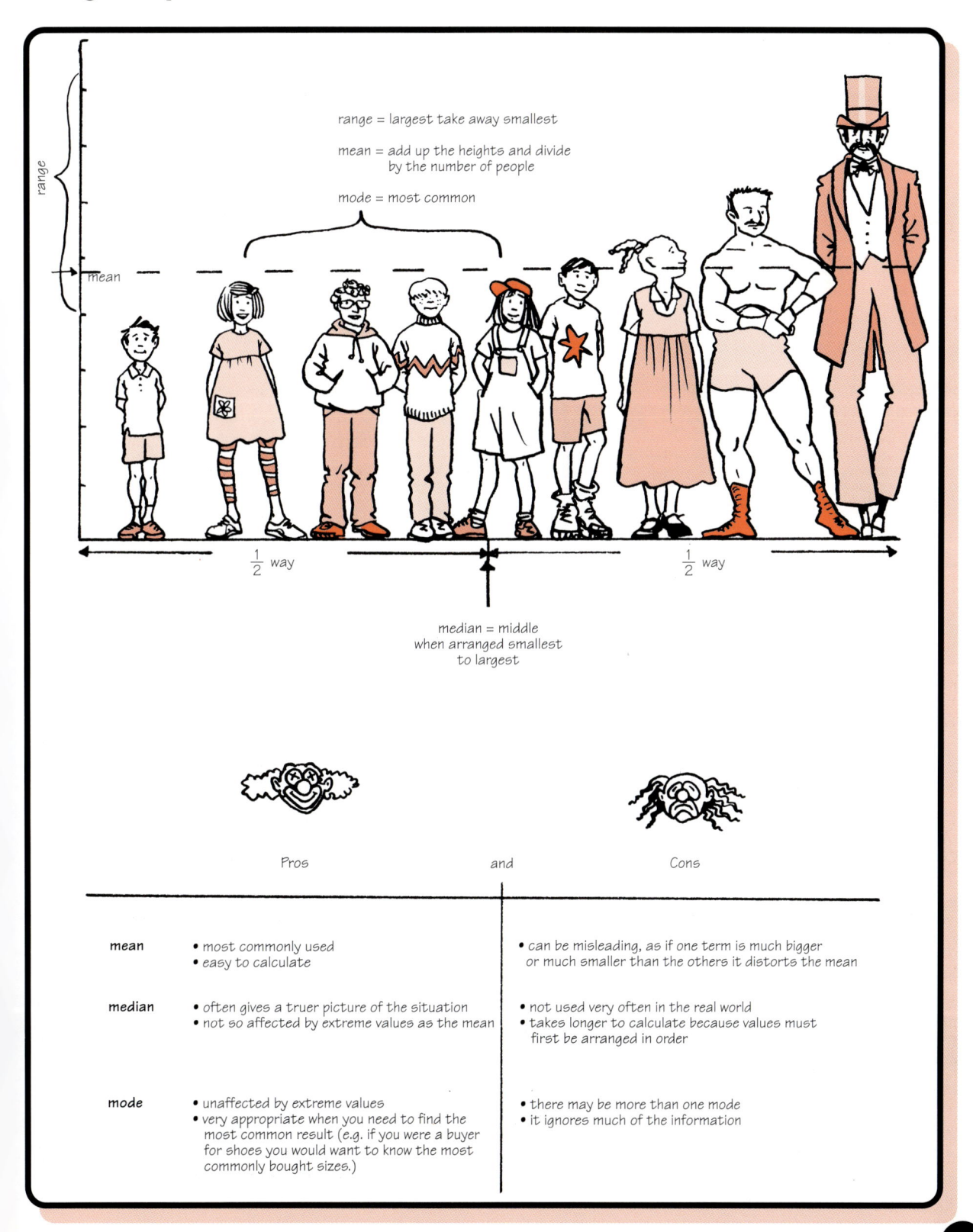

range = largest take away smallest

mean = add up the heights and divide by the number of people

mode = most common

median = middle when arranged smallest to largest

Pros and Cons

	Pros	Cons
mean	• most commonly used • easy to calculate	• can be misleading, as if one term is much bigger or much smaller than the others it distorts the mean
median	• often gives a truer picture of the situation • not so affected by extreme values as the mean	• not used very often in the real world • takes longer to calculate because values must first be arranged in order
mode	• unaffected by extreme values • very appropriate when you need to find the most common result (e.g. if you were a buyer for shoes you would want to know the most commonly bought sizes.)	• there may be more than one mode • it ignores much of the information

Rules of probability

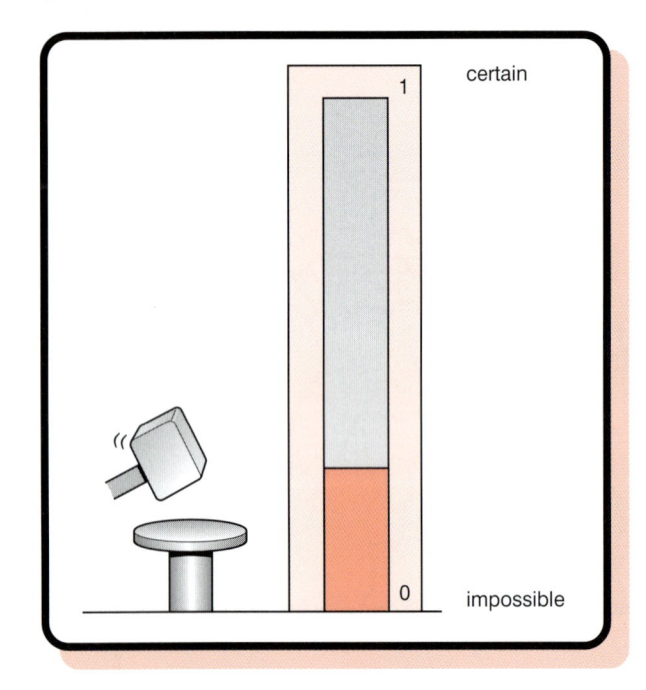

1. Each event's outcome can be assessed on a sliding scale from impossible to certain.
2. Impossible events have a probability of 0.
3. Certain events have a probability of 1.
4. All other possibilities are expressed as a fraction, decimal or percentage.

Calculating probability

$$\text{probability} = \frac{\text{number of required outcomes}}{\text{number of possible outcomes}}$$

Exercise 9.2

1 A spinner, as shown in the diagram, is equally likely to land on any one of its 5 edges. When it is spun it comes to rest on one edge. What is the probability that it lands on the number 4?

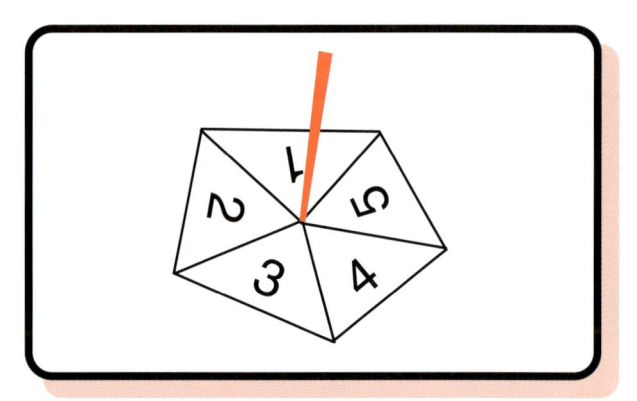

2 1000 tickets were sold in a raffle. If there were 28 prizes, what was the probability of any one ticket winning a prize? Write your answer as a fraction in its lowest terms.

3 In a box there are seven red, five blue and four green buttons.
   a) What is the probability that a button taken at random is blue?
   b) What is the probability that a button taken at random is red?

4 Crispin Syde only likes chocolates with hard centres. In a box of 30 chocolates, 12 have soft centres, 20 are milk chocolates and 5 are foil wrapped.
What is the probability of choosing one with a soft centre?

5 The diagram below shows the heights of 20 pupils in a class to the nearest centimetre.

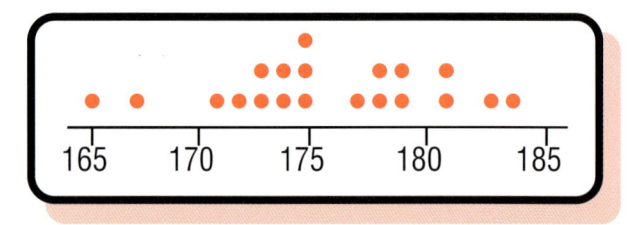

   a) What is the probability that a pupil chosen at random will be 165cm?
   b) What is the probability that a pupil chosen at random from this class will be taller than 175cm?

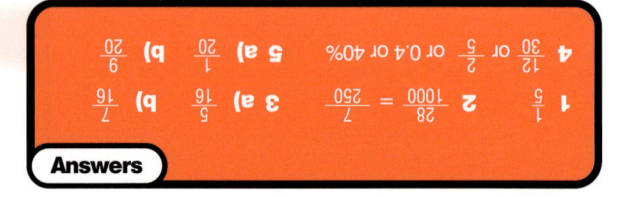

Answers

1) $\frac{1}{5}$ 2) $\frac{28}{1000} = \frac{7}{250}$ 3 a) $\frac{5}{16}$ b) $\frac{7}{16}$ 4) $\frac{12}{30}$ or $\frac{2}{5}$ or 0.4 or 40% 5 a) $\frac{1}{20}$ b) $\frac{9}{20}$

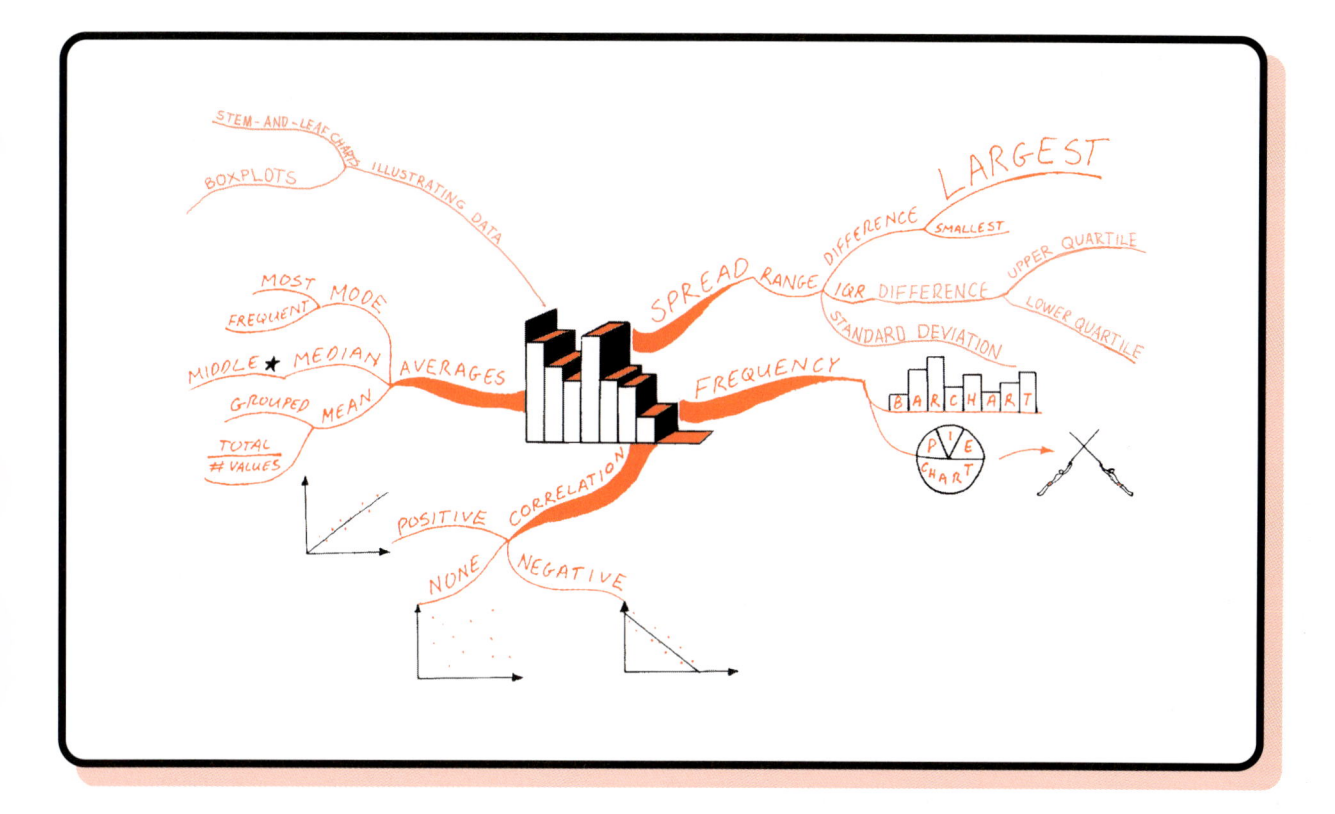

Statistics

review
How much have you learnt?

Tick off each topic in the list when you are confident you can cope with it.

- Find the mean of a set of data.
- Find the median of a set of data.
- Find the mode of a set of data.
- Find the range of a set of data.
- Draw a bar chart for a set of data.
- Draw a pie chart for a set of data.
- Draw up a cumulative frequency table.
- Find the interquartile range and semi-interquartile range of a set of data.
- Interpret scatter diagrams.
- Interpret and construct stem-and-leaf charts.
- Interpret and construct boxplots.
- Calculate, given the formula, the standard deviation of a set of data.
- Find the probability of a simple event.

Statistics review

1. Find the mean, median and range for the following sets of data.
   a) 9.6, 10.1, 8.4, 9.8, 6.9, 11.4, 7.2
   b) 104, 116, 102, 14, 144, 100
   For the second set of data, which is a better measure of the average, the mean or the median? Give a reason for your answer.

2. a) The marks of 15 pupils in a test in class 1C are displayed below in a stem and leaf diagram.

   ```
   1 | 2 4 8
   2 | 3 5 7 9
   3 | 5 6 9 9        1|2 means 12
   4 | 2 4 7 9
   5 |
   ```

   How many pupils scored 39?

   b) The marks of 15 pupils in the same test in class 1D are shown below.

   27, 26, 34, 47, 50, 38, 25, 26, 10, 37, 35, 31, 21, 31, 24

   Construct a stem and leaf diagram to show the marks of the 15 pupils in class 1D.

   c) Compare the distribution of marks for classes 1C and 1D.

3. a) The boxplot drawn below shows the daily rainfall (in millimetres) recorded over a number of days. State the upper and lower quartiles.

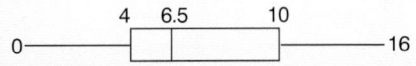

   (boxplot with values 0, 4, 6.5, 10, 16)

   b) The daily rainfall (in millimetres) for a town was recorded over **seven** days.

   The boxplot shown below was drawn for this data set.

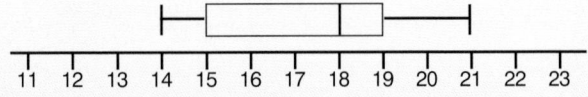

   (boxplot on scale 11 to 23)

   Write down a possible data set which fits this boxplot.

4. In a survey 720 students were asked how they travelled to school. The results are as follows.

Type of transport	Frequency
On foot	108
By car	180
By bus	252
By train	36
By bicycle	144

Statistics review

a) Draw a pie chart to represent the above information
b) What was the modal method of transport?
c) What percentage of students walked to school?

5 The table shows the distribution of absentees per class on a particular day in a secondary school

Number of absentees	Frequency
0	3
1	6
2	7
3	5
4	4
5	2
6	1

a) Make a cumulative frequency table from the above data.

b) Find the median and the lower and upper quartiles for this distribution.

6 The size of engine, length and fuel consumption of ten cars were recorded. The results are illustrated in the two scatter diagrams below. Describe the correlations shown in the two diagrams.

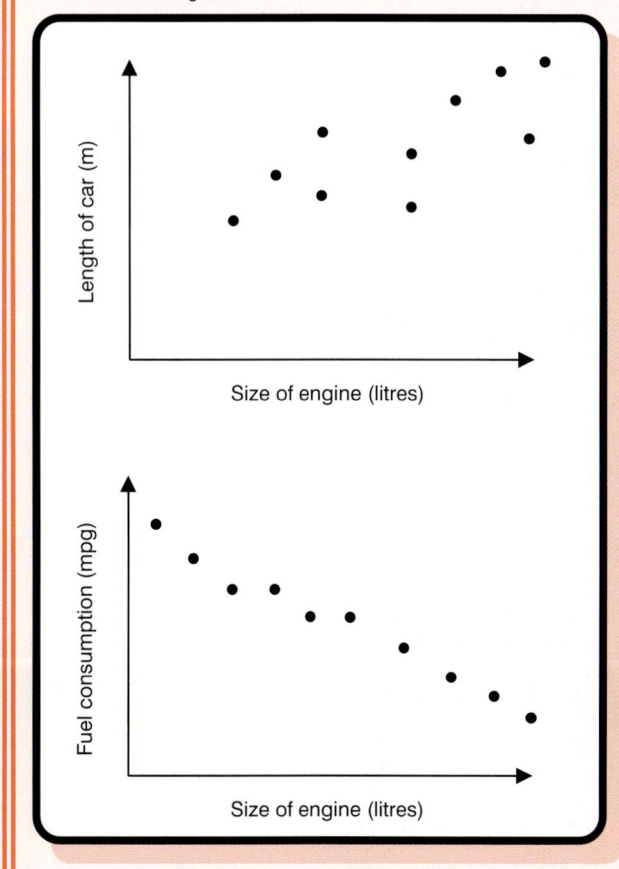

7 In a bag there are seven red, six green, two yellow and five blue marbles.
A marble is drawn, the colour noted and it is then replaced.
Giving your answer as a fraction in its lowest terms, find the probability that the marble is:
a) green **b)** red **c)** not yellow.

8 A golfer recorded the following scores for six games of golf.

69, 72, 74, 78, 73, 72

Use the formula on page 111 to calculate the standard deviation. **Show clearly all your working**.

9 a) Draw the line of best fit on the following diagram.

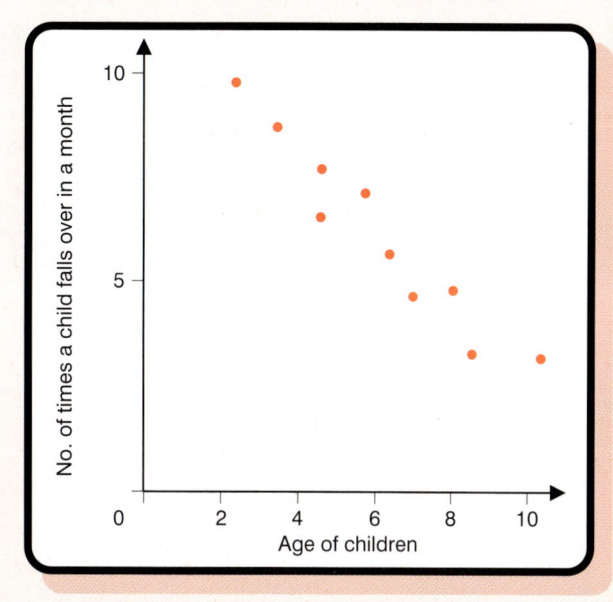

b) How would you describe the correlation in the scatter diagram?
c) Why is your line of best fit misleading when trying to predict results for babies under 2 or children over 10?

10 The sketches below and on the following page show the distributions for sets of data A, B and C.

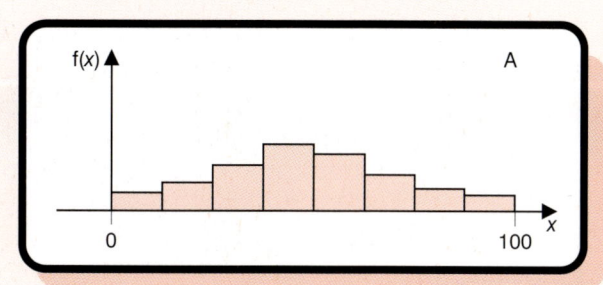

Revise Standard Grade and Intermediate Maths

[Graph B: f(x) histogram from 0 to 100, peaked left of centre]

[Graph C: f(x) histogram from 0 to 100, peaked towards left with long right tail]

a) Which set of data has the highest mean?

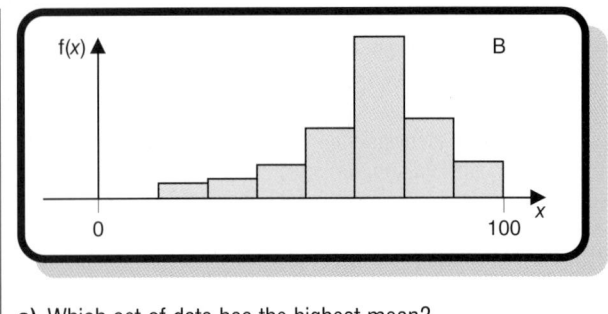

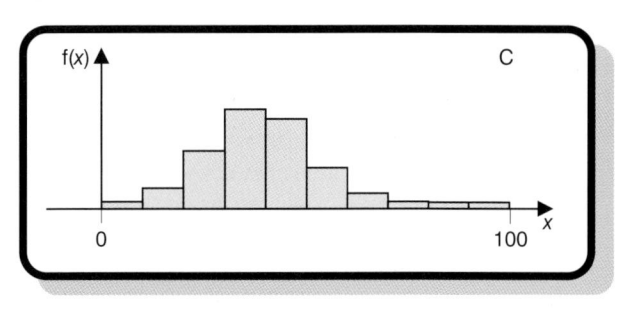

b) Which has the highest standard deviation?

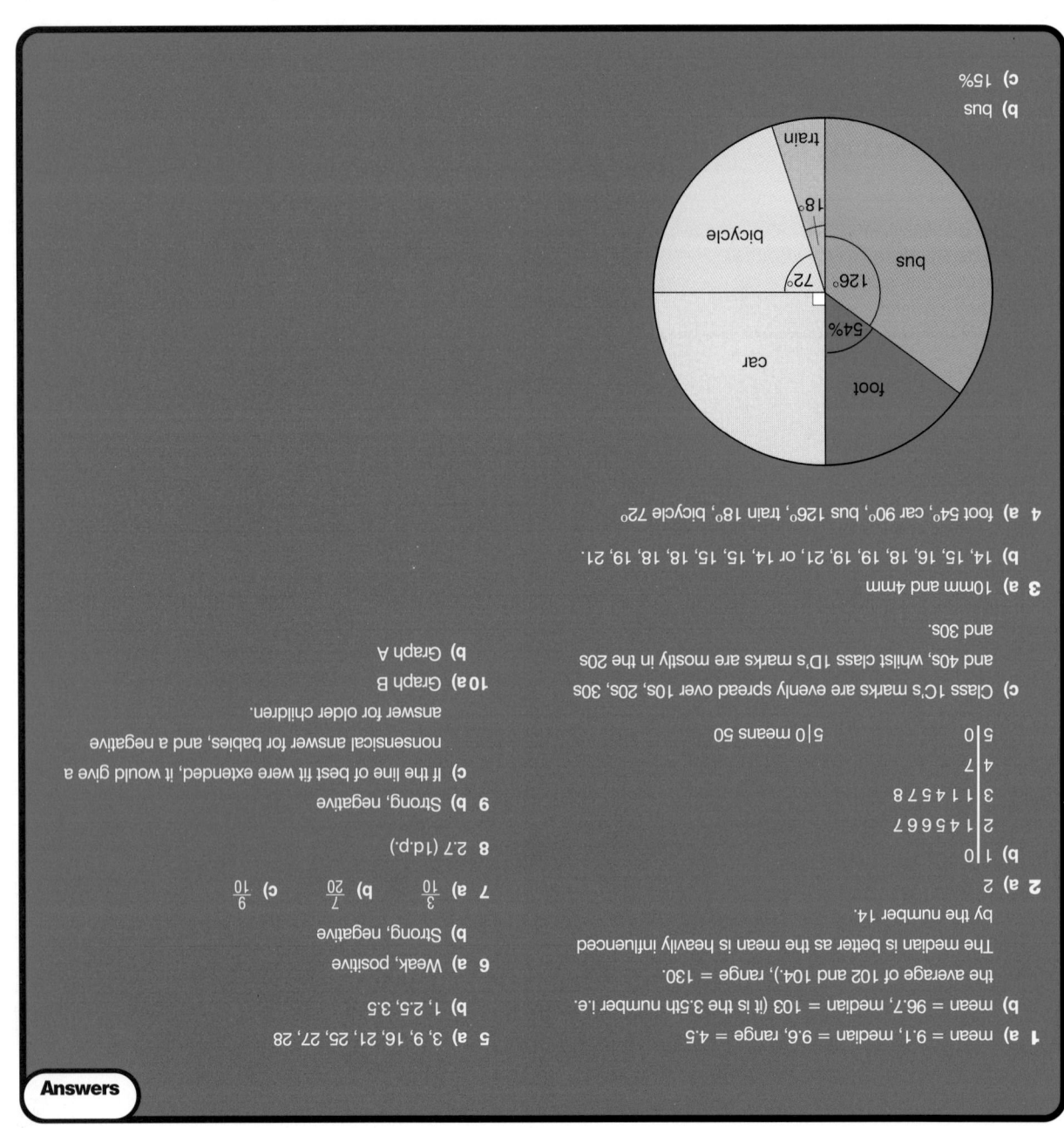

Answers

1 a) mean = 9.1, median = 9.6, range = 4.5
b) mean = 96.7, median = 103 (it is the 3.5th number i.e. the average of 102 and 104.), range = 130.
The median is better as the mean is heavily influenced by the number 14.

2 a) 2
b) 1 | 0
   2 | 1 4 5 6 6 7
   3 | 1 1 4 5 7 8
   4 | 7
   5 | 0   5|0 means 50

c) Class 1C's marks are evenly spread over 10s, 20s, 30s and 40s, whilst class 1D's marks are mostly in the 20s and 30s.

3 a) 10mm and 4mm
b) 14, 15, 16, 18, 19, 21, or 14, 15, 18, 18, 19, 21.

4 a) foot 54°, car 90°, bus 126°, train 18°, bicycle 72°

[Pie chart: foot 54%, car, bus 126°, bicycle 72°, train 18°]

b) bus
c) 15%

5 a) 3, 9, 16, 21, 25, 27, 28
b) 1, 2.5, 3.5

6 a) Weak, positive
b) Strong, negative

7 a) $\frac{3}{10}$ **b)** $\frac{7}{20}$ **c)** $\frac{9}{10}$

8 2.7 (1.d.p.)

9 b) Strong, negative
c) If the line of best fit were extended, it would give a nonsensical answer for babies, and a negative answer for older children.

10 a) Graph B
b) Graph A

Step-by-step revision

If you have a syllabus, you may find it rather daunting. Our three steps highlight the most important topics, i.e. those that crop up most often and that carry the most marks. Step 1 outlines an absolute minimum that you need to revise if you are to have any chance of achieving a pass. If you can score highly on exam questions in these topics you will be well on the way to passing.

Step 1

Number
1. X-Direct
2. Non-calculator skills
3. Rounding
4. Standard form or scientific notation

Algebra
1. Substituting numbers into formulae
2. Solving equations

Shape
1. Area and circumference of a circle
2. Pythagoras' theorem and trigonometry

Statistics
1. Mean, median and mode
2. Probability
3. Stem-and-leaf charts, boxplots

As you can see, this is a very short list. Look back in the book now if you are uncertain in any of these areas.

Step 2

These are the next most useful topics to revise. They may not appear quite as often as those in Step 1 but they still carry plenty of marks. Keep trying questions on the material from Step 1, though, while you are working through Step 2.

Number
1. Ratio ruler

Algebra
1. Equations, simple and simultaneous
2. Formula rearrangement
3. Simplifying and factorising
4. Gradient and equation of a line

Shape
1. Area and volume
2. Bearings
3. Sine rule and Cosine rule
4. Arcs and sectors of a circle
5. Similar figures
6. Graphs of $\sin x$ and $\cos x$, trig equations

Statistics
1. Standard deviation, cumulative frequency
2. Scatter diagrams and line of best fit.

Step 3

If you have completed Step 2, congratulations! You are almost there. Look back at the chapter reviews and tick or highlight all of the topics with which you feel confident. There may still be a few items outstanding. Try to make time to fill these gaps because they could make all the difference and help you get a higher grade.

Checklist

Avoid these banana skins!

1. What is an easy way of calculating 29 x 7 (without your calculator)?
2. What is the difference between significant figures and decimal places?
3. If you have 17 numbers, which one would be in the median position?
4. What do the interquartile range and range describe?
5. When shouldn't you use X-Direct?
6. When using Pythagoras' theorem and finding one of the shorter sides, what must you remember?
7. What three points should you remember when finding a bearing?
8. When is a stem-end-leaf chart useful?
9. What does a boxplot show?
10. Give the formulae for the area and the circumference of a circle.
11. What should you check on your calculator before starting trigonometry?
12. Why do we calculate standard deviation?
13. What should you remember when working in algebra with inequalities?
14. Is 1.3×10^{-7} a small or large number?
15. What is the difference between using `SIN` and `INV SIN` on your calculator?
16. What shapes does the net of a cylinder consist of?
17. Draw a freehand sketch of the graph of $y = \sin x°$
18. Would you use the Sine rule or the Cosine rule if you know two sides and the included angle in a scalene triangle?
19. What three letters can help you remember the rules for corresponding, opposite and alternate angles?
20. When is the mean an unsuitable measure of the average?

You may want to add some of your own banana skins at this point.

Revise Standard Grade and Intermediate Maths

Answers

1. $30 \times 7 = 210$
   $210 - 7 = 203$
2. If you are unclear on this, turn to page 16.
3. The 9th number.
4. How widely apart the data is spread.
5. Inverse proportion – it can drive you MAD!
6. For Shorter Sides Subtract.
7. Look north, turn clockwise, and always write the bearing with three figures.
8. When there are a lot of numbers and you want to find the median and quartiles.
9. The minimum and maximum and the median and quartiles.
10. area = πr^2, circumference = $2\pi r$ or πd
11. Check that it is set to degrees.
12. To find out how well the data is spread over the range.
13. The inequality reverses when you:
    a) swap the inequality around, or
    b) multiply or divide both sides by a negative number.
14. A very small number.
15. Use sin if you want to find a length, use inv sin if you have the sine and want to find an angle.
16. Two circles and a rectangle
17. [graph showing sine curve from 0 to 360, amplitude 1 to –1]
18. Cosine rule.
19. F, X and Z respectively
20. When a small part of the sample is much bigger or much smaller than the rest.

Specimen examination papers

Here's a chance to try out all your new skills on two practice papers. We have tried to make them as close to the real thing as possible, but all examiners have their own funny little ways, so it is a good idea to do as many past papers as possible. No doubt your Maths teacher will keep you busy.

Before you start on Paper 1, though, Ringo has a few hints to help you avoid that awful sinking feeling.

1. Work right through the paper, doing as many questions as you can. Leave out any questions you can't do straight away, then come back to them.

2. If you are working on a question and you get a sudden brainwave about another question, jot it down somewhere (perhaps the inside cover) to use later.

3. A lucky guess might gain you some marks. A blank page never does. If you attempt at least part of a question, there is a chance that you will get some marks.

4. Don't get bogged down in any one question. It's better to move on and come back later if you have time.

5. Always show your working. It's surprising how many marks you can pick up, even if you get the wrong answer.

And finally, if you really don't know where to start, remember:

Read the question.
Identify the problem, i.e. what are they asking?
Note the information, i.e. what do I know already, what information are they giving me?
Get on with it.
Or go back and attempt the question again later if you have time.

Foundation level Paper 1 (Non-calculator)

1. Calculate
   a) 387 + 29 + 456
   b) 1020 − 293
   c) 2.3 + 7.9
   d) 6.7 × 5
   e) 8.5 ÷ 5
   f) 10.2 × 10
   g) $\frac{1}{6}$ of £72
   h) 20% of £130

2. The scale below shows speed in miles per hour and kilometres per hour.

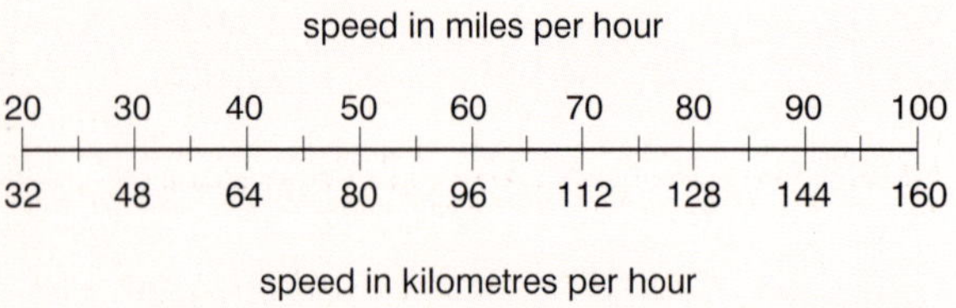

   speed in miles per hour

20	30	40	50	60	70	80	90	100
32	48	64	80	96	112	128	144	160

   speed in kilometres per hour

   a) Use the scale to change 64 kilometres per hour into miles per hour.
   b) Use the scale to change 75 miles per hour into kilometres per hour.

3. Two towns are 40km apart.
   On a map they are 8cm apart.
   Complete:
   The scale of the map is: 1cm represents …

4. How many more grams must be placed on pan Y to make the scales balance?
   (Pan Y: 800g; other pan: 1½ kg)

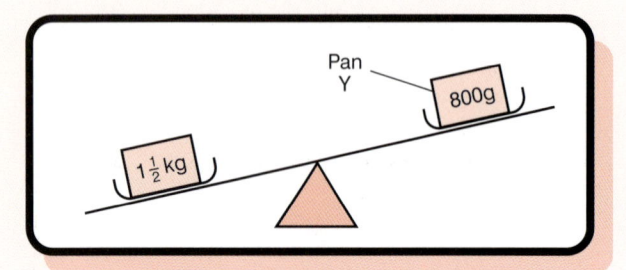

5. Calculate the size of the angle x.
   (Triangle with angles 45°, 62°, and x)

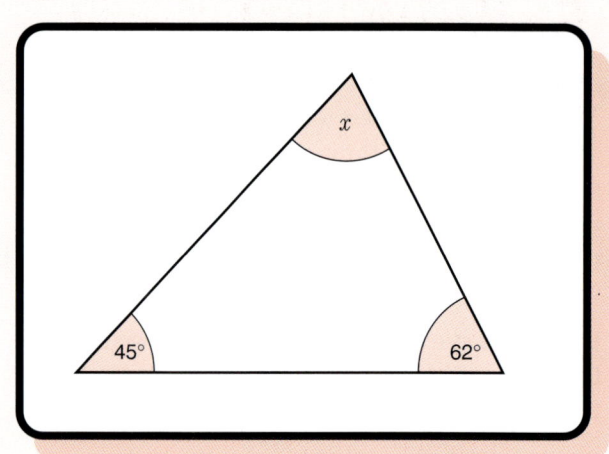

6. It is evening and this is the station clock:

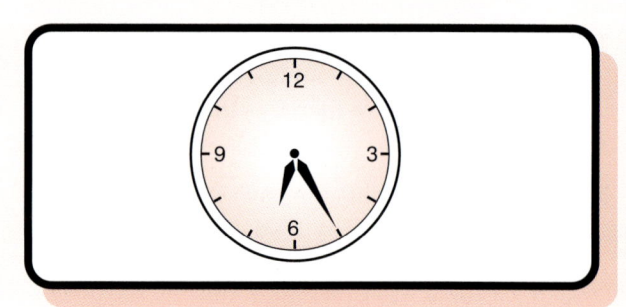

   John's train leaves at 19.05.
   How long does he have to wait?

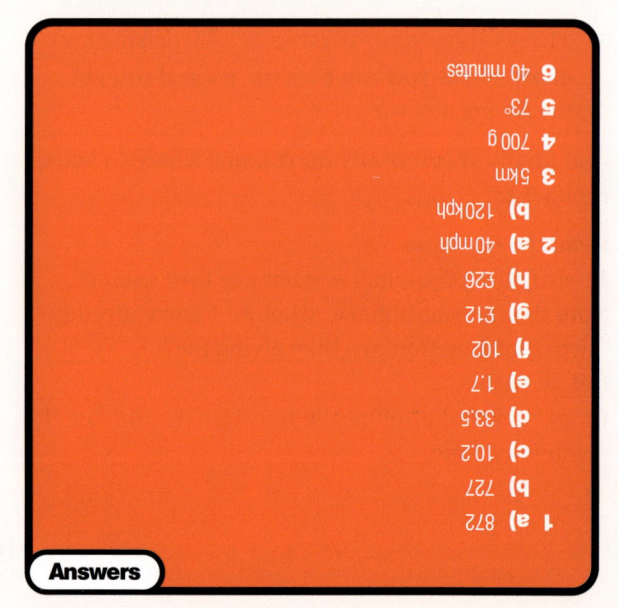

Answers

1. a) 872
   b) 727
   c) 10.2
   d) 33.5
   e) 1.7
   f) 102
   g) £12
   h) £26
2. a) 40mph
   b) 120kph
3. 5km
4. 700 g
5. 73°
6. 40 minutes

Foundation level
Paper 2

1

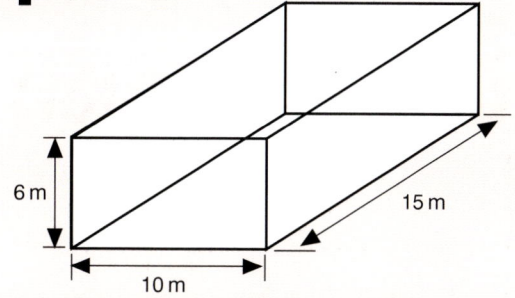

A room is 15 m long, 10 m wide and 6 m high. Calculate its volume in cubic metres.

2 A car runs for 100 miles on 2 gallons of petrol. How far will it run on 7 gallons?

3 Four circular table mats of the same size and as large as possible are cut from a square piece of wood with sides 20 cm long. Calculate the diameter of each mat.

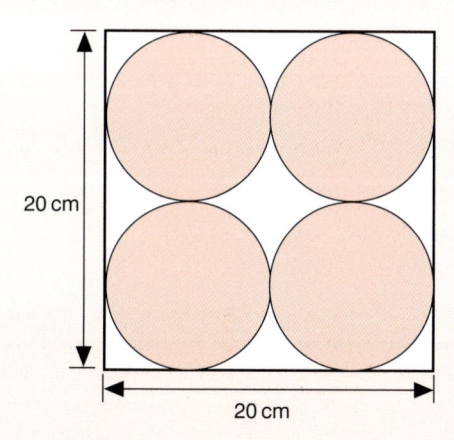

4 Four matchboxes contain 38, 41, 42 and 43 matches. Calculate the average number of matches per box.

5 Pupils in a first year class were asked to name the school subject which they liked best.

The answers were:

English	3 pupils
Mathematics	6 pupils
Games	10 pupils
Art	7 pupils
Science	1 pupils

Complete the bar chart to show these results.

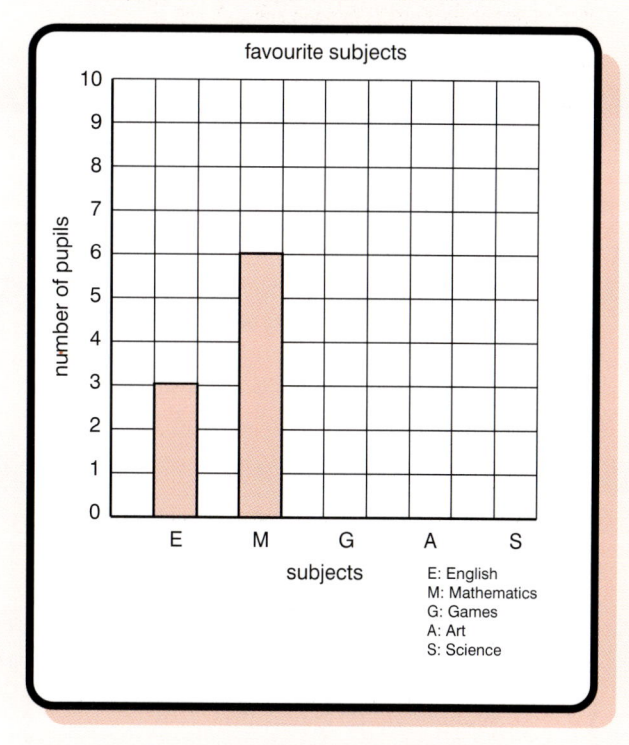

favourite subjects

E: English
M: Mathematics
G: Games
A: Art
S: Science

6 A motor bike can be bought by making a deposit of £150 and paying £15.60 a week for 50 weeks.

What is the total cost of the motorbike?

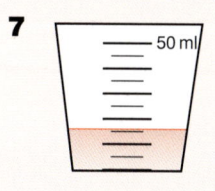

7 This drawing shows a 50 ml measuring jug holding 15 ml of water.

Shade this drawing to show the jug holding 35 ml of water.

8 How many of the small cubes like B would exactly fill box A?

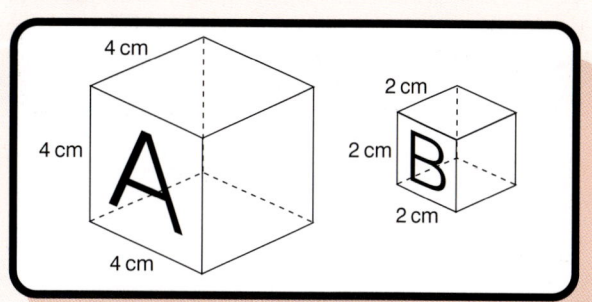

127

9 Which of the following diagrams are nets of cubes? (Answer YES or NO in each case.)

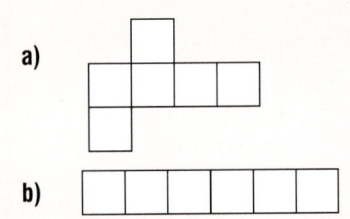

a)

b)

10 a) The graph shows a journey which was made up of three parts:
(i) walking from home to the bus stop
(ii) waiting at the bus stop
(iii) going by bus.

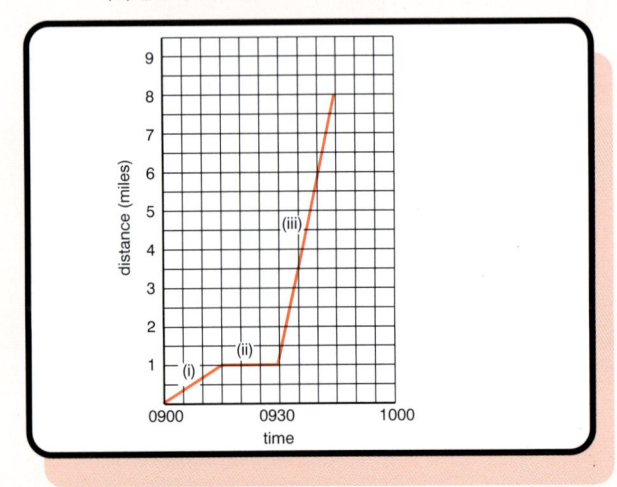

How long did the whole journey take?

b) How far was travelled by bus?

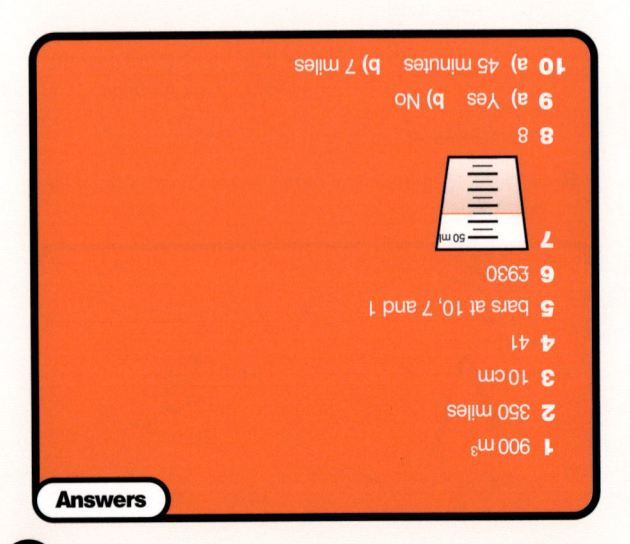

General level (Intermediate 1)
Paper 1 (non-calculator)

1 Calculate

a) 28×11

b) $\frac{2}{3}$ of 48

c) $\frac{1}{2} + \frac{3}{4}$

d) $\frac{1}{2} \times \frac{1}{6}$

e) 30% of £12

f) $4 \times (-5)$

2 a) Find the mean, the median and the range of these numbers: 7, 8, 3, 9, 6, 30.

b) Is the mean or the median a better indicator of the average?

3 The thickness of a layer of oil is measured and found to be 2.7×10^{-6} millimetres.
Write this number out in full.

4 Solve the equation $3 + 5x = 31$

5 Simplify $3(4x - 8) + x$

6 Solve $2x - 9 > 16$

Answers

1 a) 308
b) 32
c) $1\frac{1}{4}$
d) $\frac{1}{12}$
e) £3.60
f) −20
2 a) mean = 10.5, median = 7.5, range = 27
b) The median is better, as the mean is distorted by the one much bigger value.
3 0.0000027 mm
4 $x = \frac{28}{5} = 5.6$
5 $13x - 24$
6 $x > 12.5$

Answers

1 900 m³
2 350 miles
3 10 cm
4 41
5 bars at 10, 7 and 1
6 £930
7 50 ml
8 8
9 a) Yes **b)** No
10 a) 45 minutes **b)** 7 miles

128

General level (Intermediate 1) Paper 2

1 In a sale, a shop reduced all its prices by 15%.

  a) Find the new price of an article which originally cost £55.00.

  b) Find the original price if the reduced price is £102.

  c) In the week before the sale, the average number of customers per day was 250. During the sale this number increasd to 370. What was the percentage increase?

2 Find the angle marked x below, to the nearest degree.

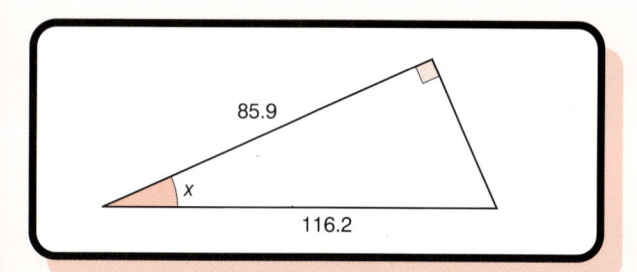

[Right-angled triangle with hypotenuse 85.9, base 116.2, angle x at left]

3 A fish tank is made in the shape of a cuboid. with a base measuring 60 cm by 40 cm. If it contains 72 litres of water, how deep is the water in the tank?

4 In the diagram below calculate:
  a) AB   b) BC   c) the area of triangle ACD.

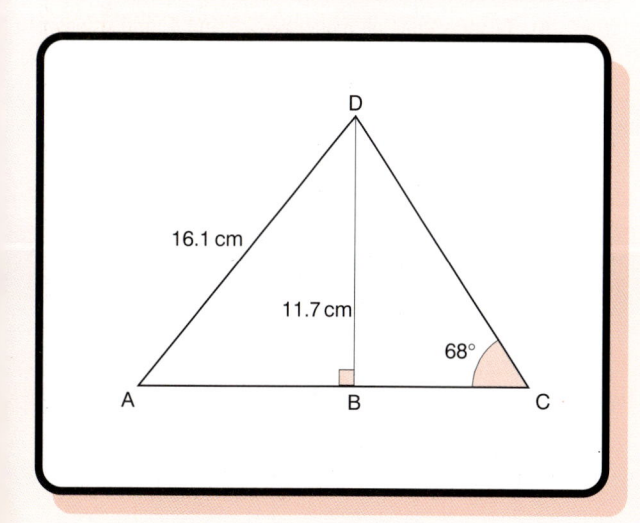

[Triangle ACD with D at top, B on AC. AD = 16.1 cm, DB = 11.7 cm, angle at C = 68°]

5 A cylindrical tank with a lid has a base radius of 1.7 m, and a height of 3.4 m.
  a) Find its volume.
  b) Find its surface area.

6 Two judges were scoring students in a public speaking competition. Each judge awarded marks out of 100. Here are the marks for 6 students who took part:

Contestant	Judge A	Judge B
Morag	51	60
Chris	23	37
Sami	66	68
Russell	40	51
Claire	34	44
Angus	75	76

  a) Draw a scatter graph for these marks.

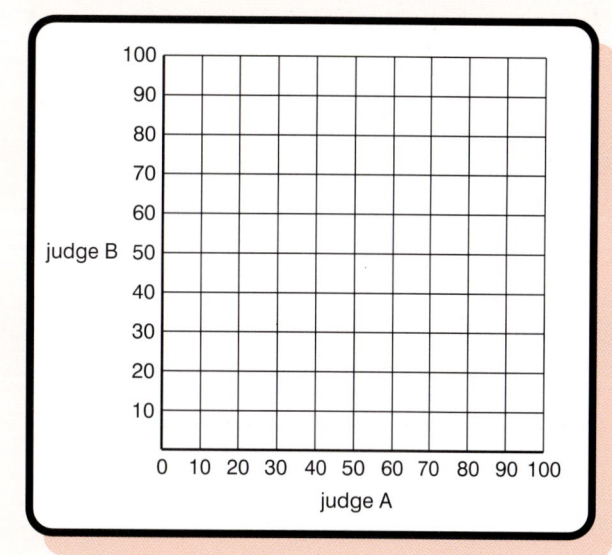

[Blank grid, judge B (vertical, 0–100) vs judge A (horizontal, 0–100)]

  b) Draw a best-fitting straight line on your graph.

  c) Ruth's talk was given 60 marks by Judge A, but Judge B did not hear it. Use your line to estimate the most likely mark that Judge B would have awarded Ruth.

7 23 members of a swimming club take part in a sponsored swim.

The frequency table shows the number of lengths completed by the members.

Number of lengths	Number of members
16	2
17	4
18	3
19	5
20	9

a) Find the median number of lengths completed by the members.
b) Calculate the mean number of lengths completed by the members to 2 d.p.
c) Find the probability that a member has completed exactly 19 lengths.

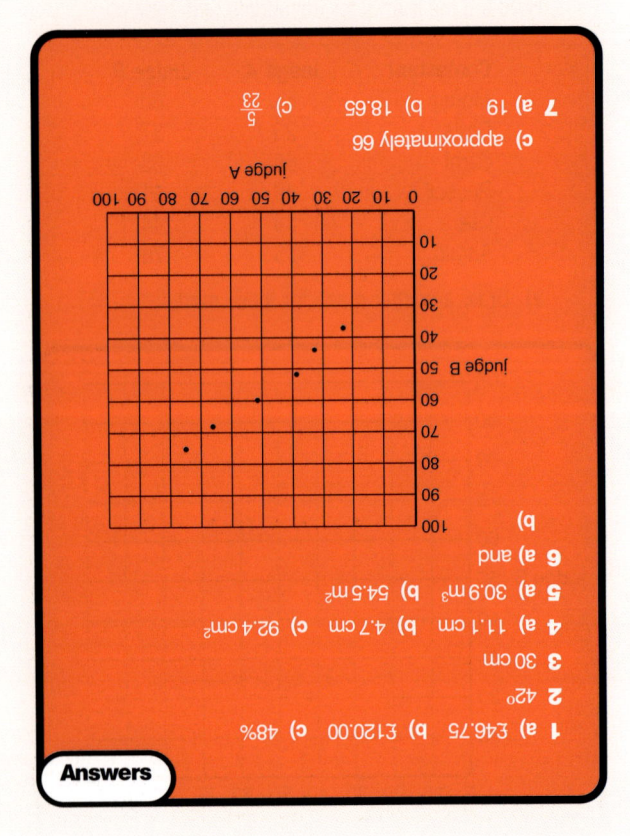

Credit level (Intermediate 2)

Paper 1 (non-calculator)

1 Calculate
  a) $2\frac{1}{3} - 1\frac{1}{5}$
  b) $3\frac{1}{2} \times 2\frac{1}{4}$
  c) $\frac{3}{7} \div \frac{1}{3}$

2 Evaluate the following, when $x = -5$, $y = -3$ and $z = 4$.
  a) $x + y$
  b) $y - z$
  c) xy
  d) $3x^2$

3 Solve the following equations.
  a) $10x + 3 = 12x - 7$
  b) $4x + 2 = 2x - 12$
  c) $4(x - 3) = 2 - x$
  d) Use an algebraic method to solve the following simultaneous equations.
   $5x + 2y = 29$
   $2x + 5y = 41$

4 a) The following table gives some values for the equation $y = 2x - 4$. Fill in the rest of the table.

x	−2	−1	0	1	2	3	4
y	−8			−2		2	

  b) Taking values of x between −2 and 4, and values of y between −8 and 8, draw the graph of $y = 2x - 4$.
  c) Hence or otherwise, find the gradient and the y-intercept.

5 An employer advertised a part-time job at the rate of £50.00 per week plus £5.75 per hour.
  a) If w stands for the wage in pounds, and h stands for hours worked, write a formula in terms of w and h to show this information.
   Begin the formula: $w =$
  b) Rearrange the formula to make h the subject.
  c) If an employee earned £165.00 in a week, how many hours would have been worked?

6 Match the labels to the graphs opposite.
  a) $y = x^3$ b) $y = -x$
  c) $y = x^2 + 2$ d) $y = 2x - 3$

Answers

1 a) £46.75 b) £120.00 c) 48%
2 42°
3 30 cm
4 a) 11.1 cm b) 4.7 cm c) 92.4 cm²
5 a) 30.9 m³ b) 54.5 m²
6 a) and b)

[scatter graph with axes labelled judge A (0 to 100) and judge B (0 to 100)]

c) approximately 66
7 a) 19 b) 18.65 c) $\frac{23}{5}$

i)

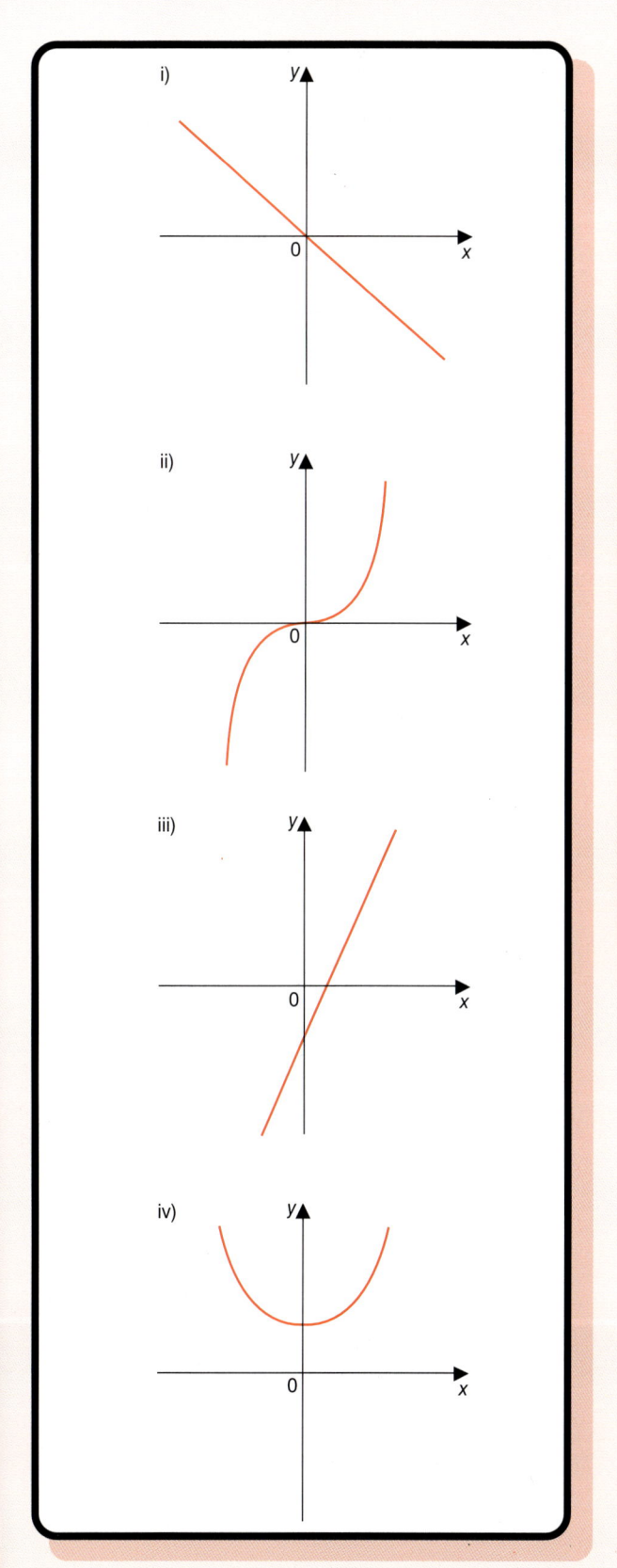

(graph: line with negative gradient passing through origin)

ii)

(graph: cubic-like curve through origin)

iii)

(graph: line with positive gradient, positive y-intercept)

iv)

(graph: parabola opening upwards, vertex above x-axis)

Answers

1 a) $\frac{17}{15}$ or $1\frac{2}{15}$ **b)** $\frac{63}{8}$ or $7\frac{7}{8}$ **c)** $\frac{9}{7}$ or $1\frac{2}{7}$

2 a) -8 **b)** -7 **c)** 15 **d)** 75

3 a) $x = 5$ **b)** $x = -7$ **c)** $x = 2.8$ **d)** $x = 3, y = 7$

4 a)

x	-2	-1	0	1	2	3	4
y	-8	-6	-4	-2	0	2	4

b)

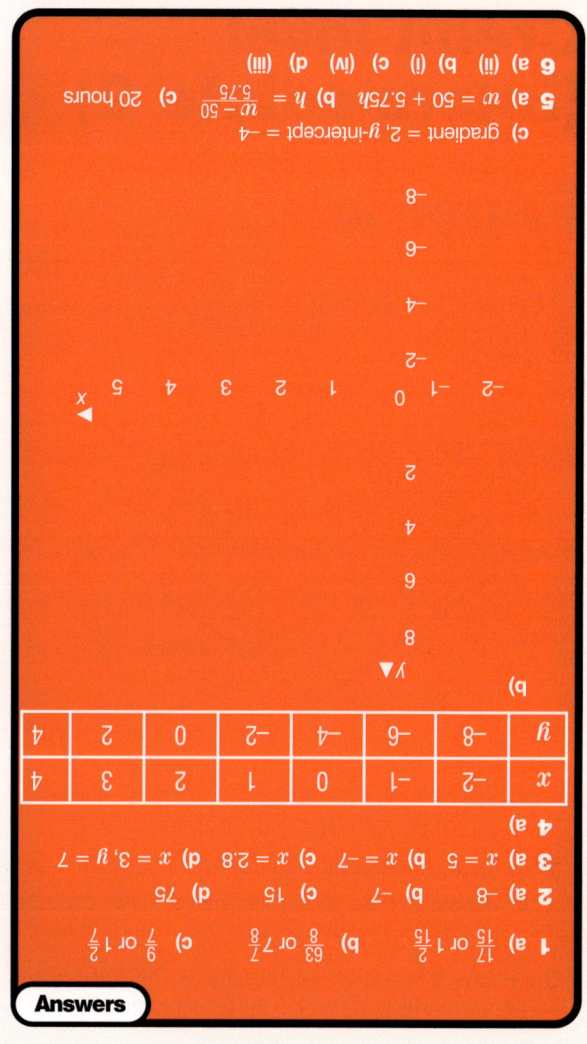

(graph with y-axis from -8 to 8 and x-axis from -2 to 5)

c) gradient $= 2$, y-intercept $= -4$

5 a) $u = 50 + 5.75h$ **b)** $h = \frac{u-50}{5.75}$ **c)** 20 hours

6 a) (ii) **b)** (i) **c)** (iv) **d)** (iii)

Credit level (Intermediate 2)

Paper 2

1 In the diagram below find:
  a) BC   **b)** angle CDA.

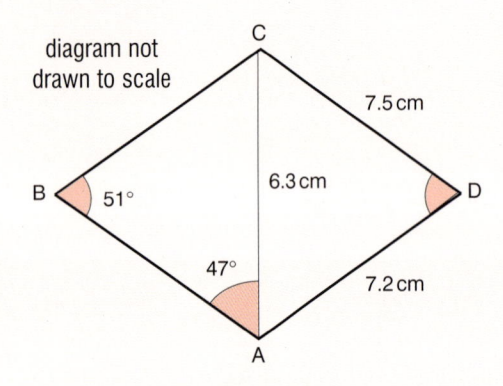

diagram not drawn to scale

c) Using the area of a triangle = $\frac{1}{2}ab\sin C$, find the area of the entire shape to 2 significant figures.

2 a) Solve by factorisation $2x^2 + 9x - 5 = 0$.
  b) Solve $3x^2 + 8x = 5$, giving your answers correct to 2 d.p.

3 Two cylinders are similar. The larger holds 152 cm³ and the smaller holds 42 cm³. If the height of the larger is 25 cm, find the height of the smaller.

4 On the diagram below, sketch the graph of $y = \cos x$.

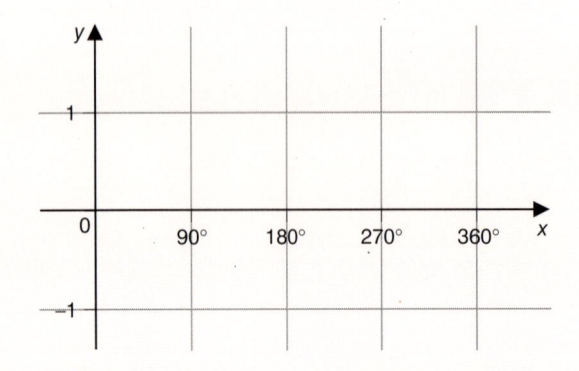

Hence or otherwise find two values of x, in the range $0° \leq x < 360°$, such that $\cos x = -0.5$.

5 Rearrange the formula $R = 3(p - q^2)$ to make q the subject.

6 Express $2^3 \div 2^5$
  a) as a power of 2   **b)** as a fraction.

7 i) Simplify where possible.
  a) $3(2x + y) - (x - y)$
  b) $5x^2 + 2x + 7x + 2y + y^2$
  ii) Find the solutions to these equations.
  a) $(x - 3)(x + 2) = 0$
  b) $x^2 + 8x + 7 = 0$
  c) $x^2 - 8x - 20 = 0$

8 a) Using the diagram, write an expression for AC².

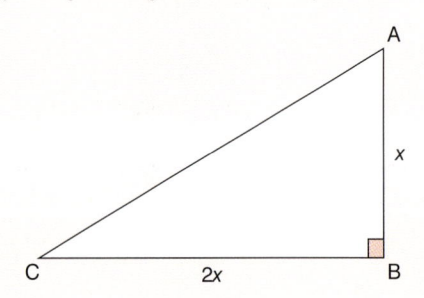

b) If $AC^2 = 20$, find the lengths of the other two sides. Show your working.

9 Find the standard deviation of this random sample of digits, showing all the necessary working. (Note that no credit will be given for reading the standard deviation directly from a calculator.)

5 7 2 6 8

10 The pattern for a skirt consists of part of the sector of a circle.

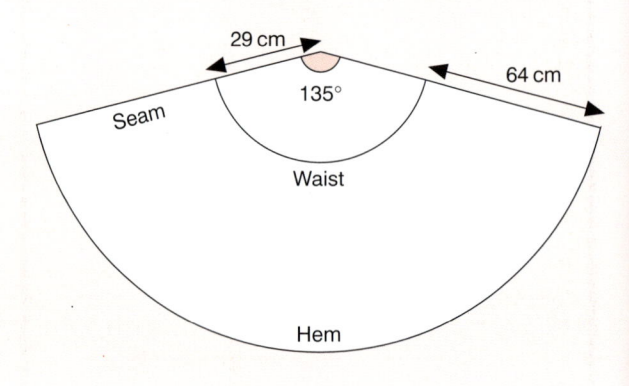

Calculate the length of the waist shown on the pattern above.

11 The diagram shows a glass bowl with two chop-sticks resting on the rim at points A and B. The lengths of the parts of the chop-sticks inside the bowl are 10 cm and 13 cm respectively, and the angle between them is 115°.

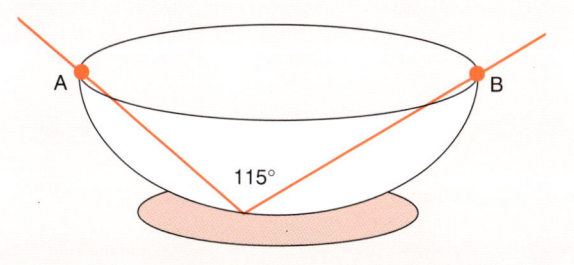

Find the length of AB to 3 significant figures.

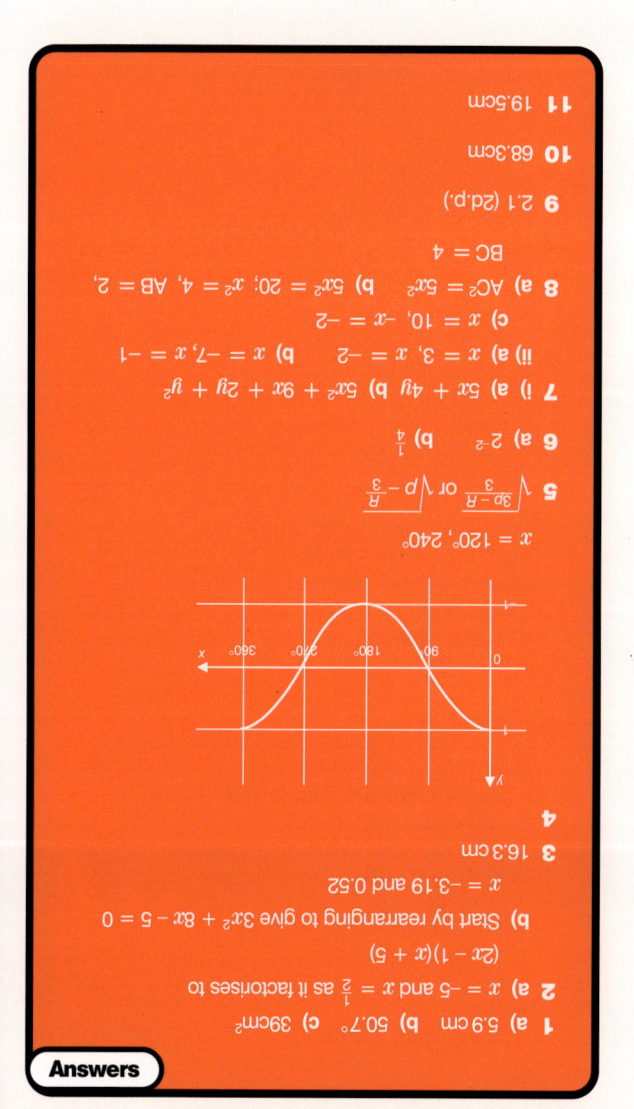

Answers

1 a) 5.9 cm b) 50.7° c) 39cm²
2 a) $x = -5$ and $x = \frac{1}{2}$ as it factorises to $(2x-1)(x+5)$
   b) Start by rearranging to give $3x^2 + 8x - 5 = 0$
      $x = -3.19$ and 0.52
3 16.3 cm
4
$x = 120°, 240°$
5 $\sqrt{\frac{3p-R}{3}}$ or $\sqrt{p - \frac{R}{3}}$
6 a) 2^{-2} b) $\frac{1}{4}$
7 i) a) $5x + 4y$ b) $5x^2 + 9x + 2y + y^2$
  ii) a) $x = 3$, $x = -2$ b) $x = -7$, $x = -1$
      c) $x = 10$, $-x = -2$
8 a) $AC^2 = 5x^2$ b) $5x^2 = 20$; $x^2 = 4$, $AB = 2$,
      $BC = 4$
9 2.1 (2d.p.)
10 68.3cm
11 19.5cm

Index

Angles
   depression 75
   elevation 75
   labelling of 100
Area
   circle 91
   parallelogram 94
   surface 94
   triangle 94
Averages
   mean 110, 112, 113
   median 110, 111, 112, 113
   mode 110, 113

Bearings 75
Brackets
   double, using FOIL 35
   single 28

Circles
   area 91
   area of a sector 91
   arc length 92
   area of a segment 92
   circumference 91
Congruent triangles 101
Correlation 113, 114
Cosine rule 79
Curved graphs 58, 59

Decimal places 16
Direct proportion
   and X-Direct method 2–4

Equations
   graphical solutions 56–57
   quadratic 41
   simple 24–26
   simultaneous 33–35

Factorising
   double brackets 36–40
   single brackets 30, 31
Formula rearrangement 42–46

Gradient
   and equation of a line 54–55
   meaning of 53

Indices 17, 18
Inequalities 27
Interquartile range 110, 111
Inverse proportion 5

Joint variation 48

Karate Ken
   and isosceles triangles 67

Mean 110–112
Median 110–113
Mode 110–113

Nets 103
Non-calculator numerical skills 14–16

Percentages 6–8
Perimeter 90
Pie charts 112
Prism 94–95
Probability
   rules of 115
Proportion
   direct 2–4
   inverse 5
Pythagoras 67–70, 76–79

Quadratics 58–59
Quadrilaterals 101
Quartiles 110, 111, 112

Range 111
Ratio 8–11
Reflection 103
Rotation 104
Rounding 16

Scatter diagrams 114
Scientific notation 17, 18
Semi-interquartile range 110
Significant figures 16, 17
Similar shapes 100
Simplifying expressions 27–28
Sine rule 79
Spread 110, 111
Standard deviation 111
Standard form 18, 19
Stem-and-leaf charts 112
Straight line graphs 54–57
Surface area 94
Symmetry 103, 104

Trigonometry 76–80, 82
   and non-right angled triangles 79–81
   and right angled triangles 70–74, 76–79
   and sin, cos and tan graphs 82–84
   and equations 85–87

Variation 47–48
   joint 48
Vases and vessels
   on graphs 53
VAT 7, 8
Volume
   of a prism 94–95